THE ROD
OF AN ALMOND TREE
IN GOD'S MASTER PLAN

PETER A. MICHAS
ROBERT VANDER MATEN
CHRISTIE D. MICHAS

WinePress Publishing
MUKILTEO, WA 98275

DEDICATED TO MESSIAH YESHUA,

THE WAY, THE TRUTH, AND THE LIFE

AND TO THOSE WHO SEEK HIM

ACKNOWLEDGEMENTS

The authors want to take this opportunity to acknowledge that this work would not have been possible without God. In a real sense, this work is His, for without Him it would never have come to fruition.

I (PAM) would also like to express my utmost gratitude to all those who made this work possible, especially:

My parents, Lt. Col. Gus Michas, Ret. and Mary Michas, for their constant love and support. Thank you for supporting me through the most difficult times, as well as for sharing in my happiness and joy.

Robert Vander Maten, coauthor of this book and a special friend, for his long hours, dedication and patience, without whose collaboration this work would not have taken form and reached fruition.

Gil and Judy Loop, for their unfailing love and support, especially in times of greatest need.

Donald Kramer, who provided computer assistance whenever necessary and for his contribution to the "Foreword." Tracey Franklin, for her time and conscientious assistance to Christie during the hectic phase of preparing the second edition.

Frank Booke, for providing the funds necessary for the first edition, entitled *God's Master Plan from Aleph to Tav*.

My friends and supporters of this ministry, for their continued love and support, without which this book would never have been written.

And finally to my wife and coauthor, Christie, for uncounted hours, insight and attention to detail in the writing, editing, and final production of this work; and especially for her love and devotion.

I (RVM) would like to publicly thank my wife Joleen, and our three children Deidra, Jaclene and Joshua for supporting their dad during the writing of *The Rod of an Almond Tree in God's Master Plan*. Countless nights and many Saturdays were given up to allow Dad to go back into the garage (my office area) and work until early morning hours on the most exciting and important Bible study in which I have ever been involved.

ILLUSTRATIONS

❧

CONTENTS

EXAMINING TRADITIONAL BELIEFS

*But an hour is coming, and now is, when the
true worshipers shall worship the Father in
spirit and truth; for such people the Father
seeks to be His worshipers (John 4:23).*

Can we always rely on the truth of certain traditional beliefs? Traditional beliefs are generally accepted without examining their origin or their basis in truth. The following questions relate to matters of little real importance in life but are an excellent illustration of how commonly held beliefs may not, in fact, be true. Take the quiz and check your ability to sort fact from fiction. Who said:

1. I cannot tell a lie. I chopped down the cherry tree with my little hatchet.
2. The British are coming! The British are coming!
3. Why don't you come up and see me some time?
4. Beam me up Scotty.

Most believe the correct answers to the above are:

1. George Washington

2. Paul Revere
3. Mae West
4. Captain Kirk

In fact, the following are the true answers:

1. Joice Heth in P.T. Barnum's circus (1836)
2. From Henry Wadsworth Longfellow's 1863 ballad "Paul Revere's Ride"
3. A misquote from the 1933 movie "She Done Him Wrong"
4. This quote was never stated during any of the Star Trek episodes

Knowing the correct answers to the above questions is not of any significance with regard to the critical choices of life. However, can the same be said of matters of great importance, especially spiritual matters? The consequences of spiritual choices last an eternity. Should we not be very concerned that we are building upon spiritual truths?

God gave humankind the ability to reason—the ability to separate fact from fiction, truth from untruth. He also gave His Word that we might better know Him and understand His redemptive plan for us. Furthermore, God warned that spiritual deception abounds (Matthew 24:24-25). We must have a sound spiritual foundation in order to discern between spiritual truth and spiritual deception. What is at stake is our eternal lives and, contrary to popular belief, not all spiritual paths lead to the Creator (Matthew 7:13-14).

Incredible as it may seem, there are certain religious doctrines and traditions within Christianity that conflict with Holy Scripture. Likewise, in the time of Yeshua (Jesus), the same conflict existed. Remember Yeshua's condemnation of the Pharisees: "...why do you yourselves transgress the commandment of God for the sake of your tradition?" (Matthew 15:3). And, "This people honors Me with their lips, but their heart is far away from Me. But in vain do they worship me, teaching as doctrines the precepts of men" (Matthew 15:8-9).

Let us use our God-given ability to separate man-made doctrines and traditions from the truths and commandments of our Creator so that we may please Him. Let us not be blinded by man-made traditions and doctrines that seek to bind us to another master. And let us be free to study the Word of God unencumbered so that we might more fully comprehend and appreciate the complexity of God's Master Plan and yet the simplicity and beauty of salvation through Yeshua HaMashiach (Jesus Christ).

A Search for Truth

*Be diligent to present yourself approved to
God as a workman who does not need to be
ashamed, handling accurately the word of
truth (II Timothy 2:15).*

I (PAM) am of Greek heritage and was Greek Orthodox for thirty-three years. Then one extremely hot day in August, I stayed home from my auto parts store to move a load of gravel from the front yard to the back yard. After completing this insane task, I took a shower and was settling down for a rest when the door bell rang. It was a very tall, elderly gentleman who informed me that he had come to the neighborhood to share about Jesus. I quickly informed him that I was a Christian, that I was baptized Greek Orthodox, and did not need to know more.

Somehow he managed to keep me open-minded for the next three hours, at which time he said that he would like to have a Bible study for me and my wife. He was going to come for six weeks on Wednesdays for one hour. He ended up coming for six months for three to five hours each week. I finally told him that I believed what he was saying was correct and I accepted the Lord as my Savior.

As I continued to study the Word of God, my growth in the knowledge of Scripture was increasing in leaps and bounds. Then the next major event in my Biblical education occurred. I picked up a copy of the Bible in Greek and began to examine it by researching and studying every word in an English-Greek lexicon. I soon began to thoroughly study my Greek grammar and came to some very interesting conclusions. I realized that there were errors in the English translations of the Bible. I also realized that in many cases, the wording was extremely shallow in conveying the meaning as expressed in the original Greek. But even this was not to be the most exciting event in my studies.

Like most Christians, I had been taught that the New Testament was originally written in Greek and the Old Testament in Hebrew. However, as I continued to study, I found that the wording of the first four gospels of the New Testament seemed to be an attempt to express ideas from a language and culture other than Greek. I wondered: If the Gospels were originally written in Judea (or possibly in Antioch, the largest Christian community of the earliest Church), by Jews, about a Jew in Jewish culture, could it be that the Greek was, in fact, attempting to express the Hebrew language and Jewish culture? This required further investigation.

I began to look in my local Christian bookstore for material and found very, very little. Then I decided to check a Jewish bookstore, the only one located some 100 miles away in Los Angeles. I ended up going into a place called Chabbad House which was run by the Lubovich, the ultra-orthodox rabbis. This was the beginning of my education in the Hebraic roots of the Bible. As my knowledge of the Hebraic context of Scripture grew, my God was being revealed to me in ways that cannot even be explained. I realize that if God had not preserved the Jewish people and their books (including the Bible), most spiritual truth and surely all the culture of Scripture would have been lost to traditions of men.

I went on to complete a course of studies at Bethesda Bible College in San Diego, after which I was ordained as a minister under Bethesda Bible College, affiliated with Assemblies of God. Later, I began my own nondenominational ministry. Since 1981, I have devoted myself to in-depth study of the Hebraic roots of the Bible, including a study of the original Greek and Hebrew.

The truth, depth, and beauty of God's Living Word is powerfully revealed when studied in its Hebraic context. Prophetic patterns and timetables emerge which confirm that the Bible is, beyond a shadow of a doubt, the inspired Word of God. This book is an attempt to provide those earnestly seeking spiritual truth an in-depth study of God's Master Plan, as it relates to His loving plan of salvation for his most beloved creation—humankind. From the earthly Paradise of the Garden of Eden to the Crucifixion and finally to the Millennial Kingdom, God's Master Plan is revealed.

REVEALING THE PATTERNS OF GOD'S WORD

*Thou wilt make known to me the path
of life; In Thy presence is fulness of joy; In
Thy right hand there are pleasures forever
(Psalm 16:11).*

I (RVM) enjoy studying the Word of God! The more I study, the more I realize how well-designed God made His creation to fit His needs; how particular He was about prophecy pointing directly to the center of attention— Jesus the Messiah; and how magnificently He has everything under control! Whenever God allows me to uncover another nugget of truth from His Word, I am able to see that events, time schedules, and places all fit together to form amazingly detailed patterns that are completely beyond the realm of chance.

I was taught about the crucifixion of Jesus from the time I was old enough to talk. I remember the flannel graphs my Sunday School teacher would use to show three crosses with Jesus in the middle. I remember going to church service with my parents and two sisters on

Thursday night before "Good Friday" to commemorate the Last Supper; then going to Sunrise Service on Easter morning, singing the great old hymn "He Arose," and seeing rows of white Easter lilies lined up in the front of the sanctuary.

These are precious memories—family memories—times that taught me about the greatest love gift mankind has and will ever know—the gift of salvation through the death and resurrection of the Lord Jesus Christ. I accepted Jesus as Savior of my life in Vacation Bible School, and even though there were times that I was mundane about my relationship with the Lord, I never changed my mind about what Jesus did for me at Calvary almost 2,000 years ago.

It was while I was in college that I was challenged to read the Bible by a friend named Glen Van Ekeren. I guess I felt I knew all I needed to know about Christianity, and didn't think that the Bible had any information that was relevant for my life in the 1970's. I thought it was just a compilation of some nice stories. I found Glen reading his Bible and I asked him if he was studying for a test. We were attending a Christian liberal arts college and were required to take religious classes. He told me that he was reading his Bible just for his personal enjoyment. I respected Glen and his relationship with Christ, so I opened my Bible to I Corinthians (this is where it fell open) and began to read.

It didn't take me long to realize that the Bible was a blueprint for living in any day and age. The principles for godly living are timeless, and the distractions to pull people away from God and into sin are also still the same as they were during Biblical days. As Solomon so wisely observed: "...there is nothing new under the sun" (Ecclesiastes 1:9).

After I received the baptism of the Holy Spirit on June 1, 1975, I noticed that my thirst for the Word was stronger than ever before. I would read and read and couldn't seem to get enough. I remember also being frustrated because I felt that I was just reading without gaining a deeper understanding of the truths that were written on the pages. However, as my love for the Lord grew, so did my belief that if my heart stayed pure He would instruct me.

I have been fortunate to have worked with Christian organizations almost all my life, and have met some great teachers of the Word. I remember thinking to myself, "I wish I knew half the things this guy's forgotten," as I would listen to one Bible teacher after another pouring out what He had learned from studying the Word of God.

I understood that salvation comes only through belief in the death and resurrection of Jesus Christ to complete the payment for my sins and I understood the importance of maintaining a godly lifestyle. However, many writings of both the Old and New Testaments were still either a mystery to me or not much more than a storybook. The Old Testament, for instance, was no more than a history book at best, with examples of how God had helped various people out of some difficult situations. It was meant to teach us that God created the world, directed people's lives, and was very hard on the Canaanites and the Philistines! The Old Testament appeared to concentrate on wars, blood sacrifices, anger, laws, and prophecies that seemed to me both boring and irrelevant.

The New Testament seemed to be more centered on love and godly instruction and was more applicable to the conduct of one's life. However, the books of Hebrews and Revelation were difficult for me to understand and therefore largely ignored.

These opinions began to change when someone introduced me to a book by Josh McDowell called *Evidence That Demands a Verdict*. The section on the fulfillment of Old Testament prophecies by Jesus the Messiah opened my eyes to the fact that the two books were connected. The Old Testament was a mirror of the New Testament and needed to be studied in order to get a better understanding of the Lord's mission while He was on earth.

Now that I saw a connection between the Old and New Testaments, more spiritual lights of understanding began to flicker on in my mind. I became even more excited about the pattern of perfection that seemed to be unfolding in the person of Jesus Christ, as His New Testament life, death, resurrection, ascension, and promised return fit the description of His Old Testament self-portrait. I also realized that I had a great desire to visit the Holy Land. By the end of 1975, I began asking God to allow me go to Israel, and in January of 1986, He granted my request.

I will never forget the thrill I felt as I walked the land of the Bible for the first time. It dramatically changed the way I read the Word of God. I have been blessed in having had the opportunity to take several groups of Christians to Israel, and now the number of times I have been on this pilgrimage are in the double digits. My trips to Israel have made the Bible a three-dimensional book to me, and have helped immeasurably in my understanding of the Scriptures. Every time I go, I learn more, and I owe this delight to the tremendously knowledgeable tour hosts whom I have been privileged to serve.

Two of these hosts have been particularly instrumental in challenging me to go deeper in my scriptural dig for the truth. One is Evangelist Perry Stone from Cleveland, Tennessee and the other is Peter A. Michas of Messengers of Messiah International Ministries in Troy, Illinois. Both men showed me connections between the Old and New

Testaments that I had no idea even existed. Moreover, they showed me that the Bible is a Hebrew book and thus can be better understood if the student also understands the background of Hebraic law, traditions, and history. This meant becoming familiar with such books as the Mishna, the Talmud, the Midrash, and others.

Because we will be using information from some of this outside material, let me share something else that I have learned as a rigid premise that must never be compromised. The Bible is the unerring Word of God (in its original Hebrew and Greek). Other resource materials must be viewed as supplements but never substitutes for Holy Scripture. Some of this material can be so fascinating that it can lead a person to believe that the Bible must be wrong if discrepancies surface. This is a terrible mistake that has been made by more than one well-meaning, over-eager student who has forsaken his/her first love by getting bogged down in a law from which we have been set free through Christ Jesus.

However, if these outside sources do not contradict the Word of God, they can be valuable tools to use in gaining clarification and a deeper understanding of the Bible. In some cases, Scripture seems to take for granted that we know things that most of us do not know unless we have studied Hebraic law and customs. For instance, Scripture assumes that we know what the law states about the purification of the Jews and the significance of the six stone water pots that are mentioned in John 2:6 at the wedding in Cana of Galilee. Without this understanding, we could not fully appreciate the great symbolism of this first miracle of Christ, Who revealed Himself as the ultimate Purifier of humanity through His blood.

Another example is an understanding of the *tallit,* or prayer shawl, and its Biblical significance. The tallit is referred to in Numbers 15:38 ("garments") and Mark 5:27

("cloak"). This outer, seamless and four-cornered garment was worn by all adult Israelite males. Scripture explains that a tassel (*tzitzit*) was attached to each of the four corners as a symbol and reminder of the 613 commandments God had given to His People. From Jewish sources, we know that Hebrew letters represent numbers as well as letters. In this light, the numerical value of the word *tzitzit* plus the total number of the tassel's strands and knots is highly significant—613—the number of commandments God gave the Israelites.

Taking this understanding with the Talmud's teaching that an unclean person could be stoned to death if he or she were out in public during the day, the story of the woman with the issue of blood (Mark 5:25-34) comes to life in our mind's eye with much more clarity. This woman was unclean according to the Law and yet was out in public during daylight hours. She touched the hem of the Lord's cloak (prayer shawl) and was miraculously healed. However, she was not too eager to tell everyone about her miracle because, by law, she could have been stoned to death! Suddenly, we gain a much deeper appreciation of how the woman touched the symbol of the Law but was healed by the Giver of the Law, and why she was so afraid to testify about her healing.

There are many other examples but I think the point is clear. These additional resources are very helpful in gaining a richer understanding of Scripture when they are used with wisdom in supporting, rather than superseding, the Biblical writings. It is in this spirit of an honest quest for truth that Hebraic roots resource materials have been included in this book.

Occasionally, other resources can at first appear contradictory to Scripture. However, upon closer examination, the discrepancy is usually found to be in traditional thought rather than in Scripture. Also, I have come to realize that the original language of the Bible is inerrant but subsequent translations may not be. Thus, in many cases, it is critical to refer to the original Hebrew and Greek in order to have a clearer understanding of the originally intended meaning.

We owe Bible translators a tremendous debt of gratitude for the sacrifices they made to translate the original Hebrew and Greek into the English language. It is this labor of love that has allowed the Word of God to be understood by all English-speaking people (including me). However, there are occasions when translator bias or incomplete understanding may be written into the translation, especially if the Hebrew or Greek word used has more than one English meaning. As you read this book, this will become evident.

The centerpiece of *The Rod of an Almond Tree in God's Master Plan* is the crucifixion, resurrection, and ascension of Yeshua the Messiah (the Hebrew name of Jesus is "Yeshua," meaning "Salvation," Matthew 1:21). In examining these events, many new ideas will be revealed. Some of these ideas conflict with traditional teaching, but the intent of this research is not to generate controversy for the sake of controversy. Rather, it is to demonstrate that the events leading to the crucifixion were divinely orchestrated. Thus, it becomes abundantly clear that every detail fits into the prophetic picture that is painted in the Old Testament. This picture is a masterpiece of precision beyond anything humanly possible and leaves no doubt that Yeshua is the Messiah.

Many of the conclusions derived use a method of logical thinking called deductive reasoning. My children's school math books often use this type of reasoning in problem-solving. Squares are shown with numbers in them, and some of the squares are left blank. However, the numbers are laid out in a developing pattern so the student can reasonably assume that the numbers fitting the blanks fit the pattern set forth in the rest of the numerical sequence.

Example:
1) 1 2 3 [__] 5 [__] [__] 8 9 [__] 11
2) 1 3 [__] [__] 9 [__] [__] 15 17 19 [__]
3) 2 3 5 [__] 17 [__] [__] 129 [__] [__] [__]

In example number 1, the pattern is to add each number by one. In example number 2, the pattern is to list odd numbers sequentially. These are two fairly easy patterns to decipher. The third example requires the problem-solver to multiply the preceding number by 2 and subtract one to arrive at the next number. It may not be as easy, but there is still a pattern that has been set up to guide the student in correctly completing the missing pieces to the puzzle.

Answers:
1) 1 2 3 [4] 5 [6] [7] 8 9 [10] 11
2) 1 3 [5] [7] 9 [11] [13] 15 17 19 [21]
3) 2 3 5 [9] 17 [33] [65] 129 [257] [513] [1025]

This "pattern" approach was used in arriving at some of the deductions expressed in this book. Occasionally, there was no research material available to explicitly answer all our questions. Some of the answers in the "squares" were missing, so we had to study the patterns given to us by God in His Word. We could then make deductions as to what fit those patterns and prophecies in order to fill in the blanks. Some of the patterns became quite complex, but perseverance was rewarded with understanding. When the patterns were understood, it became clear what answers would fit into the "blanks," because God does not change.

For I, the Lord, do not change... (Malachi 3:6).

... coming down from the Father of lights, with whom there is no variation, or shifting shadow (James 1:17).

Patterns are very important to God. In Exodus 25:9, God told Moses emphatically that He wanted the Tabernacle built exactly after the pattern that He would show him. God repeated this command in verse 40 and again in Exodus 26:30. Hebrews 9:22-25 also points out the importance of patterns in revealing truth. Yeshua predominantly taught in parables, which is a method of teaching a truth using an example or pattern. As Matthew 13 states:

> v. 34 All these things Jesus spoke to the multitudes in parables, and He did not speak to them without a parable,
>
> v. 35 so that what was spoken through the prophet might be fulfilled, saying, "I will open My mouth in parables; I will utter things hidden since the foundation of the world."

Therefore, if some of the answers are not specifically stated in Scripture, we used the divinely ordained patterns that were given to the children of Israel from which to draw our own conclusions.

There will likely be critics of this work because some of the traditions and assumptions that have been handed down for generations are being challenged. However, in following the Biblical command to "present yourself approved to God" (II Timothy 2:15) and to use the Word of God for "teaching, for reproof, for correction, for training in righteousness..." (II Timothy 3:16), we have spent countless hours and reams of rough drafts in formulating our ideas to follow the Biblical descriptions.

Our desire now is to paint a picture which mirrors illustrations we have gleaned from the instruction manual—the Bible. Too often, we found that the traditional teachings did not match all aspects of Scripture, which caused us to write this book. If the research and conclusions that we have presented adhere more closely to the Biblical writings than do the traditional teachings, then the burden of proof shifts to those who would adhere to these traditions rather than to the patterns found within Scripture.

The argument might be presented that questions why we should "stir things up." Most Christians seem to be content, for instance, in believing the crucifixion happened within the framework of traditional thinking. Why write something that might create waves and which could possibly cause division and hard feelings among believers?

I want my family to have the same precious memories that I spoke of at the beginning of this preface, but I would like those memories to be built on an accurate portrayal of the Biblical record. If God felt it was important to structure times, events, and places so precisely to point to His Son, I do not believe it is within our right to alter them so as to accommodate our traditions. We must make the change—not God!

Occasionally, Peter Michas, his wife, Christie, and I will compare our ideas with opposing viewpoints, but it is not our intent to address every idea that conflicts with ours in order to justify our viewpoint. The book would become too long and cumbersome. In most cases, we will simply state our deductions and let them stand on their own merit, to be critiqued by the reader.

With regard to the overall content of the book, Peter, Christie, and I agree on the major points and on most points of relatively minor significance. In those few areas where our opinions differ, Peter's views have taken precedence as he has done the majority of the research.

The reader will note that we use the Hebrew spelling of the Lord—Yeshua—instead of Jesus. This is a preference of Peter Michas. We lean so heavily on Hebraic sources in this book that he felt it would be appropriate in this setting, and I agree.

It is our sincere hope that there will be others who will build on the foundation of our research. We trust that they will either add to the knowledge gained, or find new evidence that will ultimately either solidify the deductions expressed or fine-tune them where necessary.

Have your Bible ready because several of the supportive scriptures are simply referenced rather than quoted. If we quoted every scripture used, this would quickly become a book of quotes rather than ideas. Therefore, we felt it would be better to point the reader to the passages upon which our ideas are built, so one can study both the references and related scriptures in order to come to one's own conclusions.

There are certain key foundational doctrines of faith that Peter Michas, Christie, and I agree upon and we want to state them here so there is an understanding of the basic tenets of faith before entering into this study.

Statement of Beliefs

We believe that the Hebrew and Greek Scriptures are the inspired and the only authoritative Word of God. We follow the Bible as God's only loving plan for the salvation of humankind.

We believe in one, true God, who is omnipotent, omniscient, and omnipresent. We believe in the unity of Father, Son, and Holy Spirit.

We believe in the deity of Yeshua (Jesus), the one and only Messiah and Lord. We believe in His virgin birth, in His sinless life, and in His miracles.

We believe in the redemptive work of His own blood, in His descending into Sheol Paradise, in His bodily resurrection, in His ascension to the right hand of the Father, and in His future return in power and glory with His Bride.

We believe that salvation for lost and sinful humankind is by grace alone, through the blood of Yeshua in atonement for sin, by the work of the Holy Spirit.

We believe in the present and continuous ministry of the Holy Spirit, whose presence within each true believer enables the believer to live—free of guilt and condemnation—a life on earth in a balanced godly way.

We believe that water immersion by one's own self in the presence of witnesses, as performed by John and continued into the second century, is a personal witness of one's own rebirth in Yeshua HaMashiach (Jesus Christ). However, we do not believe that baptism itself is a prerequisite of salvation.

We believe that God is sovereign and in complete control of healing by His grace.

We believe in the resurrection of the saved and their eternal life with God. We believe in the resurrection of the lost and their eternal separation from God.

We believe in the spiritual unity of all true believers in Yeshua—Messiah, Lord, and Savior. (Galations 3:28 "There is neither Jew nor Greek, there is neither slave nor free man, there is neither male nor female; for you are all one in Christ Jesus.")

The purpose of this book is not to challenge any of these foundational cornerstones of the Christian faith.

The purpose of this book is to rightly divide the Word of Truth; to clarify not only what Yeshua did but how and why He did it; and to understand how He made our glorious, eternal future possible.

With this understanding established, let's open the Bible and enjoy examining the beautiful master plan of the Creator, designed to point to Yeshua and His payment for the sins of mankind! We will start with the book of Genesis...

DEFINITIONS

GEMARA: The Gemara is the second and supplementary part of the Talmud, providing a commentary on the first part (the Mishna).

YESHUA: Yeshua is the Hebrew name of the Messiah, meaning "Salvation." "Jesus" is the English transliteration of the Greek name.

MIDRASH: The Midrash is a rabbinical commentary that studies and interprets the legal, ethical, and devotional aspects of Scripture. The *Midrash Halakhah* deals with the derivation of laws from the Bible. The *Midrash Haggadah* deals with the ethical and devotional ramifications of the Bible. It was written beginning sometime after the Exile and before the 6th century and completed in the 12th century.

MISHNA: The Mishna forms the basis of the Talmud. It is a collection of Jewish law and ethics and represents four centuries of Jewish religious and cultural activity in Palestine. It is divided into six parts known as *sedarim* (orders) which are subdivided into tractates, named after the principal subject discussed. The Mishna was compiled and edited by Rabbi Yehudah ha-Nasi and his colleagues at the beginning of the 3rd century.

PENTATEUCH: The Greek name for the first five books of the Bible.

SEPTUAGINT: A translation into Greek of the Hebrew Scriptures made several centuries B.C.E. and completed by the end of the 2nd century B.C.E.

TALMUD: The Talmud is a collection of rabbinical laws, law decisions, and comments on the Mosaic law. It represents the tradition, or oral Torah, that had been passed down by word of mouth from generation to generation. The oral law was believed to be based upon information that God orally conveyed to Moses from Mount Sinai, but which had not been recorded in the first five books of the Bible.

There are two versions of the Talmud, the Babylonian and the Palestinian, which consist of the Hebrew Mishna and the Aramaic Gemara. The Babylonian Talmud is more comprehensive than the Palestinian Talmud and is the one referred to in this book. At the end of the 3rd century, the Babylonian Talmud teachings began to be recorded. The *Halakhah* includes the commandments of the law. The *Haggadah* deals with the spiritual significance of the laws and also relates many historical events.

TANACH: The Tanach refers to the Hebrew Bible (Old Testament), including the Law or Instruction (Torah), the Prophets, and the Hagiographa ("writings," referring to the third and final part of the Jewish Scriptures).

TORAH: The Torah refers to the first five books of the Bible, as they were originally written in Hebrew. It is the inspired Word of God as given to Moses and is 100% accurate as written in the original language. This accuracy has been preserved in subsequent Hebrew copies recorded down through the generations to the present time. The Torah contains the history of the world's creation; the laws of Adam, Noah, and Moses; and the history of the formation of the nation of Israel and how they came to be the Chosen People.

THE TORAH ANTHOLOGY: *The Torah Anthology* was written by Rabbi Yaakov Culi, one of the greatest Sephardic sages of his time, and first published in 1730. It is considered to be one of the best commentaries ever written on the Torah—in any language—and is a veritable encyclopedia of Jewish knowledge. In 1967, Rabbi Aryeh Kaplan began an English translation which was completed by Rabbi Eliyahu Tonger after Rabbi Kaplan's death.

The Biblical translations in *The Torah Anthology* are highly accurate. There is also a high degree of accuracy concerning Hebrew historical events, but there is also a great deal of legend material. Many rabbis believe that the legend material contains a great deal of accurate information. The authors of this book doubt the overall accuracy of much of the legend material but realize that it does contain certain accurate elements of truth which must be critically ascertained in the course of research and study.

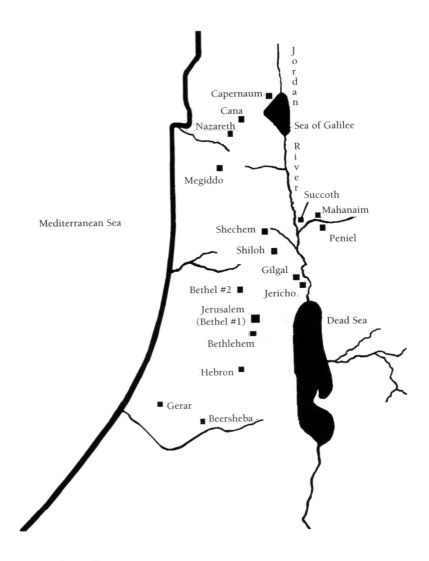

Map of Israel

1

THE LIGHT OF THE MESSIAH

*Then God said, "Let there be light"; and
there was light. And God saw that the light
was good; and God separated the light from
the darkness (Genesis 1:3-4).*

In Genesis 1:3-4, the Word of God is as magnificent as it is simple in expressing how God began to form our world. The moment God spoke, a metamorphosis of universal proportions was set into motion.

However, as one reads and examines the entire account of Creation, an undeniable question arises. Genesis 1:3 states that God created light on the First Day of creation. Yet, the sun, moon, and stars which provide light to our planet were not created until the Fourth Day (Genesis 1:14-19). The question is: How could there be light before the sun existed?

Some feel that the answer is simply a mystery beyond the comprehension of humankind and will be left a mystery until God decides to reveal it. It is true that there is much we cannot comprehend yet must accept as fact because we believe in the infallibility of God's Word (in its original Hebrew and Greek). The Bible is the unshakeable standard of truth. Indeed, the Scriptures speak of the profound and infinite knowledge and wisdom of God: "How unsearchable are His judgments and unfathomable His ways!" (Romans 11:33).

Notwithstanding, we have a mandate to "Be diligent to present yourself approved to God as a workman who does not need to be ashamed, handling accurately the word of truth" (II Timothy 2:15). Certainly, we will not have all knowledge in this lifetime (I Corinthians 13:12). Realizing this, we should never discard our trust in God simply because we do not understand everything about Him. Furthermore, we are commanded to continue to study the things that are written in the Word of God because they were put there for our instruction and understanding.

THE FIRST LIGHT OF CREATION

The light of creation and its relationship to subsequent events of creation is a mystery that has baffled both Christian and Jewish scholars. For the believer, it is one of those mysteries accepted as truth, yet remaining incomprehensible.

The Torah Anthology highlights two differing perspectives related to the events of creation.[1] These two viewpoints were expressed by two rabbis in a discussion among the Sages concerning the order of creation. According to Rabbi Yehudah, the Torah (first five books of the Bible) was to be interpreted literally with the understanding that the events of creation took place in six literal days. A contrasting opinion was offered by Rabbi Nehemiah, who believed that creation was spoken into existence in the first instant of God's words. According to this concept, successive days of creation merely revealed the specifics of what had already been initiated at the moment of creation.

The authors believe that both of these great scholars of God's Word were correct in their ideas of the order of creation. Rabbi Yehudah was correct in stating that the universe was created in six days. However, Rabbi Nehemiah was also correct in his belief that all the plans, blueprints, purposes, structure, timing, etc. for this creation were composed on Day One. In other words, the intangible plans were completed on Day One but the physical manifestation of these plans began on Day Two. Certainly, it would be impossible to comprehend the magnificence of God's creation without coming to an understanding of the light that was revealed on that First Day.

THE LIGHT'S BRILLIANCE

The light that was revealed on Day One of creation was completely unlike any other light in its brilliance and qualities. Rabbinic literature refers to it as the "Primeval Light" and that it was spiritual in nature.[2] One opinion concerns the intensity of the Primeval Light as being seven times brighter than the sun.[3] In this regard, it is interesting to note that Isaiah 30:26 refers to a light seven times brighter than that of the sun that will illuminate the world when the Messiah returns. Some rabbis interpret the Isaiah passage to refer to a literal and miraculous "increase in the radiance of the heavenly luminaries."[4]

However, a prophecy given by Yeshua in Matthew 24 sheds further light on this matter:

> v. 29 "But immediately after the tribulation of those days THE SUN WILL BE DARKENED, AND THE MOON WILL NOT GIVE ITS LIGHT, AND THE

> STARS WILL FALL from the sky, and the powers of the heavens will be shaken,
>
> v. 30 and then the sign of the Son of Man will appear in the sky, and then all the tribes of the earth will mourn, and they will see the SON OF MAN COMING ON THE CLOUDS OF THE SKY with power and great glory."

Could it be that this light, seven times brighter than the sun, is none other than the Light of the Messiah, the Light of the world, and the Light spoken of in Genesis 1:3-4? If so, would not all the peoples of Earth witness the Light of the Messiah when He returns?

Regardless of the exact intensity of this light, it is certain that it was spectacular in its illuminating qualities, vastly exceeding any other source of light in the universe. How exciting to know that this wondrous light will be given to the righteous in the hereafter (Colossians 1:12). It would appear that the righteous have a very bright future indeed!

THE NATURE OF THE LIGHT

What was the nature of this light? Let us examine the Hebrew in context for a deeper insight. First, let us consider the light spoken of in verses 3-5 of Genesis 1:

> v. 3 Then God said, "Let there be light"; and there was light.
>
> v. 4 And God saw that the light was good; and God separated the light from the darkness.
>
> v. 5 And God called the light day, and the darkness He called night. And there was evening and there was morning, one day.

The Hebrew word, *or*, is translated "light" in the above verses.[5] The literal meaning of this word is "illumination" or "luminary." Its root word means "to be, cause, or make luminous" and "enlighten," and may be used literally and/or metaphorically.[6]

In the metaphorical sense, it refers to light of a spiritual nature. Just as the true believer is referred to as a "light" in the world (Matthew 5:14; Phillipians 2:15), so too the Messiah is referred to as "The Light" of creation. Therefore, the light referred to in verses 3-5 is a direct reference to the Messiah! God calls the Light of the Messiah "good" and sets it apart from the "darkness."

Rabbinical understanding also reveals the light of Genesis 1:4 to be associated with Messianic fulfillment. By study of the numerical equivalence of Hebrew words (gematria), the light of creation is shown to be related to the light of Torah, God's instruction according to the 613 commandments given in the first five books of the Bible.[7] In John 1:1, Yeshua is referred to as the Word, the meaning of which is identical to Torah. Again, this is a direct reference to Yeshua as the Light and the Word (Torah) of God.

The darkness referred to is not merely the absence of physical light, but is also used in the metaphorical sense to mean spiritual darkness. According to *The Torah Anthology*, the Hebrew word translated "darkness" in this passage also alludes to the Death Angel, implying a spiritual significance.[8] In essence, this conveys a picture of a spiritual void and darkness enveloping the world at this time.

Interestingly, God formed the light out of the darkness, meaning that on account of the darkness, light had to be revealed.[9] As light overcame darkness in the spiritual realm, so too this pattern became mirrored in the physical (natural) realm. That is why day follows night and why night and day are considered "one day." The Jewish timetable embodies this concept with each new day beginning at sunset, followed by daylight, and ending just before the following sunset.

In Genesis 1:16, another Hebrew word, *meorah*, is also translated as "light."[10] It refers to a "luminous body" or "luminary." This word is derived from the same Hebrew root word, *or*, discussed above. In this case, however, it refers to the moon and the sun:

> v. 16 And God made the two great lights, the greater light to govern the day [sun], and the lesser light to govern the night [moon]...

Therefore, a clear distinction can be made between the nature of the light in verse 16, as compared to the light referred to in verses 3-5. One of the most brilliant Jewish Sages, Rabbenu Malbin, raised a profound question: "Why is light of day one called 'or'—and of day four: 'meoroth'?"[11] The answer is to be found in the realization that the light of the Messiah on Day One preceded the light of the sun, and reflected light of the moon, on Day Four!

As David wrote in Psalm 104, when he described the Lord as Creator:

> v. 1 Bless the Lord, O my soul! O Lord my God, Thou art very great; Thou art clothed with splendor and majesty,
>
> v. 2 Covering Thyself with light as with a cloak, stretching out the heaven like a tent curtain.

Delving deeper into the Hebrew of Genesis 1:3, we find that there are two Hebrew words translated "let there be light." The word meaning "light" has already been discussed. The other Hebrew word literally means "let be." The word "there" does not appear in the original Hebrew but has been added for clarification. In fact, the Hebrew word that means "let be" is a masculine form and therefore refers to "him," rather than "it." Therefore, the Hebrew can validly be translated as "Let Him be Light." In this way, the Messiah is revealed in the original Hebrew words! An expanded translation of Genesis 1:3-5, including its metaphorical meanings, is:

v. 3 And Elohim said, "Let Him be Light [life, natural and spiritual; prosperity; honor; joy and all manner of happiness in this world and the next; encouragement; comfort; hope in adversity; the saving knowledge of Elohim and of the Messiah]" and He was Light.

v. 4 And Elohim saw [the revelation of] the Light that [the knowledge and wisdom of it] was good. And Elohim separated the Light from the darkness [spiritual darkness, spiritual ignorance, spiritual deception].

v. 5 And Elohim spoke, "You will be the Light" [Messiah; Word of God], until darkness [Lucifer; spiritual darkness] is defeated. And Elohim called the darkness a state of spiritual chaos and confusion. And [Lucifer] was the evening [the originator of spiritual darkness] when spiritual truth began to be obscured, and there also was the morning [the Word of God, Light, Truth] as Light dawned [prosperity and happiness] the first age.

God expressed Himself through this Primeval Light when He commanded the Light to be revealed. By His Word, God's knowledge, wisdom, and purpose for this world burst across the chaotic waters in a blinding revelation of God's glory.

THE COST OF LUCIFER'S REBELLION

How did the spiritual and physical chaos referred to in Genesis 1:2 come about? In order to find the answer to this question, we must consider Lucifer, the angel who rebelled against God. Lucifer was created by God and given the highest position among all the angels (Ezekiel 28):

> v. 12 "You [Lucifer] had the seal of perfection, full of wisdom and perfect in beauty.

> v. 14 "You were the anointed cherub who covers, and I [God] placed you... on the holy mountain of God..."

A unique aspect of Lucifer is that he was created with an anointing, meaning that he was given a special purpose. He was commissioned "to cover" or "to protect" (from the Hebrew root word *sachach*) and placed in the Garden of Eden (Ezekiel 28:13).

However, Lucifer became proud because of his unique anointing and position. He had been given the knowledge of God, knowing the difference between good and evil—light and darkness. Desiring to be equal with God, his ambition was to be worshipped as the Most High. As he rebelled against his Creator, sin originated in him. Instead of Lucifer, meaning "Lightbearer," he became known as Satan, the Adversary, and the father of darkness. Chaos quickly ensued as Satan corrupted and disrupted the natural order of God's creation.

This scenario explains why the "earth was formless and void" as described in Genesis 1:2. Though some believe that God initially created the world in a chaotic state which He later made orderly, this is inconsistent with the character of God. The Bible reveals the Creator to be orderly in everything He does. Furthermore, Scripture specifically indicates that God did not create the earth in a wasted condition (Isaiah 45:18). Therefore, a gap in time seems to exist between the events described in the first two verses of Genesis 1:

> v. 1 In the beginning God created the heavens and the earth.

v. 2   And the earth was formless and void, and darkness was over the surface of the deep; and the Spirit of God was moving over the surface of the waters.

The Hebrew words, transliterated as "*haytah tohu vabehu*" and translated as "without form and void," may indicate a subsequent event. From this Hebrew phrase, it is impossible to know how much time elapsed between the events described in verses 1 and 2. However, it can be surmised that at some point, a disruption of the orderly nature of creation occurred.

God's response to this chaos and spiritual darkness was to place His Light, Yeshua—the Word, order, knowledge, and life—into the world. As His Spirit hovered over the waters of a corrupted world, God gave this Light as knowledge of Himself. In this way, humanity could have fellowship with the Creator and understand Who was responsible for the creative work that was about to unfold.

This understanding is very powerful and exciting to an individual who has accepted Yeshua as the Messiah. As it should be, this remarkable and profound connection between the Light and the Messiah is consistent within the Hebraic context.

THE ORIGIN OF SIN

Into this newly recreated world, God would now put His new and perfect humanity, with the understanding of obedience or disobedience to His commands. However, he would also leave Lucifer, the father of darkness, in the earth realm. God's gift to Lucifer before his rebellion had been the kingdoms of this earth and "The gifts and the calling of God are irrevocable" (Romans 11:29). For this reason, Satan will remain in this world until the Final

Judgment, at which time he will be cast into the Lake of Fire with all who rebelled against God, including the kingdoms (powers) of this world.

God created Adam in His image and placed him in the Garden of Eden. We should understand that God creating man in His own image refers to the spirit of God being breathed into man, not that God has a physical body in the identical form of man. The very essence of the life-giving force of God was breathed into the soul of man. This does not make man a "little god," but an eternal living being.

Adam was created as a whole being, complete in form, containing a balance of male-female and a balance of logic-emotion. Then God separated from Adam another Adam as a helpmate (Genesis 2:21-22; Genesis 5:2). Adam named her Eve and they were designed to work together as one complete being. To Adam and Eve, God gave the knowledge and choice of obedience or disobedience to His commands.

Satan wanted desperately to regain complete control over this new world. He shrewdly chose a moment when the two were separated to deceive Eve. Satan promised Eve the very thing that he coveted when he rebelled against God—to be as the most high God:

> For God knows that in the day you eat from it
> your eyes will be opened, and you will be like
> God, knowing good and evil (Genesis 3:5).

Eve followed what Satan had instigated—disobedience and rebellion against God. Likewise, Adam followed Eve's advice and also ate the forbidden fruit. When God asked them: "Who told you that you are naked?", He knew that they had been exposed to the knowledge of good and evil, with evil presented as good and good presented as evil. Because Adam and Eve failed to act as a unit, they became vulnerable and succumbed to darkness and disobedience to God.

The human race would now need the full manifestation of the Light that God placed into the earth realm for redemption. This was God's preeminent One, the Messiah, the only One of uncorrupted truth, the Light to the world—Yeshua Himself. Not only did God provide the Messiah as the only means of salvation but He also gave each individual the choice to accept or reject the Messiah's redemptive gift.

THE LIGHT OF THE WORLD

In the New Testament, the Greek word translated as "the Light" of God is *phos*, which derives from the word *phao* ("to shine").[12] These words can also be traced to another Greek word, *phone*, meaning "voice," "saying," or "language."[13] The Septuagint (Greek Old Testament) uses the word *phos* for "light" in Genesis 1:3-5. In fact, this word refers not only to the physical brilliance of the Light but also to the Light of God's Word. Moreover, this Light refers to the Word incarnate—the Messiah Yeshua. In this, the meaning of John 1: 1-5, 14 is clearly revealed:

v. 1   In the beginning was the Word, and the Word was with God, and the Word was God.

v. 2   He was in the beginning with God.

v. 3   All things came into being by Him, and apart from Him nothing came into being that has come into being,

v. 4   In Him was life, and the life was the light of men.

v. 5   And the light shines in the darkness, and the darkness did not comprehend it....

v. 14 And the Word became flesh, and dwelt among us, and we beheld His glory, glory as of the only begotten from the Father, full of grace and truth.

There is only one thing that can save an individual from spiritual darkness: knowledge of the truth of the Creator. God's first words to the world contained the knowledge of Himself, the very essence of Himself, the Word of God. This was the light that shone so brilliantly on Day One. It was the gift of the Light of God, the Primeval Light that was revealed to a world which had been consumed in chaos and darkness.

God's Master Plan, formulated on Day One, contained every detail of God's plan in unparalleled precision. The light contained the knowledge of God, including the plan for the creation of a perfect universe, and the redemptive plan for humankind, which was implemented after the fall. This is what was meant in Colossians 1:13-23:

> v. 13 For He delivered us from the domain of darkness [void of the true knowledge of God, the end result being eternal separation from God], and transferred us to the kingdom of His beloved Son [the Light of God and eternal life],
>
> v. 14 in whom we have redemption, the forgiveness of sins.
>
> v. 15 And He is the image of the invisible God, the first-born of all creation. [The word "first-born" is translated from the Greek word *pro-totokos* which means to be preeminent in position rather than to be created or having a beginning of one's existence.[14] It indicates a birthright position over all creation, given to Yeshua by the Father.]
>
> v. 16 For by Him all things were created, both in the heavens and on earth, visible and invisible,

whether thrones or dominions or rulers or authorities—all things have been created by Him and for Him. [All things were created for the purpose of pointing humanity to Yeshua, the Messiah, Creator, and Savior of the world.]

v. 17 And He is before all things, and in Him all things hold together.

v. 18 He is also head of the body, the church; and He is the beginning, the first-born from the dead; so that He Himself might come to have first place in everything.

v. 19 For it was the *Father's* good pleasure for all the fullness to dwell in Him,

v. 20 and through Him to reconcile all things to Himself, having made peace through the blood of His cross; through Him, I say, whether things on earth or things in heaven.

v. 21 And although you were formerly alienated and hostile in mind, *engaged* in evil deeds,

v. 22 yet He has now reconciled you in His fleshly body through death, in order to present you before Him holy and blameless and beyond reproach—

v. 23 if indeed you continue in the faith firmly established and steadfast, and not moved away from the hope of the gospel that you have heard, which was proclaimed in all creation under heaven, and of which I, Paul, was made a minister.

Verse 23 clearly states that all creation proclaims the Gospel, God's Master Plan of salvation, and the Messiah as its fulfillment. God provided a path of redemption by providing knowledge of Himself through Yeshua, in order to reconcile humanity to Himself (II Corinthians 5:18-19).

The purpose of the master plan was to point humankind to its Creator and Savior, Yeshua, so that man would not lose the knowledge of God and remain in a state of darkness. This is why David wrote in Psalm 19:

v. 1   The heavens are telling of the glory of God; And their expanse is declaring the work of His hands.

v. 2   Day to day pours forth speech, And night to night reveals knowledge.

Timothy concurs, writing in I Timothy 6:

v. 15   ...He Who is the blessed and only Sovereign, the King of kings and Lord of lords;

v. 16   who alone possesses immortality and dwells in unapproachable light; whom no man has seen or can see. To Him be honor and eternal dominion! Amen.

By understanding what and Who the first light was, it is easier to comprehend other passages of Scripture. The following is a short selection:

...God is light, and in Him there is no darkness at all (I John 1:5).

Again therefore Jesus spoke to them, saying, "I am the light of the world; he who follows Me shall not walk in the darkness, but shall have the light of life" (John 8:12).

But if we walk in the light as He Himself is in the light, we have fellowship with one another, and the blood of Jesus His Son cleanses us from all sin (I John 1:7).

There was the true light which, coming into the world, enlightens every man (John 1:9).

"I have come as light into the world, that every-one who believes in Me may not remain in dark-ness" (John 12:46).

The Lord is my light and my salvation... (Psalm 27:1).

For God, who said, "Light shall shine out of darkness," is the One who has shone in our hearts to give the light of the knowledge of the glory of God in the face of Christ (II Corinthians 4:6).

Thy word is a lamp to my feet, and a light to my path (Psalm 119:105).

Jesus therefore said to them, "For a little while longer the light is among you. Walk while you have the light, that darkness may not overtake you..." (John 12:35).

"While you have the light, believe in the light, in order that you may become sons of light" (John 12:36).

The people who walk in darkness will see a great light; those who live in a dark land, the light will shine on them (Isaiah 9:2).

Arise, shine, for your light has come, And the glory of the Lord has risen upon you.

For behold, darkness will cover the earth, And deep darkness the peoples;

But the Lord will rise upon you, And His glory will appear upon you.

And nations will come to your light, And kings to the brightness of your rising (Isaiah 60:1-3).

No longer will you have the sun for light by day, Nor for brightness will the moon give you light; But you will have the Lord for an everlasting light, And your God for your glory (Isaiah 60:19).

These are just some of the Old and New Testaments passages which bear witness to this Light. The Primeval Light of God contained all knowledge. The details of a new span of time, including the plan of creation and its future, were contained in its essence. Every "i" was dotted and every "t" was crossed. Nothing was overlooked. This was the Light of God, with which nothing else could compare. Once this master plan was composed and the blueprint completed, the construction process began on the Second Day. The props were positioned in the first six days of creation, but the production of the script has continued and will continue to run its course until the entire plan is completed.

It is our pleasure to present to you some of the highlights of God's Master Plan contained in the Light of Creation: how it has been and will be revealed. Day One contained the blueprint of the prophetic timetable and the redemptive pattern. Now God's Master Plan would begin to unfold...

Notes

1. Rabbi Aryeh Kaplan, *The Torah Anthology*, Vol. 1, p. 51.
2. Rabbi Michael L. Munk, *The Wisdom of the Hebrew Alphabet*, p. 174.
3. Munk, p. 174.
4. Rev. Dr. I. W. Slotki, *The Soncino Books of the Bible: Isaiah*, p. 145.
5. James Strong, *The New Strong's Exhaustive Concordance of the Bible*, #216.
6. Strong, #215.
7. Rabbi Benjamin Blech, *The Secrets of Hebrew Words*, p. 30.
8. *The Torah Anthology*, Vol. 1, p. 54.
9. *The Torah Anthology*, Vol. 1, p. 54.
10. Strong, #3974.

11. Zvi Faier, Translator, *Malbim: Beginning and Upheaval*, p. 52.

12. Strong, #5457.

13. Strong, #5456.

14. W. E. Vine, *Vine's Expository Dictionary of Old and New Testament Words*, Vol. 2, p. 104.

2

THE LOCATION OF THE GARDEN OF EDEN

"The land of Israel is at the center of the world;
Jerusalem is at the center of the land of Israel;
the Temple is at the center of Jerusalem…"
(Midrash Tanhuma, Kedoshin 10).

On Day One, the Almighty revealed His Master Plan— the Light of His Word—throughout the universe. The Creator had intervened supernaturally to speak our new world into existence. Each subsequent day, as the plan began to unfold, earth with its water, land, and sky; vegetation; lights in the expanse of the heavens; and animals of all kinds came into existence.

God's ultimate creation was man, the only being created in the same spiritual image as the Creator. This unique spiritual nature of a human being makes possible a personal, spiritual relationship with the Creator. This should not be construed to mean that man is or has the potential of becoming a god. However, it does mean that every individual has the choice to invite the Spirit of the Holy One (Holy Spirit) to reside within his/her own spirit by accepting God's redemptive gift through Yeshua's sacrifice.

God pronounced His creation "good," meaning that it was in perfect order. Then God set aside the most fertile, exquisite place on earth, the Garden of Eden, where He could fellowship with man. There has been a great deal of conjecture as to the actual site of this unique garden.

Most scholars believe the Garden of Eden was located in Mesopotamia, where the ancient Babylonian civilization originated. Jewish legend lists the Land of Israel, Arabia, or the center of Africa as possibilities.[1] Others suggest India, where the Indus River flows. One source lists no less than nineteen possible sites proposed by scholars for this most remarkable garden.[2] Nonetheless, its exact location has never been pinpointed. Does the Bible itself provide specific information and insight that will enable us to resolve this controversy?

THE PATTERN FOR THE GARDEN OF EDEN

In this newly created world, God marked off an area of land called "Eden," and then God "... planted a garden toward [in] the east, in Eden; and there he placed the man whom He had formed" (Genesis 2:8). According to Malbin:

> *Mi-kedem* may mean 'in the east' — and it may mean 'prior to.' In respect of the last, our Sages have made the statement (Pesahim 54a): Seven things were created prior to the creation of the world... and Gan Eden [the Garden of Eden], since it says, *Mi-kedem*. The two meanings can be thought of as corresponding, respectively, to a spatial reference direction and a temporal one (or rather: one that is independent of time, being that 'prior to world' is tantamount, according to our

current understanding, to: unrelated to temporal duration). Consistent with this ambiguity in meaning — which is taken as implying that to both meanings must correspond aspects of reality — is the statement: *'Just as God created a Gan Eden on earth... He created a Gan Eden on high'* (emphasis added).[3]

The Bible indicates that certain things on Earth were patterned after things in Heaven. Examples of this are the Tabernacle and the Ark of the Covenant, which were made according to specifications given by the Creator (Exodus 25:9, 40; Exodus 26:30). Moreover, the New Jerusalem descending from Heaven, the heavenly counterpart of the earthly Jerusalem, is described in the Book of Revelation. In the same way, therefore, this fascinating concept of a dual, patterned creation may apply to the Garden of Eden.

THE LANDS OF THE EAST

Genesis 2:8 states that the Garden was positioned "toward the east." In general, Biblical references designating lands of the east apply to what is today commonly known as the Middle East. This would effectively preclude India and Africa as potential candidates for the location of the Garden of Eden.

In terms of specific references, the Old Testament mentions peoples called "sons of the east":

Then Jacob went on his journey, and came to the land of the sons of the east (Genesis 29:1).

For it was when Israel had sown, that the Midianites would come up with the Amalekites and the sons of the east and go against them (Judges 6:3).

And they will swoop down on the slopes of the Philistines on the west; together they will plunder the sons of the east; they will possess Edom and Moab; and the sons of Ammon will be subject to them (Isaiah 11:14).

Significantly, the Hebrew word, *qedem*, which translates as "east," is derived from the Hebrew word for "Eden." In fact, "*Qedem* ("East") already occurs in the Egyptian *Romance of Sinuhe* (c. 1900 B.C.) as a land near Canaan...".[4] The lands of Edom, Moab, and Ammon, as cited in Isaiah 11:14 above, were located respectively south, east, and north of the Dead Sea. This information confirms that the lands of the east and the Promised Land were closely associated.

Genesis 4:16 states that when Cain was expelled from Eden, he "settled in the land of Nod, east of Eden." Unfortunately, the location of the land of Nod is presently unknown. However, Scripture does tell us that Cain and his descendants were the first to build a city (Genesis 4:17). Archaeological evidence seems to indicate that the first city dwellers lived in the area called Canaan (for example, Jericho).

Only much later, after the Flood, did the Mesopotamian civilizations, including Babylon, develop. For this reason, it seems a likely possibility that the descendants of Adam and Eve actually settled in the area of what is today Israel and east of Israel. Given this understanding, Mesopotamia may be discarded in favor of the Promised Land, the most highly qualified and promising candidate for the location of the Garden of Eden.

THE FOUR RIVERS OF EDEN

The account in Genesis 2:10-14 gives specific information regarding four rivers in the Land of Eden. If we can locate these four rivers, our search area for the Garden of Eden will be much more clearly defined:

v. 10 Now a river flowed *out of Eden* to water the garden; *and from there* it divided and became four rivers (emphasis added).

v. 11 The name of the first is Pishon; it flows around the whole land of Havilah, where there is gold.

v. 12 And the gold of that land is good; the bdellium and the onyx stone are there.

v. 13 And the name of the second river is Gihon; it flows around the whole land of Cush.

v. 14 And the name of the third river is Tigris; it flows east of Assyria. And the fourth river is the Euphrates.

Please pay particular attention to the fact that there was a river that flowed *out of Eden*—not the Garden. The Land of Eden in fact comprised a very large area which will be described later. This particular river then flowed out of the Land of Eden to water the Garden of Eden. No information is given as to the distance from its source to the Garden.

Notice also that the next phrase "and from there" is commonly interpreted to refer directly back to the first river mentioned, meaning that the river itself directly divided into four other separate rivers. However, the single Hebrew word which translates as an English phrase "and from there" is ambiguous in the Hebrew context of the sentence. In other words, it may refer to "the garden" or it may refer back to "Eden."

Therefore, it is equally valid to interpret "and from there" as referring back to the Land of Eden rather than to the Garden of Eden. In this case, it would designate a common headwater source somewhere within the boundaries of the Land of Eden. Therefore, we should look for *four separate rivers which share a common headwater source somewhere within Eden.*

We should also recognize the possibility that this first river flowed for a certain distance within the Land of Eden before disappearing into a common underground water source from which the four rivers of Eden sprang. This concept is alluded to in *The ArtScroll Tanach Series*:

> Hirsch comments that some criticize the geographical description in this verse because it has been taken to refer to a river which divides into four streams, and no such river has been found...
> But רָאשִׁים [ra-ashe-im] *does not mean branches but four separate heads*. The river starts as a single stream... *it evidently disappears into the ground and springs up again in four different locations as four separate rivers* (emphasis added).[5]

Given the conventional interpretation of Genesis 2:10, a river that divides into four separate rivers has never been discovered. Perhaps with the insight gained from the above discussion, we will have an open mind to evaluating new possibilities. Certainly, we must also realize that the current geographical picture may be obscured. Geologists verify that many alterations in the earth's surface features have occurred over time, sometimes very rapid and dramatic transformations. Such changes could also complicate the original appearance and pattern of these four rivers.

As stated above, it is very plausible that underground waterways were involved. Indeed, the concept of underground waterways may provide an essential key to understanding the current and perhaps even past disposition of these rivers as it relates to their original source in the Land of Eden. Interestingly, Genesis 2:6 (NIV) makes reference to underground streams providing water to the surface:

> v. 6   But streams came up from the earth and watered the whole surface of the ground.

The authors have chosen the NIV translation of this passage because it more accurately translates אד as "streams." Other translations have used the word "mist" but the Hebrew word is more closely related to the word for "stream" than it is for the word "mist."[6]

Therefore, we must consider the possibility of underground waterways in an attempt to reveal the mystery of the Garden of Eden. At this point, the authors would like to propose the hypothesis that the missing Pishon and Gihon rivers are not lost at all but are instead currently flowing underground! Moreover, there is even the possibility that these rivers have been underground or partially underground since the beginning, but shared the same headwater source as the Tigris and Euphrates.

The Tigris and Euphrates Rivers

To this day, the Tigris and the Euphrates are clearly identifiable because their original names have been retained. Both rivers originate in eastern Turkey, flow southeastward, and join in southern Iraq before emptying into the Persian Gulf. The Euphrates River (about 1700 miles long) and the Tigris River (about 1180 miles long) form the extensive and historic Tigris-Euphrates River System, which has been referred to as the "Fertile Crescent."

In ancient times, this crescent-shaped region encompassed the river valleys of the Tigris and Euphrates from the Persian Gulf and curved south to the valley of the Jordan River, the land of Canaan. This extremely fertile area is also known as the "Cradle of Civilization" because it was the birthplace of the world's oldest known civilizations, including Sumer, Babylon, Assyria, Phoenicia, and Persia. Today, this region includes Iraq, Israel, Jordan, Lebanon, and Syria (Figure 1).

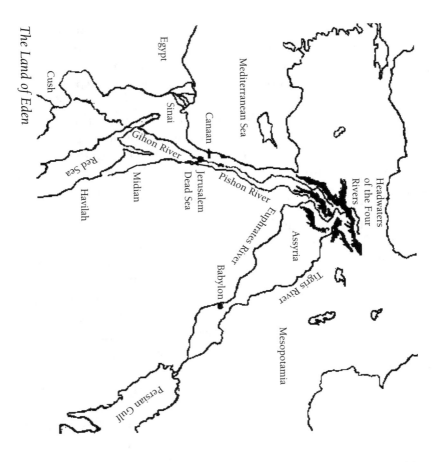

Figure 1

64

The Lost Pishon River

The other two rivers, the Pishon and Gihon, are unknown today. Their original locations have been a topic of much debate among Biblical scholars, scientists, and laymen alike. Identification of the lost Pishon and Gihon rivers would provide an essential key to unlocking the mystery of the true location of the Garden of Eden.

Genesis 2:11-12 says that the Pishon River flowed through Havilah, a land rich in gold, bdellium (fragrant resins), and onyx. Most Biblical scholars identify Havilah with southwestern Saudi Arabia.[7] In fact, an extremely rich gold mine, called the "Cradle of Gold" (Mahd edh-Dhahab), is found here, as well as remnants of an ancient mine, thought by some to be King Solomon's mine.[8] In addition, bdellium and precious stones are found southwest of this gold deposit, in what is today Yemen.[9]

Havilah connects to Canaan via the Arabah, a desert region from the Dead Sea to the Gulf of Aqaba. Interestingly, Jacob Ben Amir reported in the *Globes* newspaper that an annual flow of 140 million cubic meters of freshwater has been discovered flowing under the northern end of the Dead Sea.[10] In addition, within the past fifteen to twenty years, a tremendous water source has been discovered under the Arabah.

Experts estimate that there are approximately 75 billion cubic meters of water present under this desert! (Compare this to Israel's current water resources totaling 1.5 billion cubic meters.) Apparently, so great is the pressure of this water that it is beginning to push its way up to the surface, forming pools and promoting the growth of vegetation.

It is interesting to note that the Arabah has been a barren desert ever since Sodom and Gomorrah in the Dead Sea area were destroyed. However, before that time, this area was described as lush and green, "like the garden of the Lord" (Genesis 13:10) and capable of sustaining such large cities. Since a substantial freshwater supply is essential to sustain so much life, it seems likely there was such a source. Is it possible that the Pishon River once flowed closer to the surface through Havilah and the Arabah but subsequently became submerged, perhaps at the time of the destruction of these two cities?

As mentioned above, this underground water is now causing the desert to bloom. The prophet Isaiah foretold that this would occur, as recorded in Isaiah 35:

v. 1   The wilderness and the desert will be glad, and the Arabah will rejoice and blossom;...

v. 6   Then the lame will leap like a deer, and the tongue of the dumb will shout for joy. For waters will break forth in the wilderness and streams in the Arabah.

v. 7   And the scorched land will become a pool, and the thirsty ground springs of water; in the haunt of jackals, its resting place, grass becomes reeds and rushes.

This vast reservoir of water is now beginning to be used for irrigation to produce fruit and vegetables on what was useless land only a few years ago. The produce is not only being consumed in Israel but is also being exported to Europe in tremendous quantities. This huge, underground water source could certainly fit the Biblical description for the Pishon River!

The Lost Gihon River

The Bible tells us that the Gihon River originally flowed through the land of Cush. According to *The Zondervan Pictorial Encyclopedia*: "It would appear that originally Kush [Cush] referred to a piece of territory lying between the second and the third cataracts of the Nile."[11] Today, the Aswan High Dam is located at the first cataract of the Nile in southern Egypt. The third cataract lies in present-day Sudan, south of Egypt. Therefore, it would seem that the Gihon River was located in the area of what is today southern Egypt and northern Sudan.

Highly significant to our investigation is the possibility of an underground waterway that exists between Israel and Egypt. According to the first-century Jewish historian Josephus, there was a popular belief at that time that an underground river joined the Nile River and the Sea of Galilee. An unusual catfish (*Clarias lazera*) called "the water raven" by Josephus, is the only representative of its African family found in both the Nile and the Sea of

Figure 2

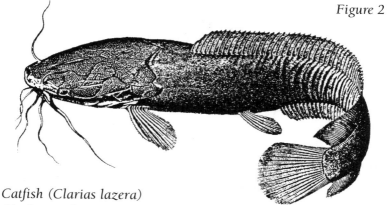

Catfish (Clarias lazera)
(Arabic Barbut, Hebrew Sfamnun, meaning Mustached Fish)

"This is an unusual fish, the sole representative of its African family.... Josephus Flavius refers to the catfish by its Greek name of "Korakinos," meaning Water Raven; he notes that it is found in the Nile. In his opinion, this fact supports the popular belief that there was an underground connection between the Nile and the lake, and that it emerged from below the ground at the largest spring at Tabgha." —(The Sea of Galilee and Its Fisherman in the New Testament by Mendal Nun, p. 10)

Galilee.[12] Apparently, this underground channel provided a conduit by which this catfish migrated from the Nile to the Sea of Galilee (Figure 2).

As confirmed by the authors, even fishermen today believe that this underground channel exists and emerges from the largest spring at Tabgha on the northwestern shore of the Sea of Galilee. It is intriguing and certainly meaningful that this was the same place where Yeshua chose his first disciples among the fishermen.

In regard to the Gihon River, there is also a tantalizing clue in Scripture that links the name "Gihon" to an underground spring in Jerusalem:

"And Zadok the priest and Nathan the prophet have anointed him king in Gihon..." (I Kings 1:45).

It was Hezekiah who stopped the upper outlet of the waters of Gihon and directed them to the west side of the city of David.... (II Chronicles 32:30).

The Gihon Spring still exists beneath the southeastern hill of Jerusalem, west of the Kidron Valley, where the "city of David" was built (Figure 3). In Old Testament times, it provided a substantial supply of water to the city.[13]

This particular water source must also have been considered unique because it was the place where Solomon was anointed (I Kings 1:32-40) and because water from this spring was mixed with the ashes of the red heifer to produce the "waters of purification." Is it just coincidence that this spring was named Gihon, or could there be a connection between the Gihon Spring and the Gihon River which watered the Garden of Eden? Is it possible that they shared the same source?

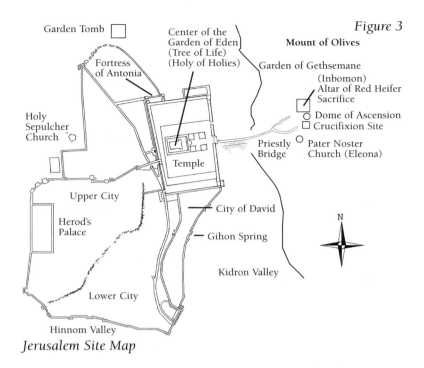

Jerusalem Site Map

JERUSALEM'S VAST UNDERGROUND WATER SOURCE

If the source of the Gihon Spring is, in actuality, the missing Gihon River, is there any evidence to show that the Gihon River currently flows beneath the city of Jerusalem?

According to an Israeli Defense film (1990), there is a vast amount of water under Israel. It is also known that an underground river runs under the city of Jerusalem. Local Arabs are aware of this water source. Five such individuals, ranging in age from mid-thirties to about mid-eighties, confirmed to one of the authors (RVM) that a river runs from the north side of the city, under the Temple Mount, and to the Pool of Siloam (into which the

Gihon spring flows). Even so, no one knows the river's origin or final destination.

One of the local Arabs was interviewed by Perry Stone and Robert Vander Maten in 1991. This gentleman makes his living by digging around and under the city of Jerusalem for hidden treasures. He described this river as a tremendous, powerful source of water that he has both seen and heard, and stated that it is located far below the streets of the city.

In addition, according to the local residents, there are no less than twenty-seven water wells located under the Temple Mount. On the northwest corner of the Temple Mount, the Sisters of Zion Church stands on the ancient site of the Antonia Fortress. Underground water constantly pours into the basement of this church and must be continually removed by pumps.

The fact that such a large source of running water flows under the Temple Mount is actually very consistent with the Biblical picture. During the time of the Temple, large amounts of running water were required for the priestly washings and animal sacrifices. For example, at the dedication of Solomon's Temple, thousands of animal sacrifices were performed (I Kings 8:63 and II Chronicles 7:5). According to Mosaic Law, the water used for such purposes could not be still (stagnant), but rather had to be "living," that is, running water.

Therefore, the existence of an underground river beneath Jerusalem is indicated. It has also been verified that a spring, called the Gihon Spring, is located beneath Jerusalem as it was in Old Testament times. Moreover, the only Biblical references for the name "Gihon" are in reference to the spring in Jerusalem and the Gihon River in the Garden of Eden. If the Gihon River does flow beneath

Jerusalem and provides the source for the spring by the same name, does the Bible provide any clues to link Jerusalem and the original Garden of Eden?

JERUSALEM AND THE GARDEN OF EDEN

The answer to this question is found in a truly remarkable reference from Ezekiel 28:13-14. It concerns Lucifer's presence in the Garden of Eden on "the holy mountain of God" (Ezekiel 28):

v. 12 "...You [Lucifer] had the seal of perfection, full of wisdom and perfect in beauty.

v. 13 "You were in Eden, the garden of God; every precious stone was your covering... On the day you were created...

v. 14 "You were the anointed cherub who covers, And I [God] placed you *there*. You were on the holy mountain of God..."

The "holy mountain of God" is a direct reference to Mount Moriah in Jerusalem! Today, Mount Moriah forms the platform for the Temple Mount. God selected Mount Moriah as the site of His Temple. Here, the first Temple was built by Solomon. After its destruction by the Babylonians, the second Temple was also rebuilt on this same site. And the Bible prophesies that the third Temple, as described by Ezekiel, will be established by the Messiah when He comes to set up His Millennial Kingdom. The prophets Ezekiel and Zechariah foretell that a tremendous amount of living (flowing) water will pour out from this Temple, the "house of God":

Afterward he brought me again unto the door of the house [Temple]; and, behold, waters issued out from under the threshold of the house eastward: for the forefront of the house *stood toward* the east, and the waters came down from under from the right side of the house, at the south *side* of the altar (Ezekiel 47:1, KJV).

And it shall be in that day, *that* living [flowing] waters shall go out from Jerusalem; half of them toward the former sea [Dead Sea], and half of them toward the hinder sea [Mediterranean]: in summer and in winter shall it be. And the Lord shall be King over all the earth: in that day shall there be one Lord, and His name one (Zechariah 14:8-9, KJV).

Therefore, the Bible clearly connects Jerusalem to the site of the original Garden of Eden, where God fellowshipped with Adam and Eve. In this regard, it is interesting that according to Jewish legend, Adam was created from the dust of Mount Moriah.[14] Furthermore, the Bible clearly shows that God will establish Jerusalem as the seat of the Messiah's Throne during the Millennial Kingdom.

Let us now summarize the information which has thus far been presented:

The four rivers of the Land of Eden shared a common headwater source. Both the Tigris and Euphrates Rivers arise from a headwater source in a mountainous area of eastern Turkey. The Euphrates River flows for a relatively short distance before connecting to a lake from which it subsequently flows and the Tigris originates very close to this same lake.

A tremendous underground water source exists beneath the area of the Arabah and the Dead Sea. Before the destruction of Sodom and Gomorrah, this area was fertile and lush. Today, this underground water source is pushing up to the surface creating a renewed fertility, as prophesied. This area fits the description of the land of Havilah, as it is mentioned in conjunction with the river Pishon. Therefore, the authors believe that this underground water does in fact represent the lost Pishon river. As such, it shared and continues to share a common source with the Tigris and Euphrates in eastern Turkey.

Evidence shows that an underground waterway flows beneath Israel, including the city of Jerusalem. In addition, it has been shown that an underground channel connects the Sea of Galilee to the Nile River in Egypt. In this regard, the underground waterway fits the description of the Gihon River which flowed throughout the land of Cush.

Significantly, it has been shown that the Bible designates the "mountain of God," Mount Moriah in Jerusalem, as the focal point of the Garden of Eden. In fact, a spring located near Mount Moriah is called the Gihon and represents an essential link to the Gihon River. This is consistent with the description of the river which watered the Garden of Eden. Because of this, the authors believe that this underground waterway represents the Gihon River and that it shared and continues to share a common source with the other three rivers in eastern Turkey.

EDEN, THE PROMISED LAND, AND THE NEW JERUSALEM

A logical conclusion based upon the previous discussion is that JERUSALEM IS THE SITE OF THE ORIGINAL GARDEN OF EDEN!

Scripture has been shown to support the concept that Jerusalem is the site of the original Garden of Eden. Indeed, Jerusalem is the only place that also fits the prophetic picture to come. The authors believe that the original Land of Eden, with Jerusalem as its center, consisted of the what is today Israel, Egypt, Jordan, Syria, Lebanon, Turkey, Iraq, western Iran, and Saudi Arabia (Figure 1). This region approximates 1500 miles square—

THE SAME DIMENSIONS OF THE NEW JERUSALEM WHICH WILL COME DOWN OUT OF HEAVEN! John describes the New Jerusalem in Revelation 21:

> v. 10 And he carried me away in the Spirit to a great and high mountain, and showed me the holy city Jerusalem, coming down out of heaven from God...
>
> v. 16 And the city is laid out as a square, and its length is as great as the width; and he measured the city with the rod, fifteen hundred miles; its length and width and height are equal.

Moreover, it is THE SAME AREA OF LAND THAT GOD PROMISED THE CHILDREN OF ABRAHAM AS AN EVERLASTING INHERITANCE! (Genesis 15:18-21; 17:8; Deuteronomy 11:24). As recorded in Genesis 15:18-21, God made a covenant with Abram:

> v. 18 ...To your descendants I have given this land, from the river of Egypt as far as the great river, the river Euphrates:
>
> v. 19 the Kenite and the Kenizzite and the Kadmonite
>
> v. 20 and the Hittite and the Perizzite and the Rephaim
>
> v. 21 and the Amorite and the Canaanite and the Girgashite and the Jebusite.

And in Deuteronomy 11:24, God promised that:

> Every place on which the sole of your foot shall tread shall be yours; your border shall be from the wilderness to Lebanon, *and* from the river, the river Euphrates, as far as the western [Mediterranean] sea.

Clearly, God promised the descendants of Abraham the land from the Mediterranean Sea to the Euphrates and from the Nile to the area that is today called Turkey. Unfortunately, Abraham's descendants broke this covenant by turning away from the only true God and turned, instead, to false gods (Deuteronomy 31:16,17; Joshua 23:16). Even so, God promised a future restoration of this land to the Israelites (Amos 9:11-15). And God promised that His Messiah would rule from Jerusalem, the center of His Millennial Kingdom.

According to rabbinical writings, God will reveal the location of the Garden of Eden during the Messianic Age.[15] If this is true, why would the Messiah choose a place other than the site of the original Garden of Eden as His seat in the Millennial Paradise?

In this regard, the actual meaning of the Hebrew word translated "garden" is revealing. The Hebrew word *gan* does not refer to a garden in the usual (European) sense of the word, i.e., a plot of ground cultivated with vegetables, fruits, flowers, or trees. Rather, it refers to a guarded enclosure, which is consistent with and supportive of the concept of Jerusalem as the original site of the Garden of Eden.[16]

This information is confirmed by the *Theological Wordbook of the Old Testament,* which lists the meaning of *gan* as "enclosure" or "garden."[17] The root word, *ganan,* means "defend," "put a shield about," or "protect." Further:

> The verb [ganan] and its derivatives occur about 130 times [in the Old Testament]. The basic idea of the verb is to cover over and thus shield from danger.
>
> *ganan* is used only in reference to the protective guardianship of God. Of its eight occurrences, six have to do with the Assyrian crisis in the days of Hezekiah. Isaiah assured the king that God

would care for Jerusalem like a mother bird hovering with wings spread over her young in the nest (Isa 31:5). God would protect Jerusalem in this crisis for his own sake and for the sake of David (Isa 37:35). The deliverance of Jerusalem would demonstrate to the world that God was faithful to his promises and mighty to deliver his people from their oppressors. Zechariah twice uses the same verb to describe the divine protection of God's people in their wars against the sons of Greece (9:15) and of Jerusalem in the last days (12:8).[18]

As explained above, all eight occurrences of the word *ganan* deal with Jerusalem. The fact that the final Scriptural usage of the word concerns Jerusalem in the last days further supports the concept that God started everything in Jerusalem and will also fulfill everything in Jerusalem. Nowhere else on earth is God more concerned, nor has He done and will continue to do more, than in Jerusalem.

Could it be that God foreknew from the moment of creation the seat of His Throne, from which He would ultimately rule and reign in the person of the Messiah after His glorious return to Earth? Did He also foreknow that the Garden of Eden would become the holy city of Jerusalem, and that the site of humankind's separation from God would become the site for its redemption and restoration to God? And is God so changeless that even the dimensions He established for the Land of Eden are equivalent not only to those of the Promised Land, but also to those of the New Jerusalem?

God is totally beyond man's finite ability to comprehend Him. He is omniscient, omnipresent, and omnipotent. He orchestrates times, places, and events magnificently and with absolute precision. It is inconceivable that

He would be haphazard in anything He does. He is the perfect, Holy, almighty God!

Additional compelling evidence that supports the concept of Jerusalem as the site of the original Garden of Eden will be discussed in the following chapters. However, let us now take a closer look at God's redemptive plan for man. Our search for deeper insight leads us to an essential piece of the puzzle: the actual site of the crucifixion...

Notes

1. Ellen Frankel and Betty Platkin Teutsch, *The Encyclopedia of Jewish Symbols,* p. 45.

2. Finis Jennings Dake, *Dake's Annotated Reference Bible*, p. 53.

3. Zvi Faier, Translator, *Beginning and Upheaval*, pp. 197-198.

4. Merrill C. Tenney, Editor, *The Zondervan Pictorial Encyclopedia of the Bible*, Vol. 2, p. 180.

5. Rabbi Meir Zlotowitz, Translator, *ArtScroll Tanach Series: Genesis,* Vol. I(a), p. 96.

6. Ehud Ben-Yehuda, Editor, *Ben-Yehuda's Pocket English-Hebrew Hebrew-English Dictionary,* Section 1, pp. 3, 86.

7. *The Zondervan Pictorial Encyclopedia of the Bible,* Vol. 3, p. 48.

8. James A. Sauer, "The River Runs Dry—Biblical Story Preserves Historical Memory," pp. 54, 57, 64.

9. Sauer, p. 64.

10. "Freshwater Was Discovered in the Northern Part of the Dead Sea," March 26, 1993.

11. Vol. 1, p. 1047.

12. Mendel Nun, *The Sea of Galilee and Its Fishermen in the New Testament,* p. 10.

13. Merrill C. Tenney, Editor, *The Zondervan Pictorial Bible Dictionary,* p. 314.

14. Alan Unterman, *Dictionary of Jewish Lore and Legend,* p. 141.

15. Frankel and Teutsch, p. 46.

16. The authors thank Israeli guide, Abraham "Pitch" Maayan, for this insight.

17. R. Laird Harris and others, *Theological Wordbook of the Old Testament*, Vol. 1, p. 364.

18. Harris, Vol. 1, p. 364.

3

THE MOUNT OF OLIVES

*And He said, "Take now your son, your only
son, whom you love, Isaac, and go to the
land of Moriah; and offer him there as a
burnt offering on one of the mountains of
which I will tell you" (Genesis 22:2).*

The Mount of Olives is a key site in both Old and New
Testament history. From the time of Adam, its summit
was ordained as a place of worship of the Most High God.
Though at times the Israelites themselves desecrated this
most holy place with the idols of false gods, God never
forgot His promise of a Messiah. And as we will see, the
Mount of Olives is the focal point in the fulfillment of
God's redemptive plan for humankind.

THE ALTAR OF SIN SACRIFICE

According to *The Torah Anthology*, Adam constructed
the first sacrificial altar.[1] Moreover, this same altar was
successively rebuilt by Abel, Noah, and Abraham.[2] In the
corresponding passages in Genesis (4:4; 8:20; 22:9), the
Hebrew word, *banah,* has been translated "built" in most

English versions. However, this word may also be translated as "rebuilt" or "restored" which, in fact, more accurately describes what actually took place.[3]

Where was this altar located and why was it so essential to God that it be maintained as the place of sin sacrifice? Only when we understand its significance with regard to God's Master Plan can we hope to answer these questions. This understanding will also lead to an even deeper appreciation for the beauty and precision of God's redemptive plan for each one of us.

Most Jewish scholars believe that, from Adam to Abraham, this particular altar was situated on Mount Moriah. However, it is clear two separate altars existed and must be differentiated. One altar is referred to in Genesis 12:

> v. 8   Then he proceeded from there to the mountain east of Bethel, and pitched his tent, with Bethel on the west...and there he built an altar to the Lord and called upon the name of the Lord.

In order to determine the location of these altars, we must first establish the identity of Bethel. Complicating the issue is the fact that the name Bethel was applied to two separate sites mentioned in the Bible. The later Bethel, 12 miles north of Jerusalem, was the site of a rival sanctuary established at the time of the divided kingdom (I Kings 12:27-29). However, the original Bethel is known to be identified with Mount Moriah in Jerusalem.[4]

Mount Moriah is profoundly significant in God's plan. Here, God fellowshipped with Adam and Eve in the Garden of Eden. Here, the Temple would be built where the Shekinah (Divine Presence) manifested inside the Holy of Holies. And here, the Messiah will seat Himself on a throne in His Temple during the Millennial Kingdom!

Most assuredly, Mount Moriah is of primary importance in God's prophetic work.

Equally important is the Mount of Olives, as we shall see. From the scripture cited above, it can be seen that Abram built an altar east of Mount Moriah (Bethel). The mountain opposite Moriah is the Mount of Olives and the authors believe that it was here that Adam built an altar of sin sacrifice. This line of reasoning is consistent in view of the fact that the Mount of Olives became the permanent site for the burning of all sin sacrifices and the place where the most holy sin sacrifice, the Red Heifer, was offered.

It also fits the pattern of the Garden of Eden as discussed in Chapter 2. For, given that the Tree of Life was on Mount Moriah, and that Adam was expelled east of the Garden, the sacrificial altar must have been built on the Mount of Olives.

Rabbinic sources confirm that the altar of sin sacrifice was located in Jerusalem opposite the "Throne of Glory."[5] The "Throne of Glory" refers to the Holy of Holies in the Temple. Since the Temple entrance was located on its eastern side, "opposite the Holy of Holies" clearly indicates the Mount of Olives (see Mark 13:3).

THE PURCHASE OF TWO ALTAR SITES

Evidence to support the idea that there were two separate and distinct yet closely associated altars can be found in I Chronicles and II Samuel. In chapter 21 of I Chronicles, David is instructed by "the angel of the Lord" to build an altar to the Lord on the threshing floor of Ornan the Jebusite:

> v. 18 Then the angel of the LORD commanded Gad to say to David, that David should go up and build [#6965, *qum*, meaning "confirm," "establish," "lift up"] an altar to the LORD

on the threshing floor of Ornan the Jebusite....

v. 22 Then David said to Ornan, "Give me the site of *this* threshing floor, that I may build [#1129, *banah*, "build," "rebuild"] on it an altar to the LORD; for the full price you shall give it to me, that the plague may be restrained from the people...."

v. 25 So David gave Ornan 600 shekels of gold by weight for the site.

v. 26 Then David built [*banah*] an altar to the LORD there, and offered burnt offerings and peace offerings. And he called to the LORD and He answered him with fire from heaven on the altar of burnt offering.

The threshing floor of Ornan purchased by David for 600 shekels of gold became the site for the Tabernacle. David's son, Solomon, would eventually replace the portable Tabernacle with the permanent Temple on Mount Moriah (II Chronicles 3:1). It is highly significant that gold was used to purchase this particular site because gold represents deity in the Bible. Indeed, the Divine Presence, as manifested by the *Shekinah* (Glory Cloud), dwelled in the Holy of Holies on top of Mount Moriah.

However, this was not the only site that David was instructed to purchase for the purpose of erecting an altar to the Lord. According to chapter 24 of II Samuel:

v. 18 So Gad came to David that day and said to him, "Go up, erect an altar to the LORD on the threshing floor of Araunah the Jebusite."...

v. 21 Then Araunah said, "Why has my lord the king come to his servant?" And David said, "To buy the threshing floor from you, in order to build an altar to the LORD, that the plague may be held back from the people."...

v. 24 ...So David bought the threshing floor and the oxen for fifty shekels of silver.

v. 25 And David built there an altar to the LORD, and offered burnt offerings and peace offerings. Thus the LORD was moved by entreaty for the land, and the plague was held back from Israel.

The threshing floor of Araunah purchased for 50 shekels of silver is separate and distinct from the threshing floor of Ornan purchased for 600 shekels of gold. The authors believe that the threshing floor of Araunah was located on the Mount of Olives and that the altar built by David was built on the same site where Abraham had offered his son Isaac.

It also became the site of the Red Heifer sacrifice and the place where all sin sacrifices were burnt. Again, there is a symbolic meaning to be found in the purchase price. With regard to the Tabernacle, silver symbolized redemption. This was to become the site of the future redemption of all humankind in the Messiah's sacrifice.

GOD'S COVENANT WITH ABRAHAM

The authors believe that Abram returned to this altar on the Mount of Olives at the time God made a covenant with him (Genesis 15). This covenant (promise) was sealed by the blood sacrifice of animals and was symbolic of the greater covenant to come—the covenant sealed by the blood sacrifice of Yeshua that is available to all who put their trust in Him. In making His covenant with Abram, God revealed significant details of His redemptive plan for humankind, including the place where the ultimate sacrifice would take place.

God promised Abram a multitude of descendants and renamed him Abraham ("father of multitudes") to reflect this promise. To his aged parents, Isaac was born in fulfillment of that promise. Years later, God called on Abraham to return with his son, Isaac, to the place where He had made a covenant with Abraham (Genesis 22):

> v. 2 ..."Take now your son, your only son, whom you love, Isaac, and go to the land of Moriah; and offer him there as a burnt offering on one of the mountains of which I will tell you."

Many scholars assume that Mount Moriah was the place God chose for this sacrifice. However, close examination of the passage reveals that God instructed Abraham to go to the "land of Moriah" and that once there God would direct him to the appropriate mountain for the burnt sacrifice.

The following example illustrates this distinction. In southern California, most residents are familiar with Mount Baldy, which has a relatively high peak with excellent ski slopes. A resident desiring to direct someone to the ski run on Mount Baldy would simple say, "Go to Mount Baldy where there is an excellent ski resort."

But if the resident wanted to direct someone to a ski run near Mount Baldy, he might say, "Go to Mount Baldy where I have some friends who can give you specific directions to another ski resort on a nearby mountain." In the same way, the authors believe that God first directed Abraham to the land of Moriah and then specifically guided him to the summit of the mountain that would later become known as the Mount of Olives.

After a three-day journey, Abraham "saw the place from a distance" (Genesis 22:4). He and Isaac left the two young men that had accompanied them thus far and took the wood, fire, and knife for the sacrifice. As they were walking (Genesis 22):

> v. 7   …Isaac spoke to Abraham his father and said, "My father!" And he said, "Here I am, my son." And he said, "Behold, the fire and the wood, but where is the lamb for the burnt offering?"
>
> v. 8   And Abraham said, "God will provide for Himself the lamb for the burnt offering, my son."

Abraham showed total trust in God. God had fulfilled His promise of a son when Abraham was 100 years old. God had also promised that Abraham's descendants would be as numerous as the stars in the sky. It is evident that Abraham trusted God to fulfill this promise as well. Perhaps he believed that God would resurrect Isaac, or perhaps he trusted God to make another provision in this special circumstance.

Since Isaac was no longer a child as is often depicted, but rather a young man in his thirties, it is clear that he voluntarily allowed his father to bind him for the sacrifice.[6] Surely, Isaac must have trusted God as much as Abraham. This picture foreshadows the willing sacrifice of Yeshua, in accordance with His Father's will. It seems that even His approximate age was indicated.

Just as Abraham took up the knife to sacrifice Isaac (Genesis 22):

> v. 11   …the angel of the Lord called to him from heaven, and said, "Abraham, Abraham!" And he said, "Here I am."
>
> v. 12   And he said, "Do not stretch out your hand against the lad, and do nothing to him; for now I know that you fear God, since you

have not withheld your son, your only son, from Me."

An interesting question regarding the angel is asked in *The Torah Anthology*: Why did the angel say, "you have not withheld your son...from Me"?[7] The authors believe the answer to this question is that the person referred to as an "angel" was no mere angel but, in actuality, a manifestation (theophany) of the Lord.

Another remarkable aspect of this event is pointed out by Phinehas Ben Zadok who states that there is an equally valid translation that can be made from the original Hebrew of Abraham's reply to Isaac concerning the lamb for the sacrifice:

God will provide Himself AS the Lamb[8]

This simple yet powerful statement contains a profound prophecy regarding the the promised Messiah. In His sacrifice was the ultimate atonement for the sins of all humankind. Yeshua, as God incarnate, fulfilled this prophecy by willingly offering Himself in our place so that the price for sin could be paid, in full, for all time!

THE PLACE WHERE GOD WAS WORSHIPPED

The first mention of the Mount of Olives by name in the Old Testament appears in the account of David's escape from Jerusalem. King David was surprised by an attempt by his son, Absalom, to seize the throne. In response, David fled the city for his life. II Samuel 15:23 states that he "passed over" the brook Kidron as he escaped Jerusalem. After crossing the Kidron Valley, David ascended the Mount of Olives.

The only way that David could "pass over" the Kidron Valley was by way of an arched stone bridge spanning the Kidron Valley, which connected the Temple Mount to the Mount of Olives[9] (Figure 4.) One thousand years later,

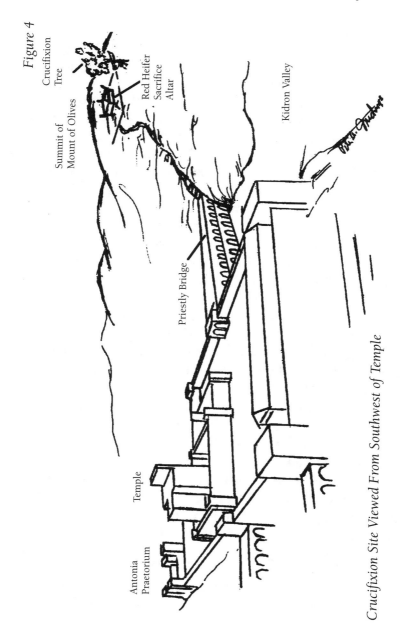

Figure 4

Crucifixion
Tree

Summit of
Mount of Olives

Red Heifer
Sacrifice
Altar

Kidron Valley

Priestly Bridge

Temple

Antonia
Praetorium

Crucifixion Site Viewed From Southwest of Temple

David's descendant, Yeshua, would also walk this same path "over" the Kidron Valley (John 18:1). Incidentally, this stone bridge provided the only ritually clean path by which the priests could take sin offerings from the Temple to the summit of the Mount of Olives, the site of the sin sacrifice altar. (The stone arch-over-arch design of the bridge ensured that the priests were protected from ritual uncleanness, such as the remains of dead bodies.)

After crossing the Kidron bridge, David followed this pathway which ascended the Mount of Olives "to the summit, where God was worshipped." In II Samuel 15:32, the Hebrew words *ha rosh* translate as "the summit." Other possible meanings are "the head," "the top," or "the skull." Any of these meanings is a direct reference to the highest point on the Mount of Olives, the site of the Red Heifer sacrifice, "the place where God was worshipped."[10]

This Old Testament clue brings to light the true meaning of one of the most important places mentioned in the New Testament—Golgotha. The Aramaic word *Golgotha* means "Place of the Skull" and is mentioned in Matthew 27:33; Mark 15:22; Luke 23:33; and John 19:17. (In Latin, the name is *Calvary*.) Note the similarity of its meaning to that of *ha rosh*, "the skull." Clearly, "the skull" does not refer to a literal skull but to a place that looks like a skull. In fact, Golgotha is the name of a specific place, the summit of the Mount of Olives, the site of the Red Heifer Altar, "the place where God was worshipped"! Even Hebrew translations of the New Testament use the words *ha rosh* to refer directly to the crucifixion site.

THE PLACE "OUTSIDE THE CAMP"

There are many Old Testament references to a designated place called "outside the camp." This is where sin sacrifices were burned:

But the flesh of the bull...you shall burn with fire outside the camp; it is a sin offering (Exodus 29:14).

"He shall carry the bull outside the camp, and burn it as he burned the first bull; it is the sin offering for the assembly" (Leviticus 4:21, RSV).

"The bull of the sin offering and the goat of the sin offering, whose blood was brought in to make atonement in the holy place, shall be taken outside the camp; their skin and their flesh and their dung shall be consumed in fire" (Leviticus 16:27, RSV).

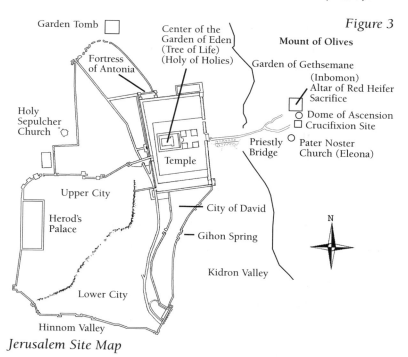

Jerusalem Site Map

The place "outside the camp" indicates a specific location ordained by God. During the time the Israelites lived in the wilderness, "outside the camp" was located directly east of the Tabernacle entrance, at a distance of 2000 cubits.[11] Here all sin sacrifices were burned, including those animals sacrificed inside the Tabernacle. It was also the place where the Red Heifer was sacrificed and burned, its ashes then used in purification rites.

Once the Israelites settled in Jerusalem, the Temple was built as a permanent sanctuary to replace the portable Tabernacle. The place called "outside the camp" retained the same specific designation in reference to the location of the sanctuary—2000 cubits east of the Temple. Marking the distance (3000 feet, a little over one-half mile), one comes to the summit of the Mount of Olives, at the site of the Red Heifer altar (Figures 3 and 4).

In addition, the place "outside the camp" was closely associated with a location referred to as "a clean place":

'...he shall... carry the ashes out to a clean place outside the camp' (Leviticus 6:11, RSV).

Then someone who is clean shall gather up the ashes of the heifer, and deposit them outside the camp in a clean place; and they shall be kept for the congregation of the Israelites for the water for cleansing. It is a purification offering (Numbers 19:9, RSV).

These both refer to the area of the altar on the Mount of Olives.

In the New Testament, there are only two references to this location:

For the bodies of those animals whose blood is brought into the sanctuary by the high priest as a sacrifice for sin are burned outside the camp (Hebrews 13:11, RSV).

Let us then go to Him outside the camp and bear the abuse He [Yeshua] endured (Hebrews 13:13, RSV).

Plainly, the place where sin sacrifices were burned was the same during the time of Yeshua as it was during Old Testament times. Not only that, verse 13 makes a direct reference to the place where Yeshua Himself suffered, the summit of the Mount of Olives. Quoting the entire passage in Hebrews from verse 11 through verse 13 (RSV), this fact is explicitly stated:

v. 11 For the bodies of those animals whose blood is brought into the holy place by the high priest as an offering for sin, are burned outside the camp.

v. 12 Therefore Jesus also, that He might sanctify the people through His own blood, suffered outside the gate.

v. 13 Hence, let us go out to Him outside the camp, bearing His reproach.

In the above passage, Paul refers to the particular place well-known to all Jews at the time as "outside the camp." Additional support that the Mount of Olives is indicated can also be found in the descriptive phrase "outside the gate" in verse 12. It refers to the Eastern gate which was directly east of the Temple entrance and opposite the Mount of Olives. Unmistakably, the crucifixion took place on the summit of the Mount of Olives, close to the altar used to burn all sin sacrifices!

IN THE PRESENCE OF GOD

The place of Jewish executions for blasphemers, which is what Yeshua was judged to be, was also "outside the camp":

Take the blasphemer outside the camp; and let all who were within hearing lay their hands on his head, and let the whole congregation stone him (Leviticus 24:14, RSV).

Then the LORD said to Moses, "The man shall
be put to death; all the congregation shall stone
him outside the camp" (Numbers 15:35, RSV).

According to Jewish Law, a person accused of committing the sin of blasphemy had to be tried, convicted, and killed "in the presence of God." Since God's presence resided in the Holy of Holies of the Temple, the only appropriate execution ground was the summit of the Mount of Olives. From this high point, the condemned man had a clear, unobstructed view of the only entrance to the Temple, on its eastern side. Thus, Yeshua died facing the Temple "in the presence of God" (Figure 3).

Beyond doubt, Yeshua was led like the Red Heifer (the holiest sin sacrifice) from the Temple through the Eastern gate, across the Kidron bridge, and up the ascent of the Mount of Olives to the summit. This was the only path from the Temple to the summit that afforded ritual purity necessary for an acceptable sacrifice. And, just as the Red Heifer's face was turned toward the entrance of the Temple as it was sacrificed, so too Yeshua died—the ultimate holy sacrifice—His face turned toward the Temple!

There is further scriptural evidence to show that the crucifixion occurred on the Mount of Olives. Scripture records that at the moment of Yeshua's death, the veil of the Temple was torn from top to bottom. This event was witnessed by the centurion (and others), who was so convicted that he confessed Yeshua as the "Son of God." As this veil was attached to the front of the Temple, the witnesses had to be on the Mount of Olives, the only place in Jerusalem affording the crucial vantage point required to witness this event (Chapter 11).

IN A GARDEN

Scripture identifies the place of the crucifixion as a garden (John 19):

v. 41 Now in the place where He was crucified there was a garden; and in the garden a new tomb, in which no one had yet been laid.

v. 42 Therefore on account of the Jewish day of preparation, because the tomb was nearby, they laid Jesus there.

The Greek word translated "garden" in verse 41 does not refer to a garden in the Western sense, but rather describes a "tree orchard." During the time of Yeshua, olive tree orchards covered a large area of the Mount of Olives, including the place called Gethsemane, where an olive oil press was located. Therefore, the Mount of Olives fits the actual Biblical description of the place where Yeshua was both crucified and buried.

Figure 5

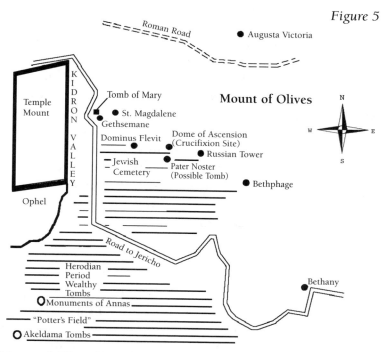

Mount of Olives Site Map

In addition, it is known that Jewish tombs were predominantly located on the Mount of Olives during the time of Yeshua (Figure 5). According to certain reliable sources, all Jewish tombs at this time were located on the Mount of Olives.[12] If this is the case, this factor alone confirms the Mount of Olives as the only possible site of both the crucifixion and burial.

HISTORICAL EVIDENCE

Historical records confirm that the earliest Christians knew that the Mount of Olives was the place of the crucifixion and resurrection. Eusebius, a church historian (264-340 C.E.), confirmed historical records written one hundred years earlier to this effect.[13]

Indeed, the Mount of Olives was the only place considered holy to the early Christians. The summit of the Mount of Olives, its highest point, became known as *Inbomon*. The word was derived from the Greek *en bommo,* meaning "high place" or "altar."[14] The site of the crucifixion is located very close to this place on the Mount of Olives.

Prior to the time of Constantine, Christians came from all over the world as pilgrims to a cave-crypt near the crucifixion site. This crypt was recognized as the tomb where Yeshua was buried and resurrected.[15] Because of its importance to Christians, the Eleona Church was built on top of this cave-crypt about three hundred years after the crucifixion.

Following its destruction by the Neo-Persians (614 C.E.), a chapel was rebuilt during the Middle Ages. According to tradition, this site marks the place where Yeshua taught the disciples the Lord's Prayer. In commemoration, a church was built in 1868 and named Pater Noster, Latin for "Our Father."[16] (See Figure 6 and Appendix I.)

Figure 6

Tomb Under Pater Noster Church

Now that the place of Yeshua's sacrifice for the sin of humankind has been firmly established, let us examine the origin of the first sin in the Garden of Eden. Central to this study is the Tree of Knowledge of good and evil...

Notes

1. Rabbi Aryeh Kaplan, Translator, Vol. 1, p. 281.

2. *The Torah Anthology*, Vol. 1, pp. 287, 375; Vol. 2, p. 332.

3. James Strong, *The New Strong's Exhaustive Concordance of the Bible*, #1129.

4. Ellen Frankel and Betty Platkin Teutsch, *The Encyclopedia of Jewish Symbols*, p. 81. Rabbi Meir Zlotowitz, Translator, *The ArtScroll Tanach Series: Genesis*, Vol. 1(b), pp. 1238-1239.

5. *The Torah Anthology*, Vol. 2, p. 332.

6. *The Torah Anthology*, Vol. 2, p. 321.

7. Vol. 2, p. 315.

8. *Which Day Is the Passover?*, p. 35.

9. Mishna, Parah 3:6.

10. Mishna, Tractate Parah.

11. Mishna, Tractate Parah.

12. Abraham Maayan and Chaim Melech, Israeli tour guides.

13. Ernest L. Martin, *Secrets of Golgotha*, p. 67.

14. Martin, p. 62.

15. Martin, p. 80.

16. Jack Finegan, *The Archaeology of the New Testament*, p. 97.

4

THE TREE OF THE KNOWLEDGE OF GOOD AND EVIL

When the woman saw that the tree was good
for food, and that it was a delight to the
eyes, and that the tree was desirable to make
one wise, she took from its fruit and ate; and
she gave also to her husband with her, and
he ate (Genesis 3:6).

In this chapter and the next, the significance of the Tree of Life and the Tree of Knowledge of good and evil will be discussed. Given that God created a literal Garden of Eden, it follows that the Tree of Life and the Tree of Knowledge were real trees in that Garden. Some consider the Biblical account of an earthly paradise with a Tree of Life and Tree of Knowledge as a purely metaphorical picture. However, if the Garden of Eden were an actual and not merely a figurative place, then the two trees mentioned actually lived and grew in the Garden.

If these trees actually existed, is it possible to know what kind of trees they were? Is is also possible to determine where they were located within the Garden? And most importantly, how does the literal reality of the trees, their type and location in the Garden, tie in to the symbolic meanings of God's Master Plan?

THE TREES OF THE GARDEN

New evidence recently discovered by geologists and archaeologists supports the view that at one time the land around Jerusalem was very heavily forested with many varieties of trees. Genesis 2 refers in general to the great variety of trees found in the Garden of Eden and in particular to the Tree of Life and the Tree of Knowledge of good and evil:

> v. 8   And the LORD God planted a garden toward the east, in Eden; and there He placed the man whom He had formed.

> v. 9   And out of the ground the LORD God caused to grow every tree that is pleasing to the sight and good for food; the tree of life also in the midst of the garden, and the tree of the knowledge of good and evil.

This passage specifies that the Tree of Life was located in the "midst" or center of the Garden of Eden. On the other hand, the Tree of Knowledge is merely mentioned without noting its particular position. Genesis 3:3, however, does define a spot for this equally important tree:

> v. 3   ...the tree [of knowledge] which is in the middle of the garden...

Note that the Hebrew word *tavek*, translated as "middle" in verse 3, can also be translated as "within," or "within the boundaries of," as well as "middle" or "midst."[1] This same Hebrew word appears in Genesis 2:9, where it has been translated "midst" as it refers to the location of the Tree of Life. Apparently, for the sake of consistency, *tavek* has been translated as "middle" or "midst" in the above passages of the English versions. It is the authors' opinion, however, that the Tree of Knowledge was within the boundaries, but not at the exact center, of the Garden.

Had the Tree of Life and the Tree of Knowledge been located together—either side by side or interwoven together—at the center of the Garden, it seems likely that Scripture would have noted this close relationship. Evidently, the two trees were relatively close to each other but not next to each other. This critical distinction will become evident as the authors continue to discuss the significance of these two trees. The Tree of Knowledge of good and evil will now be considered.

THE FIG TREE AND THE ORIGIN OF SIN

The forbidden fruit of the Tree of Knowledge of good and evil is generally portrayed as an apple. But is this an accurate representation, or can it be traced to another source?

It is known that in Greek mythology, the apple represented knowledge and was associated with Athena, the goddess of wisdom. Certain ancient statues of Athena even show her holding the apple in her hand. Therefore, it seems probable that the notion of the apple being the "forbidden fruit" of knowledge originated from Greek mythology rather than Hebraic sources. In order to determine the actual type of fruit involved, let us examine Biblical and Hebraic references.

As a result of eating the fruit of the Tree of Knowledge, Adam and Eve knew good from evil. They realized that they were "naked" which, according to the *ArtScroll Tanach Series*:

> ...signifies that they realized that they had
> stripped themselves of even the one precept with
> which they were entrusted [i.e. they were naked of
> obedience]...[2]

Further:

> Having eaten from the forbidden tree, Adam
> and Eve lost the consistent inner purity that
> enabled them to treat all bodily organs and func-
> tions as tools in the service of God. To this extent
> they had 'dishonestly' appropriated their bodies
> for the use of evil impulses, and found it necessary
> to clothe themselves to help control their new-
> found lust.[3]

Consequently, Adam and Eve's behavior immediately after
eating of the tree can be understood in terms of both a
physical and a spiritual nakedness.

Scripture states that they were ashamed and hastily
sewed fig leaves together to hide their nakedness (Genesis
3:6-7). It is the authors' conjecture that they picked the
closest leaves available to them at the time—fig leaves
from the tree of which they had just eaten! It does not
seem likely that Adam and Eve went running through the
Garden in their haste and shame looking specifically for a
fig tree because of the size of its leaves. Certainly there
had to have been many varieties of leaves to pick from,
including even larger ones. From this we may deduce that
the Tree of Knowledge of good and evil was actually a fig
tree. (Consistent with the concept of Jerusalem, not
Mesopotomia, as the site of the Garden of Eden is the fact
the the fig tree is indigenous to the Land of Israel, not to
Mesopotamia.[4])

The Torah Anthology confirms that the Tree of
Knowledge was a fig tree:

> When Adam and Eve ate the fruit, they realized
> that they were naked. Since the fruit they had eaten

was a fig, they made loin clothes out of fig leaves.[5]

In response to their disobedience (Genesis 3):

v. 22 Then the Lord God said, "Behold, the man has become like one of Us, knowing good and evil; and now, lest he stretch out his hand, and take also from the tree of life, and eat, and live forever"—

v. 23 therefore the Lord God sent him out from the garden of Eden, to cultivate the ground from which he was taken.

v. 24 So He drove the man out; and at the east of the garden of Eden He stationed the cherubim, and the flaming sword which turned every direction, to guard the way to the tree of life.

Adam and Eve had been given the freewill choice to obey or disobey God. They had chosen to disobey and the result was spiritual separation from their Creator. Neither they nor God could continue to enjoy the same perfect relationship because they had become sinful, and any object or person corrupted by sin must be expelled from the presence of the holy God.

God's denial of access to the Tree of Life under the circumstances was actually merciful for it prevented eternal separation from God and a world eternally engulfed in sin. Though physical and spiritual death had become a part of humankind's existence because of sin, God provided a way to bridge the gap and give each individual the choice between eternal life with the Creator or judgment and eternal separation.

THE TABERNACLE AS A PATTERN FOR THE GARDEN OF EDEN

The Tabernacle can be used as a pattern of the Garden of Eden. Note that the Tabernacle was the portable sanctuary containing the Ark of the Covenant during the time the Israelites were in the wilderness. The Temple, patterned after the Tabernacle, was later built on Mount Moriah in Jerusalem as the permanent sanctuary.

As the central reference point, let us choose the Holy of Holies, the inner sanctuary where God manifested His presence. The only entrance to the Tabernacle (and the Temple) was at its eastern side and the Holy of Holies was inside, at its western side.

Building upon the concept of Jerusalem as the center of the Garden of Eden, the Tree of Life grew on Mount Moriah in the exact spot of the Holy of Holies of the Temple! Here God had manifested His presence as He fellowshipped with Adam and Eve before they had sinned. Given this point of reference, Adam and Eve were expelled east of Mount Moriah, to the Mount of Olives:

According to *The Torah Anthology*:

> Adam was placed to the east [of Eden] and it was surrounded by angels of destruction, who would frighten him off if he attempted to reenter the Garden of Eden. Adam was placed to the east because, as the Talmud teaches, the Divine Presence is to the west. Since the entire intent of repentance is that one's eyes be lifted to God in a petition for atonement, God placed Adam to the east, so that he would gaze toward the west.[6]

The Divine Presence, as stated above, was located "to the west." Given that the Divine Presence was located on Mount Moriah, Adam and Eve would have been expelled to the east on the Mount of Olives.

It is known that Adam erected a sacrificial altar after he and Eve sinned. The authors believe this altar was placed on the summit of the Mount of Olives, eventually becoming the place where all sin sacrifices were burned

(Chapter 3). This site could be considered analogous to the Brazen Altar of the Tabernacle, where sin sacrifices were burned.

Inside the Tabernacle perimeter, the Brazen Altar was placed on its eastern side. It can be interpreted to represent the site of the Red Heifer sacrifice on the summit of the Mount of Olives, where Yeshua became the ultimate sacrifice for the atonement of sin. Although Adam and Eve were no longer allowed on Mount Moriah, no doubt they gazed toward the west, remembering the place where they had fellowshipped with God. Certainly, when they offered sacrifice for sin on the summit of the Mount of Olives, they must have looked toward the Divine Presence on Mount Moriah in repentance and hope.

Continuing to follow the Tabernacle pattern, and moving from east to west (towards the Holy of Holies), we move from the Brazen Altar to the Brazen Laver. The Brazen Laver contained the waters of purification and can be seen to symbolize the river of life (Gihon).

Then moving from the Laver toward the Holy of Holies, we come to the outer veil of the Holy Place, which may be seen to represent the eastern side of Mount Moriah. Past this point, another veil embroidered with cherubim formed the partition in front of the Holy of Holies. The veil with its cherubim symbolically represents the real cherubim who guarded the Tree of Life that grew at the site of the Holy of Holies.

Inside the Holy of Holies of the Tabernacle/Temple was the Ark of the Covenant, covered by the Mercy Seat where God manifested His presence. In the Garden, the Tree of Life grew in this same place and was where God manifested His presence to Adam and Eve! The Holy of Holies also marks the future Throne of the Messiah Yeshua when He returns to set up the Millennial Kingdom on earth.

(For an in-depth discussion of the Tabernacle and Temple, see *The Zondervan Pictorial Encyclopedia of the Bible*.)

THE FIG TREE AND THE MOUNT OF OLIVES

We know that the Tree of Knowledge of good and evil was located within the boundaries of the Garden of Eden. Given Jerusalem as the site of the Garden, let us look to Scripture for clues as to the possible position of this particular fig tree.

The area of Jerusalem was known to produce fig trees. In particular, the New Testament refers to a city called Bethphage ("house of unripe figs") that was located on the Mount of Olives.

Moreover, when Yeshua entered the city of Jerusalem the week of Passover, He singled out a particular fig tree and cursed it. He stated that He never wanted anyone to eat of its fruit again (Mark 11):

> v. 13 And seeing at a distance a fig tree in leaf, He went *to see* if perhaps He would find anything on it: and when He came to it, He found nothing but leaves, for it was not the season for figs.

> v. 14 And He answered and said to it, "May no one ever eat fruit from you again!"

As stated in verse 13, it was not yet "the season for figs." There are two seasons for figs: the winter season (May and June) and the summer season (August and September). However, the Jerusalem fig bears ripe fruit about one month later due to the cooler climate.[7] Since it was just prior to Passover, which generally falls toward the end of March or beginning of April, it was too early for ripe figs.

Of course, Yeshua knew it was too early for ripe fruit. His cursing of the fig tree was purely symbolic in nature.

The authors believe Yeshua cursed the tree whereby sin had entered the world—the fig tree! The authors also believe that the reason Yeshua singled out this particular fig tree was because it grew in the same place as the fig tree from which Adam and Eve ate, when they committed the first sin!

Yeshua, the Lamb of God, had come to break the curse of sin (Revelation 22:3). The only acceptable means of atonement for sin was through blood sacrifice as ordained by God (Genesis 3:21). And Yeshua knew when He cursed the fig that His time to fulfill His redemptive role was at hand.

The fig He cursed was on the Mount of Olives, where sin first came into the world and where He would shed His blood in atonement for all sin! As we can see, even the most intricate details were included in God's Master Plan, and every word and action of Yeshua pointed to His mission of redemption.

THE FIG TREE AS A SYMBOL OF ISRAEL

God chose Israel to be the caretaker of the Law. As Romans 9:4 states:

> who are Israelites, to whom belongs the adoption as sons and the glory and the covenants and the giving of the Law and the *temple* service and the promises,

Because of sin, God had to show humankind through laws and sacrifices what was required to have a relationship with Him. Furthermore, it was through the Law that humankind understood what sin was in the sight of God: "...through the Law comes the knowledge of sin" (Romans 3:20). The fig tree represents the nation of Israel in the role of the caretaker of the Law. In this connection, a relationship may be seen between the Law and the Tree of Knowledge since they both imparted a knowledge of good and evil.

In Luke 13:6-9, Jesus used the parable of the fig tree to represent Israel:

v. 6 And He *began* telling this parable: "A certain man had a fig tree which had been planted in his vineyard; and he came looking for fruit on it, and did not find any.

v. 7 "And he said to the vineyard-keeper, 'Behold, for three years I have come looking for fruit on this fig tree without finding any. Cut it down! Why does it even use up the ground?'

v. 8 "And he answered and said to him, 'Let it alone, sir, for this year too, until I dig around it and put in fertilizer;

v. 9 and if it bears fruit next year, *fine*; but if not, cut it down.'"

During His ministry, Yeshua had waited to see a change in Israel. He had waited to see if the nation of Israel would "bear fruit," that is, remain faithful to its calling and use the Law and the prophets to point the world to the Messiah.

We should remember that the first believers were Jews who recognized and accepted their Messiah. However, the nation of Israel, as a whole, did not recognize and accept the Messiah. Nevertheless, God has not rejected the nation of Israel, nor is He in any way finished with the Jewish people. If this were true, no one—Jew or Gentile—could ever be redeemed because "all have sinned and fall short of the glory of God" (Romans 3:23).

Because Yeshua had come to fulfill the Law (Matthew 5:17) and to set us free from the law of sin and death (Romans 8:2), salvation would never again be attainable through the Law. Yeshua's sacrifice provides full payment for sin for Jew and Gentile alike. This is why "there is neither Jew nor Greek, bond nor free, male nor female. We are all one in Christ Jesus" (Galatians 3:28). Romans 10:12-13 emphasizes this truth: "For there is no distinction between Jew and Greek [Gentile]; for the same Lord is Lord of all, abounding in riches for all who call upon Him; for WHOEVER WILL CALL UPON THE NAME OF THE LORD WILL BE SAVED."

In the Old Testament, it is stated that Israel was sole possessor of salvation. This was because they were entrusted with the knowledge of the plan through the Law (Deuteronomy 4:8). However, non-Jews could be "grafted in" by becoming proselytes—submitting themselves to the Mosaic Law, which was celebrated in anticipation of the Messiah. Therefore, salvation was not granted to an individual because of national origin, but because of belief in the one true God and obedience to the Law.

In the New Testament (New Covenant), both Jew and Gentile can possess salvation through the Fulfiller of the Law. The Law was not the perfect solution for sin because mankind could not achieve the demands of the Law. The perfect solution for sin was the fulfillment of the Law through Yeshua. The book of Hebrews emphatically states that we now have a new covenant (Hebrews 7:22; 8:6; 13:20). Yeshua invites each person to partake of this new covenant (Luke 22:20) stating that: "I am the way, and the truth, and the life; no one comes to the Father, but through Me"(John 14:6).

THE FIG TREE AND THE RETURN OF YESHUA

In Matthew 24, Yeshua taught the parable of the fig tree to explain the season of His return to earth:

> v. 32 Now learn the parable from the fig tree: when its branch has already become tender,

and puts forth its leaves, you know that summer is near;

v. 33 even so you too, when you see all these things, recognize that He is near, right at the door.

Understanding that the early season for figs symbolically represents the first harvest of believers at Pentecost (May/June), we may also understand that the final harvest of believers will occur during the late season for figs.

Given the insight that the Biblical Feast (Holy) Days God ordained represent a prophetic timetable, it is virtually assured that Yeshua's second coming will coincide with one of the Feast Day periods. Since the Jerusalem fig ripens in late September or early October, it seems probable that the Lord will return during one of the fall Festivals, Rosh HaShanah or Sukkot (Tabernacles). However, it is impossible to determine the exact day because both feasts span a period of more than one day.

Now that we have a fuller understanding of the Tree of Knowledge of good and evil, let us turn our attention to the Tree of Life. The Tree of Life is central to God's redemptive plan for humankind and its remarkable history can be traced from the Garden of Eden to the most important event in human history...

Notes

1. James Strong, *The New Strong's Exhaustive Concordance of the Bible*, #8432.

2. Rabbi Meir Zlotowitz, Translator, *ArtSroll Tanach Series: Genesis*, Vol. 1(a), p. 121.

3. Zlotowitz, Vol. 1(a), p. 124.

4. Nahum M. Sarna, Commentator, *The JPS Torah Commentary: Genesis*, p. 26.

5. Rabbi Aryeh Kaplan, Translator, *The Torah Anthology*, Vol. 1, p. 262.

6. *The Torah Anthology*, Vol. 1, p. 276.

7. Merrill C. Tenney, Editor, *The Zondervan Pictorial Encyclopedia of the Bible*, Vol. 2, p. 534.

5

THE TREE OF LIFE

*So He drove the man out; and at the east of
the garden of Eden He stationed the cherubim, and the flaming sword which turned
every direction, to guard the way to the tree
of life (Genesis 3:24).*

Out of all the trees of the Garden of Eden, the Tree of
Life and the Tree of Knowledge of good and evil were
the only trees to be singled out by name. As discussed in
the previous chapter, the Tree of Knowledge played a central role, both literally and symbolically, in humankind's
sin and spiritual separation from God.

In contrast, the Tree of Life will be seen to have played
the central role, both literally and symbolically, in
humankind's redemption and spiritual restoration with
God. From the day it was planted in the garden, its
unique purpose was to provide fruit which would give
humankind eternal life! What type of tree was the Tree of
Life and can we discover what happened to it? What significance does it hold in relation to God's Master Plan?

BETHEL AND THE ALMOND TREE

Of key importance to our investigation is a place called Bethel, where Jacob came face to face with the God of Abraham and Isaac. After receiving Isaac's blessing, Jacob made a journey. According to Genesis 28:

v. 11 …he came to a certain place and spent the night there…

v. 12 And he had a dream, and behold, a ladder was set on the earth with its top reaching heaven; and behold, the angels of God were ascending and descending on it.

v. 13 And behold, the Lord stood above it and said, "I am the Lord, the God of your father Abraham and the God of Isaac; the land on which you lie, I will give it to you and to your descendants."

v. 16 Then Jacob awoke from his sleep and said, "Surely the Lord is in this place, and I did not know it."

v. 17 And he was afraid and said, "How awesome is this place! This is none other than the house of God, and this is the gate of heaven."

v. 18 So Jacob rose early in the morning, and took the stone that he had put under his head and set it up as a pillar, and poured oil on its top.

v. 19 And he called the name of that place Bethel; however, previously the name of the city had been Luz.

What was this place that Jacob called "the house of God"? The place had been called Luz, but he renamed it Bethel, meaning "House of God." It seems that this site was very holy indeed and of particular significance to God. It was here that God repeated His promise to Jacob, the same promise He had made to Abraham and Isaac: this land was to belong to their descendants, His Chosen People.

Mount Moriah in Jerusalem is identified with the site of Jacob's dream.[1] From Genesis 28:19, we know that Mount Moriah was called Bethel at this time but at an earlier time had been known as Luz. Therefore, we know that Bethel and Jerusalem occupied the same site,[2] the site of the Garden of Eden.

This Bethel must not be confused with another city of the same name (I Kings 12:28-29), established north of Jerusalem by King Jeroboam (930-909 B.C.E.). The latter city was, in fact, a counterfeit of the original Bethel and intended to supplant the holy city God had ordained. The original city of Bethel later became known as Jerusalem, and the Temple—"the House of God"—was built on Mount Moriah, the same place where Jacob saw the ladder to Heaven in a dream or vision![3]

An essential clue relating to the Tree of Life is found in the earliest known name for Mount Moriah, *Luz*. It means "almond tree" in Aramaic, Arabic, and Ethiopic.[4] According to *The Torah Anthology*, the city of Luz was associated with an immense almond tree. In addition, it was thought that God, from the time of creation, had determined that the Death Angel would not have any power in this place so that its inhabitants would never experience death.[5]

This apparently symbolic picture may trace back to a real place which coincides with the concept of Jerusalem as the original Garden of Eden. Here, the Tree of Life—an almond tree—and the water of life (Gihon) which nourished it, were located in the center of the Garden. The Death Angel had no power in this place until Adam and Eve disobeyed God.

Later, God instructed Solomon to build His House, the Temple, where He had fellowshipped with Adam and Eve. The Holy of Holies was built directly over the place where the Tree of Life had grown! And the veil, embroidered with the two cherubim and placed in front of the Holy of Holies, was patterned after the actual cherubim assigned to guard the Tree of Life!

THE TRANSPLANTING OF THE TREE OF LIFE INTO THE GARDEN

Returning to the Garden, it is remarkable that rabbinic Sages accepted a concept of God transplanting the Tree of Life into the Garden of Eden. (See Chapter 2 for a discussion concerning the existence of both an earthly and a heavenly Garden of Eden.) According to Genesis 2:9, "And out of the ground the Lord God caused to grow every tree that is pleasing to the sight and good for food; the tree of life also in the midst of the garden, and the tree of the knowledge of good and evil." Malbin explains:

> The term 'planting' (*netiyah*) means, in the case of the trees, placing their seeds in the earth. Our Sages explain that the seeds which God had implanted were like locust horns, by which they are telling us that the seeds which were placed in the earth were very large. [As I have explained elsewhere, planting of large seeds can be described either by the term seeding (*zriyah*) or implanting (*shtila*). On the other hand, the verb 'to make grow' (*zmihah*) reveals in this verse that the trees matured as soon as they were planted, within the hour sprouting leaves and producing ripe fruit. The verse also stresses that He made it grow 'out of the ground' — which prompted our Sages to

deduce that the planting had not been done in this soil of the garden, but elsewhere. (Their declaration that the trees were implanted, can also be taken as saying that they were transplanted — the word *shtila* meaning the latter, as well)].[6]

This concept of transplantation of the Tree of Life is highly significant, for it ties into another profound possibility: that even a branch from this tree could be successfully transplanted (Chapter 6).

THE ROD OF GOD—A BRANCH FROM THE TREE OF LIFE

A fascinating connection may exist between a branch from the Tree of Life and a rod mentioned several times in the Bible. This rod has been variously referred to as the rod of God, the rod of Moses, and Aaron's rod (Chapter 6). According to Scripture, it miraculously budded *almond* blossoms and ripe fruit (Numbers 17:8).

According to the Haggadah (narrative of the Talmud), the rod, with blossoms and fruit, was created at the twilight between the sixth day and the Sabbath of Creation.[7] Compare this with God's planting the Garden of Eden, including the Tree of Life, on the last day of creation (Genesis 2:8).

At the time of Adam's expulsion from the Garden, God gave the rod to Adam.[8] From Adam, the rod was passed down through the generations until it came into the possession of Moses.[9] Interestingly, one story claims Moses' rod as having come from the Tree of Life.[10]

Tying these various bits of information together, a link to the story of Luz and its unique almond tree emerges. The conclusion drawn by the authors is that the rod of God was in actuality a branch from the Tree of Life, which was an almond tree!

Figure 7

Menorah

In light of this conclusion, it is highly significant that the Tree of Life was represented by the menorah,[11] a seven-branched candelabrum made in the form of *almond* branches decorated with almond blossoms (Exodus 25:31-37).[12] Moreover, the golden menorah was placed in the Holy Place of the Temple on Mount Moriah, where the original Tree of Life would have grown! (Figure 7).

THE FATE OF THE TREE OF LIFE

No one knows the fate of the Tree of Life as it stood in the Garden of Eden. Perhaps the source of the water of life which nourished it was removed. We can only assume that at some point in time, the fruit which sustained eternal life was no longer present and the cherubim, therefore, no longer required to stand guard before it. God, in His mercy, did not allow Adam and Eve to eat of its fruit because the result would have been eternal, spiritual separation from Him. Instead, a plan of redemption was provided for humankind to be restored to an eternal, spiritual union with the Creator.

Whatever the fate of the Tree of Life in the Garden, Revelation 22 seems to indicate that it will reappear in the New Jerusalem:

> v. 1 And he showed me a river of the water of life, clear as crystal, coming from the throne of God and of the Lamb,
>
> v. 2 in the middle of its street. And on either side of the river was the tree of life, bearing twelve *kinds of* fruit, yielding its fruit every month; and the leaves of the tree were for the healing of the nations....
>
> v. 14 Blessed are those who wash their robes, that they may have the right to the tree of life, and may enter by the gates into the city.

In Revelation 2:7, Yeshua states: "To him who overcomes, I will grant to eat of the tree of life, which is in the Paradise of God." This scripture seems to indicate that at the time John recorded the Book of Revelation, the Tree of Life was in Heaven and continues to be until its reappearance in the New Jerusalem. Perhaps it was the source of the Tree of Life in the earthly Garden of Eden!

In the next chapter, we will trace the history of the rod of God—a branch from the Tree of Life—as it passed through the generations of God's Chosen People.

Remembering that its source was the Tree of Life, its primary function as an instrument of God's redemption will be revealed...

Notes

1. Ellen Frankel and Betty Platkin Teutsch, *The Encyclopedia of Jewish Symbols*, p. 81.

2. Rabbi Meir Zlotowitz, Translator, *The ArtScroll Tanach Series: Genesis*, Vol. 1(b), p. 1239.

3. The research and insight of Peter A. Michas indicates that the ladder to Heaven had two legs: one leading up from the Holy of Holies on Mount Moriah and the other leading up from the Red Heifer Altar on the Mount of Olives. These two holy sites were in fact considered one composite holy place and were connected by the priestly path/bridge that led from Mount Moriah to Mount of Olives. The meeting of the two legs above Jerusalem represents "The Gate of Heaven" referred to in Genesis 28:17.

4. *The Jewish Encyclopedia*, Vol. 1, p. 434.

5. Rabbi Aryeh Kaplan, Translator, *The Torah Anthology*, Vol. 2, p. 182.

6. Zvi Faier, Translator, *Malbim: Beginning and Upheaval*, p. 203.

7. *Encyclopedia Judaica*, Vol. 14, p. 219.

8. *The Jewish Encyclopedia*, Vol. 1, p. 5.

9. *The Jewish Encyclopedia*, Vol. 1, p. 5.

10. Alan Unterman, *Dictionary of Jewish Lore and Legend*, p. 201.

11. Frankel and Teutsch, p. 106.

12. Frankel and Teutsch, p. 106. *The Torah Anthology*, Vol. 9, p. 72.

6

THE ROD OF GOD

*And David went up the ascent of the Mount
of Olives, and wept as he went…to the
summit, where God was worshipped…
(II Samuel 15:30-31).*

As mentioned in the previous chapter, God gave Adam
a branch from the Tree of Life, which was engraved
with the Ineffable Name of God (YHVH). Considering its
source, it must have been of supreme symbolic significance. But its literal history must have been of the utmost
importance as well.

Why did God give Adam a branch from the Tree of
Life and can we trace the account of this extraordinary
rod through the history of God's Chosen People? What
part does it play in God's Master Plan—past and future?
Remarkable revelations come to light as Scriptural and
historical clues are examined in the Hebraic context of
God's Word.

THE LEGACY OF THE ROD

The branch from the Tree of Life is referred to as a rod
or staff in the Bible and is known by various names: the

rod of God, Moses' rod, and Aaron's rod.[1] Tracing its history from Biblical and Hebraic sources reveals a fascinating story that links the past paradise of the Garden of Eden to the crucifixion and beyond, to the future heavenly paradise of the New Jerusalem.

According to rabbinical commentary and stories passed from generation to generation, the rod transferred from Adam successively down the line to Enoch, Shem, Abraham, Isaac, Jacob, Joseph, Moses and David.[2] According to the Midrash Yelamdenu:

> the staff with which Jacob crossed the Jordan is identical with that which Judah gave to his daughter-in-law, Tamar...[Genesis 32:10; 38:18]. It is likewise the holy rod with which Moses worked...[Exodus 4:20-1], with which Aaron performed the wonders before Pharaoh,...[Exodus 7:10], and with which, finally, David slew the giant Goliath...[I Samuel 17:40].[3]

FROM ADAM TO JOSEPH

When God gave the rod to Adam, it is logical that such a gift from the Creator would have been preserved and passed down through God's chosen line of descendants. Surely, a story concerning the rod's origin would also have been told and retold through time. Today, we have rabbinical commentary and a "legend" concerning its source and history.

Let us not be too quick to discard information based upon legend (stories passed down through the generations). Remember that the legend of Troy and the Trojan War was regarded as pure myth until Schliemann's archaeological discovery verified the existence of this city. Legends such as these actually contain certain accurate and detailed information. However, such material requires exceedingly careful evaluation and correlation to other existing information. Perhaps at some future time, a discovery will be made to verify the history of this divine rod.

It seems that the rod was handed down by Adam to Enoch and then to Methuselah. From Methuselah, it would have been transferred to Shem, the son of Noah, and perpetuator of the righteous line after the Flood. Shem was also the head of an academy teaching God's knowledge and was Abraham's tutor.[4]

Abraham acquired the rod from Shem and passed it on to his son, Isaac, as part of the birthright. Jacob then inherited the rod from his father, Isaac, and at some time gave it to Judah, one of his twelve sons (Genesis 38:18). Apparently, Judah returned the rod to his father Jacob so that it could be given to Jacob's other son, Joseph, who was the true inheritor of the Lord's blessing.

Let us briefly interject the story of Joseph as it relates to the inheritance of the rod. Joseph became a source of great envy and jealousy among his brothers, including Judah. They staged his death and sold him into slavery, whereupon he came to Egypt. Despite many tribulations, Joseph eventually rose to the level of Pharaoh's Viceroy. He alone was able to interpret Pharaoh's dream, thus ensuring Egypt's survival of a forewarned famine. When Joseph's brothers came to Egypt for grain during the famine, they were reconciled. Consequently, Jacob was reunited with the son he thought he had lost and before he died he gave the rod to Joseph.

FROM JOSEPH TO MOSES

After Joseph's death, however, there is a temporary break in the rod's possession. According to one account:

On Joseph's death the Egyptian nobles stole some of his belongings, and, among them, Jethro

121

appropriated the staff. Jethro *planted the staff in his garden*, when its marvelous virtue was revealed by the fact that nobody could withdraw it from the ground; even to touch it was fraught with danger to life. This was because *the Ineffable Name of God was engraved upon it*. When Moses entered Jethro's household he read the Name, and by means of it was able to draw up the rod, for which service Zipporah, Jethro's daughter, was given to him in marriage (emphasis added).[5]

What makes this account so remarkable is the reference to *planting the rod engraved with the Ineffable Name of God (YHVH)*. Considering the prior reference to God's transplanting the Tree of Life in the Garden of Eden, it seems of great consequence that a reference is made to planting a branch from this same tree in another garden. The concept of planting will become of paramount importance in the almond rod's ultimate redemptive purpose.

By God's intervention, Moses was empowered to remove the rod from the garden where it had been planted. Later, after Moses related the miracles God performed through the rod during the Exodus, Jethro, a Midianite priest, became convinced that "the Lord is greater than all the gods" (Exodus 18:11).

THE ROD OF MOSES

Moses was chosen by God to lead the Israelites out of captivity in Egypt. Before his calling, he had fled Egypt and spent forty years in the land of Midian as a shepherd of Jethro's flocks. As previously mentioned, Moses recognized the Divine Name of God on the planted rod in Jethro's garden and was able to withdraw it from the soil. Because of this, Jethro recognized Moses was chosen by

God for some great purpose and he gave his daughter, Zipporah, to be Moses' wife (Exodus 2:21).

For forty years, Moses lived in Midian. Most scholars think that Midian refers to an area of Arabia, east of Aqaba.[6] Greek, Roman, and Arabic sources place Midian in Arabia, as well as on the shore of the Red Sea, and Josephus confirms this area as the Biblical Midian.[7] Recent archaeological and scientific evidence shows that Mount Sinai is actually located in this same area, not in the Egyptian Sinai peninsula, the traditional location.[8] Scripture itself explicitly states that Mount Sinai is located in Arabia (Galatians 4:25).

It is on Mount Sinai (also called Horeb) that Moses encountered the Living God at the burning bush (Exodus 3). At this time, God gave Moses his mission to deliver the Israelites out of bondage in Egypt. When Moses asked by what sign the people would believe him, God commanded him to cast the rod on the ground, whereupon it was transformed into a serpent. Then God commanded Moses to pick it up by the tail, whereupon it was transformed back into a rod (Exodus 4:3-4). This miracle-producing rod would be instrumental in the deliverance and continued survival of God's Chosen People.

Moses' request to free his people was, of course, denied by Pharaoh (Exodus 5:2). Subsequently, the rod was used to perform miracles to induce Pharaoh to relent. It was transformed into a serpent as proof of God's power before Pharaoh and his court. After Pharaoh's sorcerers were able to duplicate this miracle (through the power of Satan), the greater power of God was displayed when the serpent of Moses' rod consumed all the serpents of the sorcerers' rods (Exodus 7:9-12).

As Pharaoh's heart continued to harden against God's will, the ten plagues of Egypt were sequentially initiated through the use of the rod. In addition, Moses used it to part the Red Sea as the Israelites escaped the pursuing Egyptians during the Exodus (Exodus 14:16). Furthermore, water critical for survival in the desert was provided when Moses tapped a rock with the rod (Exodus 17:5-6).

While in the wilderness, dissatisfaction among the people arose concerning the authority of Aaron, brother of Moses, whom God had appointed High Priest (Numbers 16). In response to this problem, God instructed Moses to have the leaders of the twelve tribes bring their respective rods (Numbers 17:2-6). Moses was further instructed to place these rods, along with Aaron's, inside the Tabernacle overnight. The next morning, it was discovered that Aaron's rod had budded, producing blossoms and ripe almonds (Numbers 17:7-8). This settled the question once and for all by whose authority Aaron held his position. Moreover, the rod continued to maintain live shoots throughout summer and winter as a sign to be understood and respected.[9]

According to God's command, this perpetually budding almond rod, which became known as Aaron's rod, was to be placed "before the testimony" (Numbers 17:10). This meant that it was to be placed *in front* of the Ark, which contained the "testimony," that is, the tablets of the covenant (Ten Commandments). Notice that other Old Testament references confirm that only the tablets were kept inside the Ark (Exodus 25:16; 40:20; I Kings 8:9).

Unfortunately, due to a mistranslation of Hebrews 9:3-4, the traditional belief is that Aaron's rod was placed *inside* the Ark. This passage has been translated:

v. 3   And behind the second veil, there was a tabernacle which is called the Holy of Holies,

v. 4   having a golden altar of incense and the ark of the covenant covered on all sides with

> gold, in which *was* a golden jar holding the
> manna, and Aaron's rod which budded, and
> the tablets of the covenant.

However, the original Greek grammar indicates that the subject of this passage is the Holy of Holies. Accordingly, the items described refer to those contained inside the Holy of Holies, not inside the Ark itself.

This understanding clarifies additional information given in the above passage. Firstly, it is known that the manna (like the rod) was placed in front of, not inside, the Ark (Exodus 16:33-34). Secondly, what is referred to as the "altar of incense" is actually the Mercy Seat, the gold lid of the Ark. In the original Greek, the phrase "of incense" does not appear. In fact, the actual altar of incense is known to have been placed inside the Holy Place, not inside the Holy of Holies (Exodus 40:26). Therefore, apparent discrepancies are resolved by a translation that better reflects the intended meaning of the original Greek text of this passage:

v. 3   Behind the second veil is the tabernacle that is called the holy of holies,

v. 4   in which is placed the ark, covered on all sides with gold, with an altar [mercy seat], also in the [holy of holies] is the golden pot having the manna and the rod of Aaron that budded, also the tablets of the covenant.

Clearly, God's command to place the rod "*before* the testimony to be kept as a sign" was obeyed. The placement of the miraculously budding almond rod before the Ark of the Covenant is of the greatest significance and will become very evident. At this time, it should be understood to represent the Tree of Life—both literally and symbolically. We should also note that though the rod was kept inside the Tabernacle, Moses still had the authority to remove it when necessary to perform a miracle, as we will see.[10]

THE STANDARD FOR THE SERPENT

While in the wilderness, the Israelites sinned by complaining about the conditions and the food (Numbers 21:4). God sent fiery serpents with a fatal bite as a judgment which caused them to cry out to their mediator, Moses, for God's forgiveness and healing.

Figure 8

The Serpent on the Standard

In response, God directed Moses to fashion a copper (symbolizing judgment) serpent and set it upon a pole. *The Book of II Kings* indicates that the serpent on this pole was fashioned out of Moses' own property.[11] Knowing that God's redemptive work had thus far been accomplished through the rod of Moses, it seems logical to assume that the rod was again used for this purpose. Moreover, known as the rod of God, it symbolized God's authority and judgment.

A picture on the cover of *The Midrash Says* depicts the serpent, attached to a crossbar, mounted on a rod. The serpent represented the sin that led to sickness and death.[12] It was raised up so that all the people who had been bitten could easily see it. By looking up to it, they were symbolically looking to God, thus demonstrating their faith (total trust) that He would forgive and redeem them from death (Figure 8).

Knowing that this rod was from an almond tree, it is interesting to note that "almonds, in connection with a prophecy or miracle, symbolize that the Almighty will bring about His decree in a hurry."[13] The Hebrew word *shkdeem*, meaning "almond," is derived from *shakad*, meaning "hurry." Also in connection with this meaning, it is significant that the almond tree is the first tree to blossom in the spring. Obviously, those looking to the serpent on the standard needed a miracle of healing and forgiveness "in a hurry."

FROM MOSES TO DAVID

From the time of Moses (1446-1406 B.C.E.) until the time of David (1010-970 B.C.E.), the rod of Aaron was kept in front of the Ark of the Covenant in the Tabernacle. Eventually, the Tabernacle was moved by David to the top of Mount Moriah. In this way, the miraculous almond branch had come full circle: from the Tree of Life in the Garden of Eden and back—to Mount Moriah, where the original Tree of Life had grown in the midst of the Garden!

From Adam, the almond rod passed through succeeding generations, following the ancestral lineage chosen by God to be the eventual bearer of His Messiah, Yeshua. It is significant that though Joseph had received the blessing of the birthright along with the rod, Judah had been promised by God that the scepter of authority, represented by the rod of God, would go to his descendant (Genesis 49:10).

It is possible that the transfer of the rod back to the line of Judah occurred through Samuel. Samuel, a descendant of Joseph and last of the judge-rulers, was directed by God to anoint David. Therefore, it seems plausible that he would have also transferred the rod to David.

According to the Midrash Yelamdenu, David carried the rod into battle against Goliath.[14] The Biblical account makes a direct reference to the rod in I Samuel 17 (NIV):

> v. 40 Then he [David] took his *staff* in his hand, chose five smooth stones from the stream, put them in the pouch of his shepherd's bag and, with his sling in his hand, approached the Philistine.
>
> v. 41 Meanwhile, the Philistine, with his shield bearer in front of him, kept coming closer to David.
>
> v. 42 He looked David over and saw that he was only a boy, ruddy and handsome, and he despised him.
>
> v. 43 He said to David, "Am I a dog, that you come at me with sticks?" And the Philistine cursed David by his gods.
>
> v. 44 "Come here," he said, "and I'll give your flesh to the birds of the air and the beasts of the field!"
>
> v. 45 David said to the Philistine, "You come against me with sword and spear and javelin, but I come against you *in the name of the Lord* Almighty, the God of the armies of Israel, whom you have defied" (emphasis added).

David deliberately chose not to wear protective armor offered by King Saul, nor did he carry the typical weapons of battle. In contrast, his opponent, the giant Goliath, was fully armed and armored. Undoubtedly, David's victory was proof of God's miraculous intervention. The rod, engraved with the Ineffable Name, bore witness to the authority by which this miracle of redemption had been performed.[15]

After David united the twelve tribes of Israel, he established Jerusalem as the Kingdom's permanent capital and placed the Tabernacle on Mount Moriah. However, it was not until his son, Solomon, that the Temple was constructed.

Thereupon, the Ark containing the Ten Commandments was placed inside the Holy of Holies of the Temple.

But there is no mention of Aaron's rod or the golden jar of manna at this time (II Chronicles 5:4-10). Furthermore, there are no other direct scriptural references as to the whereabouts of the rod from this time forward.

What happened to this miraculous rod, which was an implement of God's redemption and a symbol of His authority? Many have been fascinated by the search for the Ark of the Covenant. Even more fascinating is to trace the rod of God and search out its essential role in the universal redemption of humankind.

THE ROD REPLANTED ON THE MOUNT OF OLIVES

Subtle scriptural clues, understood within the context of the Law, seem to indicate that the rod planted by Jethro was replanted by David. As the rod had been preserved until the Exodus to become the instrument of redemption for the nation of Israel, the authors believe it was likewise preserved until the crucifixion to become the instrument of redemption for all humankind. Let us examine a pivotal event which seems to mark this crucial replanting of the divine almond rod.

It is known that David's son, Absalom, attempted to usurp his father's authority. King David was caught off guard and was forced to flee for his life. As he did so, he fled over the Kidron Valley and continued the ascent up to the summit of the Mount of Olives (II Samuel 15):

v. 23 ...The king [David] also passed over the brook Kidron...

v. 24 ...Zadok also came, and all the Levites with him carrying the ark of the covenant of God...

v. 25 And the king said to Zadok, "Return the ark of God to the city. If I find favor in the sight of the Lord, then He will bring me back again..."

> v. 30   And *David went up the ascent of the Mount of Olives,* and wept as he went, and his head was covered and he walked barefoot...
>
> v. 31   ...*coming to the summit, where God was worshipped...*(emphasis added).

Note that as David fled, Zadok and the Levites followed with the Ark. The roadway taken would have been the one that led from the Eastern gate of the Temple Mount over the arched stone bridge spanning the Kidron Valley and connecting to the roadway that led up to the summit of the Mount of Olives (Figure 3).

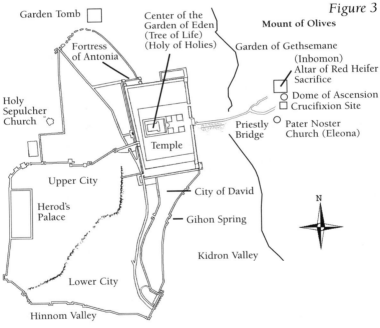

Figure 3

Jerusalem Site Map

From previously quoted scripture, it is known that Aaron's rod was positioned in front of the Ark in the Holy of Holies. Also, whenever the Ark was moved, the rod was moved in conjunction with it. Furthermore, it is known that the area contained within a radius of 2000 cubits from the Ark was considered holy. In fact, whether the Ark was moving or stationary, this 2000-cubit perimeter was carefully maintained.[16] This idea is supported by Joshua 3:4 and Numbers 35:5.

Surely the rod would have been kept within this holy perimeter surrounding the Ark, whatever the Ark's position. Therefore, it is reasonable to assume that the Ark and the rod could not be separated from each other by a distance exceeding 2000 cubits (about 3,000 feet, a Sabbath day's journey).

As King, David was vested with the responsibility of preserving the rod and the authority to carry the rod.[17] The authors believe that David took the rod under God's direction at the time he fled. If this is the case, it explains why Zadok and the Levites followed David with the Ark. In this way, the legal 2000-cubit distance requirement could be maintained.

According to II Samuel 15:5, David instructed Zadok to return the Ark to its position inside the Holy of Holies of the Tabernacle. However, he did not return at this time but continued to flee after pausing near the summit of the Mount of Olives. Remember, however, that he must have left the rod near the summit so that it was not taken outside the holy area as designated by the Ark's location. Significantly, the summit, which was "the place where God was worshipped," was just over this 2,000 cubit limit.[18] This place was well-known as the site of the Red Heifer sin sacrifice.[19]

David wept as he ascended the Mount of Olives (II Samuel 15:30). In Psalm 22, he reveals a clear, prophetic picture of the future crucifixion scene. He describes One who is "a reproach of men, and despised by the people"

(v. 6). All who see Him sneer and say " let Him [the Lord] deliver him...because He delights in him" (v. 8). The One in anguish says: "they pierced my hands and my feet. I can count all my bones...They divide my garments among them, and for my clothing they cast lots" (vv. 16-18).

How was David able to precisely detail an event one thousand years in the future, if not by divine revelation? His descendant, Yeshua—God's ultimate sin sacrifice— would walk this same path to His crucifixion. Was David given a vision of these events and then directed by God to plant the rod, knowing it would become the instrument of redemption for all humankind?

It is remarkable that Psalm 23, which follows the description of the crucifixion in Psalm 22, includes a reference to the comfort given by God's rod and staff: "Your rod and Your staff, they comfort me." According to *The ArtScroll Tanach Series*, "Radak notes that both words,... rod and...staff, refer to the same stick...".[20] The commentary goes on to make an interesting remark that:

> God provides an equal balance of affliction and support, blending them skillfully to achieve the desired effect. This follows the idea mentioned previously that the affliction itself is a support.[21]

For David, the rod was a source of affliction—as he was given a vision of the crucifixion—but the rod was, at the same time, a source of comfort and support—as he was given knowledge of its redemptive purpose.

THE NEXT THOUSAND YEARS

David was not overthrown by Absalom but instead was succeeded by his son Solomon. It was King Solomon who built the first Temple and was known for his great wisdom. Unfortunately, even this great man was led away from the one, true God by his many pagan wives. To please them, he allowed idols to be brought into the Temple, and trees, sacred to the goddess Ashtoreth (Astarte), to be planted on the Mount of Olives (I Kings 11:1-8).

As King Solomon fell away from uncompromised worship of the one, true God, so too did the Israelite nation. They turned the Mount of Olives, "where God was worshipped," into a place of idolatry. Soon after Solomon, the Kingdom disintegrated into the ten northern tribes (Israel) and the two southern tribes (Judah). During this time, idolatry ran rampant under the kings of Israel and the kings of Judah.

As judgment for their idolatry, the Northern Kingdom fell to the Assyrians and the ten tribes were dispersed (722 B.C.E.). As for the Southern Kingdom, not until the righteous King Hezekiah of Judah (715-686 B.C.E.) was there an end, for a time, to the abomination on the Mount of Olives. At this time, he cut down the Asherah groves and destroyed the copper serpent which hung from Moses' rod (II Kings 18):

> v. 4 He [Hezekiah] removed the high places and broke down the sacred pillars and cut down the Asherah. He also broke in pieces the bronze [copper] serpent that Moses had made, for until those days the sons of Israel burned incense to it; and it was called Nehushtan.

Notably, the copper serpent is mentioned in the same passage as the Asherah groves. It seems to place the serpent on the Mount of Olives, the same place where the authors believe David planted the rod. The authors believe that the serpent had never been removed from the rod and, therefore, must have remained attached to the almond tree as it grew. Subsequently, the serpent was removed and destroyed, but the almond tree was left intact.

The prophet Jeremiah (626-585 B.C.E.) continued to warn the tribes of Judah and Benjamin of the judgment that would follow because of continued idolatry. In one of Jeremiah's revelations from God, he makes a remarkable reference to the rod of an almond tree (Jeremiah 1):

> v. 11 And the word of the Lord came to me saying, "What do you see, Jeremiah?" And I said, *"I see a rod of an almond tree."*
>
> v. 12 Then the Lord said to me, *"You have seen well, for I am watching over My word to perform it"* (emphasis added).

Significantly, the Hebrew root word for "watching" in verse 12 is *shaqad*, which is derived from the root word *shaqed*, meaning "almond tree."[22] It appears that God was watching over this particular almond tree in reference to His Word, Yeshua, to perform His redemptive work at the appointed time yet to come!

Unfortunately, the prophets' warnings were rejected by the people and judgment fell as the Babylonians conquered Jerusalem, destroyed the Temple, and took the people into captivity (586 B.C.E.). Seventy years later, they returned to the land and rebuilt the Temple. In the fourth century B.C.E., Alexander the Great subdued this region in his pursuit to Hellenize the world.

After Alexander's short-lived empire, the Israelites experienced terrible persecution under Antiochus Epiphanes (167 B.C.E.), but returned to autonomous rule after the Maccabean revolt (160 B.C.E.). However, self-rule soon came to a halt as the Roman Empire continued its inexorable expansion throughout the Mediterranean (63 B.C.). During the centuries of turmoil and instability, however, this special tree was being preserved for the most important event in human history (Chapter 7).

THE SCEPTER OF AUTHORITY

When Yeshua returns, He will set up His Throne in Jerusalem (Ezekiel 43:7). At this time, it is thought that the prophet Elijah will return the rod—a branch from the Tree of Life—to the Messiah.[23]

The Book of Revelation (19:15) indicates that Yeshua will rule with "a rod of iron" during the Millennial Kingdom. The word "iron" comes from the Greek word *sithiros* and is translated in a metaphorical sense to signify "absolute authority" (Psalms 2:9).[24] The authors believe His scepter of authority will be none other than a branch from the Tree of Life!

The Messiah will seat Himself on the Mercy Seat in the Holy of Holies on Mount Moriah. He will replace the Ark that had symbolized Him, in the place where God had first fellowshipped with Adam and Eve, the same place the Divine Presence dwelt among His People! Just as a branch from the Tree of Life was kept before the Ark, He will set the almond rod before Himself on the Throne of God, where the Tree of Life had grown in the Garden of Eden!

Assuredly, the Creator guaranteed the preservation of the rod of God until He would use it as an instrument of His ultimate redemptive work. God had planted the original Tree of Life in the Garden of Eden. Under His guidance, a branch from this almond tree was planted in a garden by Jethro. Once again, it was replanted by King David, in another garden—on the Mount of Olives. And a tree grew from this almond rod...

Notes

1. Merril C. Tenney, Editor, *The Zondervan Pictorial Encyclopedia of the Bible*, Vol. 1, p. 5.

2. *The Jewish Encyclopedia*, Vol. 1, pp. 5-6.

3. *The Jewish Encyclopedia*, Vol. 1, pp. 5-6.

4. Rabbi Aryeh Kaplan, Translator, *The Torah Anthology*, Vol. 1, p. 432.

5. *The Jewish Encyclopedia*, Vol. 1, p. 5.

6. *The Zondervan Pictorial Encyclopedia of the Bible*, Vol. 4, p. 222.

7. *Encyclopedia Judaica,* Vol. 11, p. 1506.

8. Larry Williams, *The Mountain of Moses.*

9. Rabbi Moshe Weissman, *The Midrash Says*, Vol. 4, p. 239.

10. Rabbi Aryeh Kaplan, *The Torah Anthology: The Passover Haggadah*, p. 59.

11. Rabbi A. J. Rosenberg, Translator, *The Book of II Kings*, p. 375.

12. Weissman, Vol. 4.

13. Weissman, Vol. 4, p. 239.

14. *The Jewish Encyclopedia*, Vol. 1, p. 5.

15. An interesting symbolic picture is revealed in the account of David and Goliath. King Saul had only his earthly armor to offer David as protection. In contrast, David carried the rod of God which bore the Name of God and symbolized His power and protection. Goliath symbolized the might and power of the world and he laughed at the young man who carried only a staff and a sling shot. As David held the power of the Name of God on the staff, he loosed the stone from the sling and Goliath was struck between the eyes. As Goliath fell to the power of the Name of God, so too every knee will bow to the name of the Lord when Messiah comes to set up His Kingdom. A parallel to this story can also be seen in Daniel 2:31-45, in which a stone is used to bring down the great statue in King Nebuchadnezzar's dream. The statue represents the empires of the world that will be crushed by the Messiah who carries the Name of the Lord. David represents a type of Messiah.

16. Rabbi Nathan Bushwick, Translator, *The Torah Anthology: The Book of Joshua*, pp. 75-76.

17. Weissman, Vol. 4, p. 239.

18. Alfred Edersheim, *The Temple: Its Ministry and Services* (1994 hardcover edition), p. 7.

19. Mishna, Tractate Parah.

20. Rabbi Avrohom Chaim Feuer, Translator, *The ArtScroll Tanach Series: Psalms*, Vol. 1, p. 291.

21. Feuer, Vol. 1, p. 291.

22. James Strong, *The New Strong's Exhaustive Concordance of the Bible*, #8245 and #8247.

23. *Encyclopedia Judaica,* Vol. 14, p. 218.

24. *The Zondervan Pictorial Encyclopedia of the Bible*, Vol. 3, p. 307.

7

THE CRUCIFIXION TREE

"And as Moses lifted up the serpent in the wilderness, even so must the Son of Man be lifted up; that whoever believes may in Him have eternal life" (John 3:14-15).

"And when they had fulfilled all that was written of him, they took him down from the tree..." (Acts 13:29, KJV).

The traditional crucifixion scene depicts three Roman crosses: Messiah in the middle and a criminal on either side. However, nowhere does Scripture state that there were three Roman crosses. In fact, there is evidence to the contrary. The reader's response may be: What difference does it make? The answer is that God's design is supremely elegant down to the smallest prophetic detail, and for the most important reason—to point unequivocally to the only true Messiah.

As God designed prophetic pictures and patterns to reveal His Messiah, He also gave His Word for man to understand their meaning and spiritual significance. Deep study of Scripture, with the Spirit of Truth to bring understanding, reveals God's beautiful and precise plan.

Knowing who our Creator is and what our Savior has done for us is a solid foundation of truth, not blind faith. Total trust in God comes from knowing who He is and what He has done for us. The greater our understanding, the greater our trust will be and the closer our personal relationship with Him will be.

Therefore, as we strive to gain a deeper understanding of the prophetic fulfillment of the crucifixion, an accurate picture is essential. One of the fundamental elements is the actual crucifixion site, discussed in Chapter 3. Another aspect is the timing of the crucifixion, to be discussed in Chapter 8. In this chapter, the means of redemption will be addressed.

What light does Scripture shed on the actual scene of the crucifixion as it occurred almost two thousand years ago? And how does the Scriptural/Hebraic picture enhance our understanding of the fulfillment of Messianic prophecy?

NEW TESTAMENT REFERENCES TO THE CRUCIFIXION TREE

The traditional concept of three Roman crosses is not supported by Scripture. In fact, certain versions of the Bible, such as the KJV and NIV, more accurately translate the following scriptures by referring to a crucifixion "tree."

"The God of our fathers raised Jesus from the dead—whom you had killed by hanging him on a tree (Acts 5:30, NIV).

"We are witnesses of everything he did in the country of the Jews and in Jerusalem. They killed him by hanging him on a tree..." (Acts 10:39, NIV).

"When they had carried out all that was written about him, they took him down from the tree and laid him in a tomb" (Acts 13:29, NIV).

Christ redeemed us from the curse of the law by becoming a curse for us, for it is written: "Cursed is everyone who is hung on a tree" (Galatians 3:13, NIV).

He himself bore our sins in his body on the tree... (I Peter 2:24, NIV).

The Greek word *xulou* (or *xulon*) is translated "tree" in each of the above passages. This Greek word refers to a living tree, not a Roman cross. Even as Yeshua was going to His crucifixion, He made a direct reference to this act being carried out "when the tree is green" (Luke 23:31, NIV). The descriptive Greek word means "full of sap"; such a tree is clearly living.

One may then ask: What about the "cross" that Simon had to carry for Yeshua to the crucifixion site? In actuality, this beam was not a Roman cross but rather a crossbar that was nailed to the crucifixion tree. It was to this plank of wood that Yeshua was nailed at the wrists.[1] (Traditional depictions, showing nails through the hands, are physically impossible because the weight of the body would cause the nails to tear through the hands.) The crossbar was then nailed to the tree at which time nails were driven through the ankles into the tree trunk.

Another Greek word, *stauros*, appears in certain passages where it has been translated "cross." Its primary meaning is "upright pole" or "stake."[2] However, it can also refer to a crossbar.[3] Accordingly, the same word may refer to the crossbar, the actual pole or tree, or the crossbar/tree as a composite unit:

As they led him away, they seized Simon from Cyrene...and put the cross [crossbar] on him and made him carry it behind Jesus (Luke 23:26, NIV).

Pilate had a notice prepared and fastened to the cross [crossbar]. It read: Jesus of Nazareth, the King of the Jews (John 19:19, NIV).

The height of the tree trunk to which Yeshua was crucified can be estimated from the length of the hyssop branch, upon which a sponge soaked in sour wine was offered. As the reed was most likely about three feet in length, the height of the tree trunk was probably seven to nine feet.[4]

There is a very interesting passage which leads to another aspect of the crucifixion:

> The Jews therefore, because it was the day of preparation, so that the *bodies* should not remain on the *cross [tree]* on the Sabbath (for that Sabbath was a high day), asked Pilate that their legs might be broken, and that they might be taken away (John 19:31, NIV) (emphasis added).

Note that the word "bodies" is plural, whereas the word "cross" is singular.[5] Here, the word *stauros* is translated "cross" and refers to the tree with three attached crossbars.

Scripture indicates that the two criminals were crucified to Yeshua's right and left (Luke 23:33). However, nowhere in Scripture does it state that they were crucified on separate crosses. Suddenly the picture becomes clear: Yeshua and the two men were crucified on the same tree! One man was crucified on His right side and the other man was crucified on His left side. The symbolic picture represented by this arrangement is truly significant and will be discussed in Chapter 13.

Now we can easily understand how these men could have conversed with each other despite their agony and difficulty in speaking! Now we can clearly see that the soldiers came first to one thief, second to the next thief, and lastly to Yeshua, as they walked *around* the tree, breaking legs as necessary to hasten death!

OLD TESTAMENT REFERENCES

When referring to Yeshua's crucifixion, Paul makes the statement: "Cursed is everyone who is hung on a tree"

(Galatians 3:13). This is direct reference to Deuteronomy 21:22-23:

> v. 22 "And if a man has committed a sin worthy of death, and he is put to death, and you *hang him on a tree,*
>
> v. 23 his corpse shall not hang all night on the tree, but you shall surely bury him on the same day (for he who is hanged is accursed of God), so that you do not defile your land which the Lord your God gives you as an inheritance" (emphasis added).

A controversy existed among the rabbis (Pharisees) as to whether this passage refers to a man being hanged on a tree before or after death. The rabbinic interpretation was based upon humane considerations and called for a quick death by strangulation, followed by hanging.[6] However, there is evidence from the Dead Sea Scrolls (Temple Scroll and Nahum Commentary) that this same passage was originally interpreted to mean that a man was hanged on a tree as the method of execution.

According to the Temple Scroll (Column 64), those found guilty of certain capital offenses were killed by hanging on a tree:

> If a man informs against his people, and delivers up his people to a foreign nation, and does harm to his people, you shall hang him on a tree and he shall die....And *if a man has committed a crime punishable by death,* and has defected into the midst of the nations, and has cursed his people and the children of Israel, *you shall hang him also on the tree, and he shall die* (emphasis added).[7]

According to the Sages, only blasphemers and idolaters were to be hanged on a tree, though they abided by the more humane act of hanging after death.[8] However, the Temple Scroll clearly shows that hanging could be used as the method of execution. According to Yigael Yadin:

> It is possible…that *hanging alive goes back to the Second Temple period* as the legitimate interpretation of the Bible's command to execute by 'hanging,' and that it was only the later Pharisaic halachah which gave a different interpretation, and condemned the practice of stringing up a condemned man while still alive. There is in fact proof of this in the Aramaic Targum (of a sentence in Ruth) which dwells on the four methods of carrying out judicial sentences of death. It affirms that the fourth type, which is strangulation in rabbinic terminology, is indeed 'hanging on a tree.' And the late Israeli scholar Professor J. Heinemann pointed out that this Targum *preserves an ancient pre-Tannaitic (i.e. before the mishnaic sages) tradition of punishment by actual hanging—namely, with hanging as the cause of death* (emphasis added).[9]

In addition, Yigael Yadin has reinterpreted the Nahum Commentary in light of the Temple Scroll to support the contention that the Deuteronomy passage does indeed refer to hanging men alive on a tree, as practiced in ancient Israel.[10] Crucifixion, as a form of hanging, was also practiced later in Israel's history. According to Josephus, the Hasmonean king Alexander Jannaeus crucified 800 rebellious Pharisees in the first century B.C.E.[11] With this understanding, it becomes clear what the Jewish leaders meant when they told Pilate that they had a law, and by that law He must die:

> The Jews answered him, "We have a law, and by that law He ought to die because He made Himself out *to be* the Son of God" (John 19:7).

Pilate washed his hands of the entire affair because he knew Yeshua was innocent of any charge. He then turned the matter over to the religious leaders and stated: "See to it yourselves" (Matthew 27:24). Their response indicates they understood this action as a statement made according to Jewish law, absolving him of any responsibility for this action (Deuteronomy 21:1-9). In this way, Yeshua fulfilled prophecy according to Jewish law, not Roman law (Matthew 5:17; 26:54).

It is interesting to note that Melito, the eminent Bishop of Sardis during the second century, referred to the tree as the instrument of crucifixion: "Just as from a tree came sin, so also from a tree comes salvation."[12] It seems that early Christians were well aware of the fact that Yeshua was crucified on a tree. It is also a matter of historical record that before 326 C.E., the cross did not exist as a Christian symbol, but was derived from paganism.[13]

THE CRUCIFIXION TREE AND THE TREE OF LIFE

The overwhelming evidence in support of the tree, rather than the cross, opens the door to making a profound connection between the crucifixion tree and the Tree of Life. As stated above, the Greek word *xulou* (or *xulon*) was used to refer to the crucifixion tree. (In contrast, the Greek word *dendron*, which refers to a living tree primarily known for its fruit, was never used in this way.) Significantly, the same Greek word (*xulou/xulon*) that refers to the crucifixion tree is also used to refer to the Tree of Life in the Book of Revelation:

2:7 'He who has an ear, let him hear what the Spirit says to the churches. To him who overcomes, I will grant to eat of the tree of life, which is in the Paradise of God.'

22:2 ...And on either side of the river was the tree

of life,...yielding its fruit every month; and
the leaves of the tree were for the healing of
the nations.

22:14 Blessed are those who wash their robes, that
they may have the right to the tree of life,
and may enter by the gates into the city.

22:19 ...And if anyone takes away from the words
of this book of this prophecy, God shall take
away his part from the tree of life and from
the holy city, which are written in this book.

The authors believe that the use of the same Greek
word confirms a direct link between the Tree of Life and
the crucifixion tree. That link—both literal and symbolic—has been traced from the Tree of Life in the Garden
of Eden to the crucifixion tree on the Mount of Olives.

THE LIFTING UP OF THE MESSIAH

It has previously been shown that Aaron's rod, a
branch from the Tree of Life, was planted by King David
on the Mount of Olives at the place of sin sacrifice.
Though Hezekiah later destroyed the copper serpent
attached to its trunk, the tree remained for God to work
His ultimate redemptive plan for all humankind.

Yeshua told Nicodemus: "...as Moses lifted up the serpent in the wilderness, even so must the Son of Man be
lifted up; that whoever believes may in Him have eternal
life" (John 3:14-15). Let us remember that the use of the
copper serpent affixed to the rod was to provide healing
and forgiveness to the Israelites (Chapter 6). Both symbolic
and literal meanings are evident. *Yeshua was lifted up on the
same standard!* As the serpent was lifted up high so that all
could see it, likewise Yeshua was lifted up on the highest
place in Jerusalem, so that all could see Him. And all who
look to Him find total spiritual healing and eternal life.

Jeremiah's vision of the rod of an almond tree and God's promise to watch over His Word, Yeshua, to perform the act of redemption was fulfilled at the crucifixion (Jeremiah 1:11-12). In this way, the Tree of Life, the source of the almond rod, is both literally and symbolically represented in the redemption of all humankind. Through it, God brought redemption first to the Israelites and, ultimately, to all humankind through Yeshua—the Fruit of the Tree of Life, Who gives eternal life to all who trust in Him alone!

THE ULTIMATE SIN SACRIFICE

The sin of man separates him from a spiritual relationship with his Holy Creator. God made provision for reestablishing that spiritual relationship through blood sacrifice because the penalty for sin is death (Romans 6:23) and life is in the blood (Leviticus 17:11). But animal sacrifice could provide only a temporary solution for atonement of sin.

God made the first animal sacrifice as atonement for Adam and Eve's sin of disobedience in the Garden. Understanding how God works, it is likely that the place of the first sin sacrifice by God was the same place where Adam was directed to build the first sacrificial altar. This altar was repeatedly rebuilt and reused through the generations by Abel, Noah, and Abraham (Genesis 22:9).[14] As discussed in Chapter 3, the authors believe the Mount of Olives to be the site of this altar. Furthermore, the most holy sin sacrifice, the Red Heifer, is known to have been offered on the summit of the Mount of Olives, "where God was worshipped."

With this perspective, the call of Abraham to sacrifice his only son Isaac takes on even greater significance. It is also important to understand that Isaac was not actually a child, as is so often depicted, but a young man capable of overcoming his father.[15] This pattern repeats in God's sacrifice of His only Son, Yeshua, who also willingly followed the will of His Father, in this same place. We know that God provided a substitute sacrifice in Isaac's place: a ram, whose head was caught in a thorn bush (Genesis 22:13). Two thousand years later, Yeshua, His head surrounded by the same kind of thorns (John 19:2), was provided as the ultimate substitute sacrifice for all humankind's sins.

Abraham's response to Isaac's question: "Where is the lamb for the burnt offering?" remarkably foreshadows this event, as revealed in a valid translation of the original Hebrew: *God will provide Himself as the Lamb* (Genesis 22:7-8).[16] Yes, God did provide Himself—in the God-Man Messiah—as the ultimate sin sacrifice. The evidence of this is to be found in the fulfillment of the Law in every detail (Matthew 5:17)!

In this regard, as Yeshua's blood was shed on the tree, a symbolic parallel is evident in the Yom Kippur sacrifice (Leviticus 16:14):

> Moreover, he [the High Priest] shall take some of the blood of the bull and sprinkle *it* with his finger on the mercy seat on the east *side*; also in front of the mercy seat he shall sprinkle some of the blood with his finger seven times.

Remembering that Aaron's rod was placed in front of the Mercy Seat of the Ark, it becomes clear that the sprinkling of blood would have fallen upon the rod. Remarkably, Yeshua bled predominately from seven places (head, hands, feet, back, and side) on the tree that grew from this rod. Again, the prophetic picture was fulfilled both symbolically and literally.

THE FATE OF THE CRUCIFIXION TREE

The fate of the crucifixion tree is not known; however, it can be assumed that it was eventually cut down and destroyed. Because such a tree was considered cursed, it may be that it was destroyed soon after Yeshua's crucifixion. Even if this did not occur, it is known that all trees around Jerusalem were destroyed by the Roman general, Titus, by 70 C. E.

It is possible that a branch of this tree was preserved, for it is to be returned by the prophet Elijah to the Messiah when He returns to establish the Millennial Kingdom.[17] Or perhaps another rod will come directly from the Tree of Life in Heaven.

God's Master Plan is powerfully and precisely fulfilled in the history of the almond rod. Now, for an account of unparalleled precision in the timing of prophetic events, let us examine the events of Passover in the year Yeshua was crucified...

Notes

1. Merrill C. Tenney, Editor, *The Zondervan Pictorial Encyclopedia of the Bible*, Vol. 1, p. 1041.

2. W. E. Vine, *Vine's Expository Dictionary of Old and New Testament Words*, Vol. 1, pp. 256-257.

3. *The Zondervan Pictorial Encyclopedia of the Bible*, Vol. 1, p. 1038.

4. *The Zondervan Pictorial Encyclopedia of the Bible*, Vol. 1, pp. 1041-1042.

5. Ernest L. Martin, *Secrets of Golgotha*, p. 274.

6. Yigael Yadin, *The Temple Scroll*, pp. 204-205.

7. Yadin, p. 206.

8. Yadin, p. 205.

9. Yadin, pp. 207-208.

10. Yadin, pp. 216-217.

11. William Whiston, Translator, *Josephus Complete Works*, p. 433, (*Wars of the Jews*, IV, 6).

12. Martin, p. 175.

13. For an excellent discussion of the origin and history of this symbol, see *Babylon Mystery Religion* by Ralph Edward Woodrow.

14. Rabbi Aryeh Kaplan, Translator, *The Torah Anthology*, Vol. 2, p. 332.

15. *The Torah Anthology*, Vol. 2, pp. 333-334.

16. Phinehas Ben Zadok, *Which Day Is the Passover?*, p. 35.

17. *Encyclopedia Judaica*, Vol. 1, p. 218.

8

THE TWO PASSOVERS

*'In the first month, on the fourteenth day of
the month at twilight is the Lord's Passover.
Then on the fifteenth day of the same month
there is the Feast of Unleavened
Bread...'(Leviticus 23:5-6).*

Before we attempt to reconstruct a chronology of events
from Yeshua's triumphal entry into Jerusalem through
His crucifixion to His resurrection, we must establish a
valid reference point on which to base an accurate
timetable. In this regard, the authors wish to express their
deep appreciation for the work of the late Phinehas Ben
Zadok (Hans Philip Veerman). His work, *Which Day Is the
Passover?*, provides the basis for understanding the two
Passovers and their significance in God's prophetic
timetable of the crucifixion.

The reader may wonder why a precise timetable is
essential. On the fourth day of creation, God established
a prophetic timetable: "...God said, 'Let there be lights in
the expanse of the heavens to separate the day from the
night, and let them be for signs, and for seasons, and for

days and years…" (Genesis 1:14). The word "seasons" is translated from the Hebrew word *mo'adim,* meaning *appointed times and religious feasts.*[1] Paul also taught the Gentiles that the feast days, new moons, and Sabbath days are *shadows of things to come* (Colossians 2:17).

The Jewish calendar as given by God is a lunar calendar calculated on the basis of the lunar cycle (thus the above reference to "new moons"). "Things to come are future things and shadows (foreshadows) of things to come are *prophecies,* i.e. THE WHOLE OF THE DIVINE CALENDAR IS A PROPHECY. It is the most comprehensive, *the backbone prophecy* to the whole Bible."[2]

Many false messiahs have come and gone over the course of human history. Our time especially has witnessed a proliferation of such messiahs. God knew such things would occur and has not left us in the dark as to how to identify, beyond a shadow of a doubt, the one and only true Messiah. The answer is to be found in the fulfillment of prophecies according to God's prophetic timetable. The precision of the timetable indicates a master plan beyond the control of man, for no person or persons could possibly construct, predict, and execute the complexity of events at specific times over the course of millennia.

To begin with, let us keep in mind the prophecy that Yeshua made in response to the scribes and Pharisees who asked for a sign (Matthew 12):

v. 39 …"An evil and adulterous generation craves for a sign; and yet no sign shall be given to it but the sign of Jonah the prophet;

v. 40 for just as JONAH WAS THREE DAYS AND THREE NIGHTS IN THE BELLY OF THE SEA MONSTER, so shall the Son of Man be three days and three nights in the heart of the earth."

Yeshua Himself gave this specific prophecy. Its fulfillment exactly as given is required if Yeshua is who He claims to be. Yet, the traditional concept of a Friday crucifixion and Sunday morning resurrection fails to satisfy the three night requirement.

It has been suggested that the prophecy was fulfilled according to the traditional concept because any part of a day constitutes a full day according to Hebraic thought. However, the Jews divided the day into two equal parts: night and day, with day following night. Accordingly, evening began at sunset and ended at sunrise, and day began at sunrise and ended at sunset. Based upon this Hebraic concept, any part of the daylight segment called "day" could be considered "one day" and any part of the nighttime segment called "night" could be considered "one night." Considered within this context, the traditional Friday crucifixion and Sunday resurrection fails to meet the three night requirement.

However, this does not mean that Yeshua failed to fulfill the prophecy. Instead, it is due to our failure to understand the actual timing of events during Passover week. Given an accurate timetable, it will be seen that Yeshua fulfilled both aspects of the sign of Jonah: three days *and three nights.*

In order to discern prophetic events, we must be aware of God's prophetic timetable as He established it at the moment of creation through the Biblical (Jewish) Feast Days. With regard to Passover and the Feast of Unleavened Bread, it is essential to realize there are two different dates for Passover and that there are two kinds of sabbaths. We must also be mindful that God marked the days in creation with each new day beginning at twilight, followed by daylight, and this is exactly how the Jews reckon the days of their calendar.

THE TWO PASSOVER DATES

Passover, at the time of Yeshua through today, is observed on the *fifteenth* day of the first month, according to the Jewish *sacred* calendar. The first month is called *Abib* in the Torah (first five books of the Bible). Under the influence of the Babylonian calendar during the Exile, the name was changed to *Nisan*. For our discussion, we will use the name Abib. (Note that the first month, according to the Jewish *civil* calendar begins with Rosh HaShanah, New Year, on the first of *Tishri*.)

If Passover was observed on the fifteenth of Abib, why then does Leviticus 23:5 state: "In the first month, on the fourteenth day of the month at twilight is the LORD'S Passover." Clearly, the Lord originally established Passover on the fourteenth of Abib and this date is verified in both Numbers 9:1-5 and Exodus 12:6-13 as well. When and how did a shift in this date from the fourteenth to the fifteenth occur?

We know that at the time of Ezra (about 458 B.C.E.), Passover was still being observed on the fourteenth: "And the exiles observed the Passover on the fourteenth of the first month" (Ezra 6:19). It appears that the shift of the Passover date occurred after Ezra, probably between 300 and 100 B.C.E.[3] Deuteronomy 16 provides the basis for this shift:

v. 1   "Observe the month of Abib and celebrate the Passover to the LORD your God...

v. 2   "And you shall sacrifice the Passover to the LORD your God from the flock and herd...

v. 3   *"You shall not eat leavened bread with it; seven days you shall eat with it unleavened bread...*

v. 4   "For seven days no leaven shall be seen with you in all your territory, and none of the flesh which you *sacrifice on the evening of the first day* shall remain overnight until morning."

v. 5 "You are not allowed to sacrifice the Passover in any of your towns which the LORD your God is giving you;

v. 6 but at the place where the LORD your God chooses to establish His name [Jerusalem], *you shall sacrifice the Passover in the evening at sunset, at the time that you came out of Egypt*" (emphasis added).

Note that unleavened bread was to be eaten seven days and that the lamb was to be eaten on the first day of the seven-day period called the Feast of Unleavened Bread. Notice, however, that at the time Passover was originally established and practiced during the Exodus, the lamb was eaten on the 14th day of Abib, whereas the Feast of Unleavened Bread began on the 15th day of Abib (Leviticus 23:5-6).

Actually, unleavened bread was eaten with the lamb on the 14th as well as during the seven-day Feast of Unleavened Bread beginning on the 15th (Exodus 12:8). What the Pharisees did was to combine these two separate observances into one observance, which was legitimate based upon the Deuteronomy passage.

Deuteronomy 16:6 states that Passover was to be eaten in "the evening at sunset, at the time that you came out of Egypt." The Exodus began on the evening of the 15th of Abib, the evening after they had eaten the Passover meal on the 14th (Numbers 33:3). Understanding this change, we can detect the subtle meaning of Luke's statement: "Now the Feast of Unleavened Bread, which is called Passover..." (Luke 22:1).

An extremely important consequence of this Passover shift was an accompanying shift in the Passover "preparation day." Preparation day was the day before Passover (i.e., the afternoon of the day prior to sunset of Passover) when all the lambs were sacrificed. In effect, the preparation day moved from the 13th to the 14th, in conjunction with the shift in Passover from the 14th to the 15th. This change in the calendar would prove to be of great prophetic significance.

THE SABBATHS OF PASSOVER WEEK

In order to understand the timing of events during Passover/Feast of Unleavened Bread, we must differentiate between *annual* and *weekly* sabbaths. The first and last days of the Feast of Unleavened Bread are referred to as "high holy days." High holy days are referred to as annual sabbaths and marked on the Jewish calendar in addition to the regular weekly sabbaths.

With this in mind, we can see that there were three sabbaths during Passover: the two annual sabbaths of the Feast of Unleavened Bread (first and seventh days) and one weekly sabbath within the feast period. We also know that Yeshua was buried just before the onset (at sunset) of the high holy day of the first day of the Feast of Unleavened Bread, the 15th of Abib (John 19:31):

> The Jews therefore, because it was the day of preparation [14th], so that the bodies should not remain on the cross on the [Passover] Sabbath [15th] (*for that Sabbath was a high day*)...(emphasis added).

Without this understanding, it is assumed that the preparation was for the weekly sabbath so that the crucifixion had to take place on a Friday. However, with the proper perspective, it becomes clear that the crucifixion took place on the 14th, just before the annual Passover Sabbath.

It is noteworthy that not all Jews observed the Passover meal on the 15th. The Sadducees did not agree with the Pharisees on this issue and adhered to the old tradition.[4] The more conservative Samaritans also observed Passover on the 14th, and to this day "consider the Feast of Passover and the Feast of Unleavened Bread as two distinct festivals."[5] Scripture, interpreted in the context of an accurate timetable, shows that Yeshua and His disciples followed the original Passover date.

In this way, Yeshua observed the Passover meal (Seder) according to the ordinance as originally established by God in Exodus, Leviticus, and Numbers—on the evening of the 14th of Abib. After His arrest and subsequent trial and conviction, He was crucified on the day of the 14th—"preparation day" for the rest of the Jewish population, who observed Passover on the 15th.

According to the historian Josephus, the lambs were slain between 3 and 5 p.m.[6] It seems that Yeshua, the Lamb of God, died precisely at the time the sacrifices began! Therefore, that which at first appears to be a contradiction in God's Word—namely, two different dates for Passover—in actuality reveals divine design, for no human agency could have foreknown the prophetic events that would unfold at some distant time in the future!

TIMETABLE OF PASSOVER WEEK EVENTS

The following is a summary of events according to this time frame:

14th: Tuesday evening Yeshua eats Passover meal (Mark 14:12—"on the first day of unleavened bread" refers to the first of eight days of eating of unleavened bread with the Passover as observed on the 14th, not to the first day of the Feast of Unleavened Bread, the 15th)

14th: Wednesday day Crucifixion on "preparation day," burial just before evening (John 19:31)

15th: Wednesday evening The Israelites eat their Passover meal on the first day of the Feast of Unleavened Bread—a "high holy day" or annual sabbath

15th: Thursday day Tomb sealed (Matthew 27:62-66)

16th: Thursday evening

16th: Friday day Women buy and prepare spices after the annual sabbath (Mark 16:1; Luke 23:56)

17th: Friday evening Beginning of the weekly sabbath, the women rest according to sabbath law (Luke 23:56)

17th: Saturday day, Sabbath day—Resurrection

It is remarkable that "according to an ancient church tradition, Jesus was arrested on Wednesday (cf. Epiphanius, *de fide* XXII, 1), which means that the Last Supper would have taken place on a Tuesday."[7] This ancient tradition is consistent with the above timetable and also confirmed by the Jewish calendar for the year 30 C.E.,[8] the correct year of the crucifixion.[9] All these facts are consistent with the original Greek of the Gospel accounts, which confirm a Sabbath resurrection (Chapter 12).

Therefore, counting from Yeshua's death about 3 pm Wednesday to His resurrection before daylight Saturday, there is a period of three days and three nights. Remembering that the Hebraic concept counts a part of a day as one day, the three days are: Wednesday, Thursday, and Friday. The three nights are: Wednesday night, Thursday night, and Friday night. Clearly, Yeshua fulfilled the three days and three nights of the sign of Jonah showing that He is truly the Messiah!

Now that an accurate timetable has been established for Passover week, let us examine the daily events leading

up to the trial and crucifixion of Yeshua. As we do so, we will see how He fulfilled His role as King, Priest, and Prophet, and ultimately, as God's Passover Lamb...

Notes

1. Phinehas Ben Zadok, *Which Day Is the Passover?*, p. 17.

2. Ben Zadok, p. 20.

3. Ben Zadok, p. 25.

4. Ben Zadok, p. 27.

5. *The Jewish Encyclopedia*, Vol. 9, p. 553.

6. Nahum M. Sarna, Commentator, *The JPS Torah Commentary: Exodus*, p. 55.

7. Merrill C. Tenney, Editor, *The Zondervan Pictorial Encyclopedia of the Bible*, Vol. 4, p. 609.

8. HaYom On-line Hebrew Calendar, A. G. Reinhold, 14 Fresh Pond Place, Cambridge, MA 02138-4430, Copyright © 1994. See also Jewish calendar, Jerusalem One web site.

9. *The Zondervan Pictorial Encyclopedia of the Bible*, Vol. 1, p. 1041.

9

GOD'S PASSOVER LAMB

*Now the Feast of Unleavened Bread, which is
called the Passover, was approaching. And
the chief priests and the scribes were seeking
how they might put Him to death; for they
were afraid of the people (Luke 22:1-2).*

An accurate timetable of Passover week was established
in the preceding chapter. We will now discuss the
events that transpired from Saturday, the 10th of Abib, to
Wednesday, the 14th of Abib. Many facets of prophetic
detail will be brought to light as we closely examine the
time frame and the events within the Hebraic context. As
a result, we will gain a much more accurate and beautiful
picture of how Messianic prophecy was fulfilled in Yeshua.

10TH OF ABIB (SATURDAY): ENTRY INTO JERUSALEM AS KING

Six days before Passover, Yeshua was in Bethany at the
home of Lazarus, the man He had raised from the dead
(John 12:1). The Lord and His disciples observed the
Sabbath that Friday evening with their close friends

Lazarus, Mary, and Martha. (Counting backwards from Passover on Thursday, the 15th of Abib, the sixth day falls on Sabbath.) The Sabbath before Passover is called the Great Sabbath because it commemorates the Sabbath preceding the Exodus from Egypt.[1] Significantly, the prophetical section recited after the reading of the Torah makes reference to the coming Messiah and final redemption: "Behold, I will send you Elijah the prophet before the great and awesome day of the Lord" (Malachi 4:5).[2]

The following day, Saturday, the 10th of Abib, the Passover lambs were selected by each Jewish family and brought into the home for a four-day examination period prior to the Passover sacrifice (Exodus 12:3). The lamb had to be a firstborn male without blemish in order to be an acceptable sacrifice. The four-day period allowed ample time to examine the lamb for any defect and, if necessary, sufficient time to find an acceptable replacement.

Yeshua, firstborn male and Lamb of God for the house of Israel, was about to present Himself publicly in Jerusalem as the Messiah. He too was about to begin a four-day period of examination by the religious leaders and the people—and to be found without the blemish of sin.

After leaving Bethany, Yeshua had his disciples obtain a mount, a donkey colt that had never been ridden, from Bethphage (Mark 11:1-7). Significantly, Yeshua rode from this point, the official entry point into the holy city.[3] They followed the Jericho road from the eastern to the western slope of the Mount of Olives, over the Kidron bridge, and through the Eastern Gate to the Temple (Figure 5).

A great multitude met Him, paving His path with their own garments and palm branches, freshly cut from the Mount of Olives (John 12:13). The garments laid on the Messiah's path were actually prayer shawls, which were worn. The word "garment" is translated from the Greek word, *chiton*, which refers to a seamless garment.[4] The tallit, or prayer shawl, was a seamless garment with four corners, a tassel attached to each of the four corners (Numbers 15:38-40).[5] It symbolizes the Law of God and represents the totality and covering of God. Upon its collar (mantle), the Hebrew letters spell "Lord of lords and King of kings," a symbolic reminder of the promised Messiah. By laying their tallits down, the people were acknowledging Yeshua as God's promised Messiah.

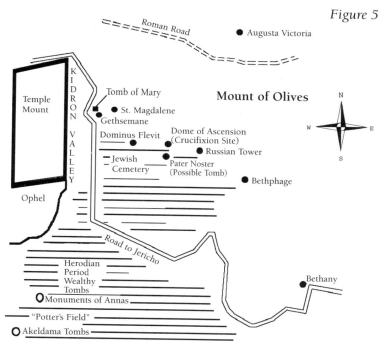

Figure 5

Mount of Olives Site Map

The people also waved and laid palm branches down at His path, symbolizing admiration[6] and triumphant homage to a king.[7] Significantly, the palm requires thirty years to bear fruit. Likewise, Yeshua's ministry began when He reached thirty years of age, the earliest age one could become a Rabbi (Teacher) under the Law. As they waved the palm branches, the multitudes cried out: "Hosanna [save us]![8] Blessed is He who comes in the name of the Lord (Psalms 118:26); Blessed is the coming Kingdom of our father David; Hosanna in the highest!" (Mark 11:9-10). They were witnessing the fulfillment of a prophecy made more than five hundred years before: "...Behold, your king is coming to you; He is just and endowed with salvation, Humble, and mounted...on a colt, the foal of a donkey..." (Zechariah 9:9). "King" refers to the Messiah, the son of David. The Messiah demonstrated humility by making His entry on a donkey.[9]

The Talmud notes the contrast between the Messiah coming in glory with the clouds of Heaven, as described by Daniel (7:13), and the Messiah coming as a humble person, as described by Zechariah. The Talmud also explains the reason for the difference as depending upon the worthiness of Israel. In other words, if Israel was worthy, the Messiah would come in great glory; if not, He would come as a humble person.[10]

11TH OF ABIB (SUNDAY): CLEANSING THE TEMPLE AS PRIEST

Yeshua returned to Bethany (meaning "House of the Poor") to be among His closest friends and disciples. After spending the night, Yeshua returned to Jerusalem the next day, Sunday. As He walked along the pathway to the city, He singled out a particular fig tree and said: "May no one ever eat fruit from you again" (Mark 11:13-14). Because it was not the season for figs (v. 13), it is clear that Yeshua's action was symbolic in nature.

The authors believe this fig tree represented the Tree of Knowledge of good and evil in the Garden of Eden

(Chapter 4). In addition, Yeshua was also symbolically referring to His impending sacrifice, whereby sin would be defeated once and for all. Moreover, He may have been expressing the hope that humankind would accept that sacrifice and no longer partake of the fruit of disobedience.

Afterwards, Yeshua continued along the path that led across the Kidron Valley at the southern end of the city. After crossing the valley, He ascended the steps at the Temple platform's southern entrance which led to the Stoa, or Royal Portico. Here Yeshua overturned the tables of the dishonest money-changers and ejected those buying and selling sacrifices because inferior animals were being sold for undue profit. Their impure motives and actions in the area of Temple, God's House, were an affront to Yeshua. As the ultimate High Priest, He expelled them (Matthew 21:12-13). Afterwards, He once again returned to spend the night in Bethany.

12TH OF ABIB (MONDAY): TEACHING AS PROPHET

The next day, Monday (the 12th of Abib), Yeshua and His disciples followed the same path as they had the day before into Jerusalem. Again, He singled out the same fig tree that had not borne fruit. Let us understand that the fig tree is also symbolic of Israel and that it's failure to produce fruit symbolized Israel's rejection of her Messiah (Chapter 4). This time, when Yeshua stated "No longer shall there ever be fruit from you," the fig tree instantly withered, indicating Israel's imminent destruction (Matthew 21:19-20). Indeed, historical fact verifies that Jerusalem was destroyed by the Romans in 70 C.E.

Not only did the majority of the religious leaders reject Yeshua as the Messiah, but on this particular day, they were plotting how best to discredit Him. The true Messiah represented a very grave threat to their own power and authority and could not be tolerated (John 11:48). First the chief priests and elders came to Him, challenging by what authority He acted. His answer to them was a question which they could not answer, because to do so would expose their own hypocrisy and anger the people. He then went on to tell the parables about the two sons and the wicked husbandmen, pointedly illustrating the hypocrisy and evil motives of the religious leaders (Matthew 21:28-41).

Next, the Pharisees who had joined forces with the Herodians (a political group who supported the house of Herod) sent their disciples to ask what they thought was a clever question. Their hope was to trap Him into a "politically incorrect" answer that would guarantee His death as an insurgent. The answer He gave astounded them and caused them to retreat in defeat (Matthew 22:15-22).

Finally, the Sadducees posed what they thought to be an unanswerable hypothetical question. Instead, Yeshua's response revealed their own ignorance, not only of Scripture, but also of the power of God (Matthew 22:23-33). In one final attempt, the Sadducees and Pharisees (mutual enemies) joined forces and produced a very clever lawyer (scribe) to ask a very clever question—but to no avail (vv. 34-40). Now it was Yeshua who turned the tables and asked the Pharisees a question they were unable to answer. In doing so, He showed Himself to be Who He claimed to be—Messiah and God! From this time forward, no one dared to question His authority (vv. 41-46).

The Lord then spoke to the multitudes who were gathered, exposing the hypocrisy of the religious leaders (Matthew 23:1-12). He also mourned over Jerusalem for the judgment that would follow due to the people's rejection of God's prophets and their Messiah.

Then, He left the Temple and went to the Mount of Olives, where the disciples questioned Him about His prophecies concerning the destruction of the Temple, the End-Times, and His return. Yeshua explained these things to them directly and in parables (Matthew 24 and 25). He also prophesied that in two days (Wednesday), He would be delivered up for crucifixion (Matthew 26:2).

13TH OF ABIB (TUESDAY): FELLOWSHIP AND CONSPIRACY

Yeshua spent His last day before His crucifixion among His disciples and friends in Bethany. At the house of Simon the leper, a woman anointed His head with a very costly perfume. Though the disciples thought it would have been better to sell the perfume and give the money to the poor, Yeshua again made reference to His approaching death by saying she had done a good deed by anointing Him in preparation for His burial (Matthew 26:6-13).

In the meantime, Judas Iscariot made a deal with the chief priests to deliver his Master for thirty pieces of silver (Matthew 26:14-16). In doing so, he was not aware that a five hundred-year-old prophecy was being fulfilled (Zechariah 11:12). Let us digress from the chronology long enough to understand the prophetic significance of this event.

Yeshua's Price—Thirty Pieces of Silver

According to Scripture, thirty pieces of silver from the Temple treasury was the price the chief priests paid to have Yeshua delivered to them. According to Matthew 26:

v. 14 Then one of the twelve, named Judas Iscariot, went to the chief priests,

v. 15 and said, "What are you willing to give me to deliver Him up to you?" And they weighed out to him thirty pieces of silver.

The Greek word *paradidomi* is translated as "to deliver" in verse 15. Its literal meaning is "to give up," in the sense of delivering a person or thing over to another.[11] In other passages dealing with this transaction, it has been translated as "to betray" (Matthew 27:3,4; Mark 14:44; Luke 22:48; John 18:2,5). However, the literal translation more accurately conveys the actual meaning.

The next morning, Judas felt remorse for delivering "innocent blood" and returned the thirty pieces of silver to the chief priests (Matthew 27):

> v. 3 Then when Judas, who had betrayed [delivered] Him, saw that He had been condemned, he felt remorse and returned the thirty pieces of silver to the chief priests and elders,
>
> v. 4 saying, "I have sinned by betraying [delivering] innocent blood." But they said, "What is that to us? See *to that* yourself!"
>
> v. 5 and he threw the pieces of silver into the sanctuary [Temple] and departed; and he went away and hanged himself.

It was unlawful for such "blood money" to be returned to the Temple treasury, so the chief priests decided to purchase a burial place for strangers, called "Potter's Field," which became known as the "Field of Blood" (Matthew 27:6-8).

These events fulfilled prophecy, just as Yeshua Himself said, "But all this has taken place that the Scriptures of the prophets may be fulfilled" (Matthew 26:56). According to Matthew 27:

> v. 9 Then that which was spoken through Jeremiah the prophet was fulfilled, saying, "AND THEY TOOK THE THIRTY PIECES OF SILVER, THE PRICE OF THE ONE WHOSE PRICE HAD BEEN SET BY THE SONS OF ISRAEL;
>
> v. 10 AND THEY GAVE THEM FOR THE POTTER'S FIELD, AS THE LORD DIRECTED ME."

Matthew refers to the prophecies of Jeremiah concerning Potter's Field (Jeremiah 18 and 19). However, the prophecies of Zechariah were also fulfilled (Zechariah 11):

v. 12   And I said to them, "If it is good in your sight, give *me* my wages; but if not, never mind! So they weighed out thirty shekels [pieces] of silver as my wages.

v. 13   Then the word of the Lord said to me, "Throw it to the potter, that magnificent price at which I was valued by them." So I took the thirty *shekels* of silver and threw them to the potter in the house of the Lord.

Compare the NASB translation above with a direct translation from the Hebrew in Judaica Books' *Twelve Prophets*:

v. 12   And I said to them: "If it pleases you, give [Me] My hire, and if not, forbear." And they weighed out My hire: thirty pieces of silver.

v. 13   And the Lord said to me: Cast it to the keeper of the treasury, to the stronghold of glory [Temple]—of which I stripped them. And I took the thirty pieces of silver, and I cast it into the house of the Lord, to the keeper of the treasury.[12]

This translation accurately foreshadows the price paid for Yeshua and Judas' remorseful act. The amount also represents a tragically inadequate, human estimation of the Lord's worth as Shepherd of Israel (Zechariah 11:7 shows God to be the Shepherd of Israel.)

Zechariah's Prophecy of the Edomite Shepherd

Another facet of Zechariah's prophecy involves God placing His flock, Israel, under the supervision of the shepherd, Edom. From Zechariah 11:

v. 15 And the Lord said to me: Take for yourself still another thing, the instrument of a foolish shepherd.

v. 16 For, behold! I am setting up a shepherd in the land. Those that are cut off he shall not remember; the foolish ones he shall not seek. The lame he shall not heal; the one that can stand he shall not bear. And the flesh of the fat one he shall eat, and their hoofs he shall break.

v. 17 Ho, worthless shepherd, who abandons the flock! A sword is on his arm and his right eye; his arm shall wither, and his right eye shall dim.[13]

According to the Jewish Sage, Rashi, verse 15 refers to "a sign that I [the Lord] am destined to deliver the generation of the destruction of this Second Temple into the hands of Esau." Furthermore, the kingdom of the house of Herod would become the "Shepherd" of Israel: a shepherd that does not care for its flock and, in fact, destroys it.[14]

The power of this prophecy is more fully appreciated when understood in its Biblical and historical context. Most importantly, the political power at the time of Yeshua was held by the Edomites, not the Jews. The Edomites, the descendants of Esau intermixed with the descendants of Ishmael, had always been a bitter enemy of the Jews. For a complete picture, a brief summary of relevant Biblical and historical facts is helpful.

Esau and Jacob were brothers, the sons of Isaac. After selling his birthright to Jacob (Genesis 25:29-34), Esau resented his brother and swore to kill him (Genesis 27:41-45). Subsequently, Esau's descendants intermarried with the Canaanites and occupied Edom, the area south and east of the Dead Sea.[15] The Edomites became the historical enemy of Judah, as highlighted by their rejoicing at Jerusalem's destruction by the Babylonians. Having allied themselves with Babylon, they subsequently occupied southern Judea.

During the fifth century B.C.E., Edom came under Arab control. By the fourth century B.C.E., the Edomites were overrun by the Nabateans, who pushed them out of their native lands. Eventually, some Edomites were absorbed by the Nabatean Arabs and others moved back into southern Judea, which became known as Idumea.[16]

About 120 B.C.E., John Hyrcanus, of the Hasmonean dynasty, forcibly annexed Idumea and compelled the Edomites to adopt Judaism.[17] In 63 B.C.E., Rome occupied the entire area of Palestine and installed an Edomite governor, Antipater. This same Antipater became the father of Herod the Great, who killed all male children under the age of two years in an attempt to eliminate the Jewish Messiah.

History therefore verifies that the Edomites, the descendants of Esau, were the controlling power at the time of Yeshua. In essence, the crucifixion was the result of the ancient spiritual conflict between the House of Easu and the House of Jacob, that persists to this day in the Middle East conflict. This perspective clarifies Zechariah's prophecy concerning Esau and the house of Herod. They represent the "foolish and worthless shepherd" described in Zechariah 11:15-17.

God allowed His lost sheep of the House of Esau the opportunity of reconciliation with Jacob through salvation in the Messiah, Yeshua. However, Esau rejected the only true Messiah, leaving Him for the House of Jacob, the House of Israel, and the Gentiles (Genesis 12:3; Galatians 3:13-14; Isaiah 11:10; 49:6).

In its place, the later descendants of Esau accepted Islam's counterfeit of God's covenant, i.e. that God's promise to Abraham was to come through his son Ishmael, not Isaac. As the descendants of Esau also inter-married with the descendants of Ishmael (Arabs), we can see a continuation of the battle between Jacob and Esau for the birthright blessing. The end result is that Esau, who hates his brother (Genesis 27:41-45), is cut off and eventually destroyed by God Himself (Isaiah 34:5-8; Jeremiah 49:8-22; Obadiah 1:18). THIS IS NOT TO SAY THAT AN INDIVIDUAL OF THIS LINE IS NOT GIVEN THE FREEWILL CHOICE FOR SALVATION THROUGH YESHUA. Any individual, regardless of race or any other factor, is given the oppor-tunity to accept God's One, true Messiah. Having this understanding of Zechariah's prophecies, let us now return to the chronology of events.

14TH OF ABIB (SUNSET TUESDAY TO SUNSET WEDNESDAY)

In the Upper Room

As Tuesday evening approached, the disciples fol-lowed their Master's instructions to prepare the Passover meal at the place made ready for them. It is important to point out that Yeshua ate His last Passover meal on Tuesday evening, the 14th of Abib. This was in accor-dance with the original Passover ordinance (Leviticus 23:5). The Jewish nation, however, did not eat their Passover meal until the following evening, Wednesday, the 15th of Abib, in accordance with the shifted date for Passover (Chapter 8). The symbolic significance of this will be discussed shortly.

During the Passover meal, Yeshua washed the feet of His disciples. As He did so, He revealed that one of them was unclean, i.e. would deliver Him. According to John, Yeshua designated Judas and gave him leave to do so (John 13:26-27). The other disciples were not aware of the real reason why Judas left when he did. Since Judas left, he rightly missed partaking of what followed.

As Yeshua broke the bread, He was symbolically offering Himself as the "bread from heaven" (John 6):

> v. 32 'Truly, truly, I say to you, it is not Moses who has given you the bread out of heaven, but it is My Father who gives you the true bread out of heaven.

> v. 33 'For the bread of God is that which comes down out of heaven, and gives life to the world.

> v. 34 They said therefore to Him, 'Lord, evermore give us this bread.'

> v. 35 Jesus said to them, 'I am the bread of life; he who comes to Me shall not hunger, and he who believes in Me shall never thirst.'

When the Israelites were in the wilderness, God had miraculously provided manna from Heaven. They were to collect no more than their daily need, except the day before Sabbath when they were allowed to collect twice as much so that they would not have to work on Sabbath. (Exodus 16:16, 22). By following God's instruction, the people showed their faith (trust) that He would provide for their daily needs. The amount collected was called an *omer* and provided total and complete sustenance.[18]

The omer also symbolically represents the Messiah. In this regard, it is highly significant that Aaron was instructed to keep one omer of manna in a jar in the Holy of Holies, in front of the Ark of the Covenant, as a sign to all the generations of God's providence (Exodus 16:33). The omer of manna represented Yeshua, the spiritual "Bread from Heaven." In Him, all of an individual's spiritual needs are met.

After offering the disciples the bread, Yeshua offered them the wine (Matthew 26):

> v. 27 And when He had taken a cup and given thanks, He gave it to them, saying, "Drink from it, all of you;
>
> v. 28 for this is My blood of the covenant, which is poured out for many for forgiveness of sins.
>
> v. 29 "But I say to you, I will not drink of this fruit of the vine from now on until that day when I drink it new with you in My Father's kingdom.

Yeshua offered His disciples the Third Cup of the Seder (Passover meal). The Third Cup symbolizes redemption. Yeshua's blood, symbolized by the wine, provides that redemption. When Yeshua says that He will not drink of the wine again until He drinks it with believers in Heaven, He refers to the Fourth Cup of the Seder. The Fourth Cup symbolizes praise and will be drunk by the Bride at the Marriage Supper of the Lamb, a time of great praise and celebration!

Clearly, Yeshua intended the symbolic meaning of the bread and wine. The bread symbolizes His body: it was unleavened, meaning without sin. The wine symbolizes His blood: it was shed in atonement for humankind's sin (Matthew 26:26-28). This was indeed one of the most memorable occasions experienced by the disciples, although, at the time, they did not comprehend its full meaning. Yeshua intended that this symbolic remembrance and understanding of His sacrifice of love would be continued by believers for generations to come.

At Gethsemane

After the Passover meal, Yeshua and His disciples went to a garden (tree orchard) on the Mount of Olives, where they had often enjoyed one another's companionship. This time, however, it was not a pleasurable time of relaxation, for Yeshua felt the crushing weight of what He was about to endure. He selected His closest disciples to come away from the group in order to pray. Then, He moved apart from them to pray to His Father to spare Him, if possible, from the terrible suffering to come. Nevertheless, He asked that the will of the Father be done, knowing that the only way to bring salvation to humankind was through His own sacrifice (Matthew 26:36-39).

Sadly, when Yeshua needed the support of those nearest Him, they fell asleep. Knowing that His time was at hand, He woke His disciples. Immediately, Judas Iscariot and an armed, angry mob approached. This mob included the Temple Guard, which consisted of Levites and priests, not Roman soldiers.[19] Their purpose was to take Yeshua to the the High Priest on the Temple Mount.

Note that the word "Roman" in the NASB version of John 18:3, 12 appears in italics, indicating that this word is not in the original Greek text. Other English versions do not even include the word "Roman." Also, the word translated "cohort" comes from a Greek word that actually means "mob." Luke mentions the High Priest's slave as well as the chief priests and officers of the Temple, which confirms this was the Temple Guard, not a Roman cohort (Luke 22:50-52). This distinction is important because Yeshua fulfilled Messianic prophecies according to Jewish, not Roman, law.

Knowing their purpose, Yeshua faced them and asked whom they sought. When they replied "Jesus the Nazarene," His response was: "I am" (John 18:5). Though most versions translate this as "I am He," the original Greek can be translated as "I Am (the) I Am" and "I Am (the One that) will be." Clearly, Yeshua is referring to Old

Testament scripture which recorded Moses' face to face encounter with God at the burning bush. At that time, Moses asked God His Name, to which came the reply: "I AM WHO I AM; and He said, 'Thus you shall say to the sons of Israel, I AM has sent me to you' " (Exodus 3:13-14). The original Hebrew of this passage translates as: "I will be who I will be."[20] By this statement, Yeshua identified Himself as the great "I AM"—the One who is Eternal, the One who was promised to come as the Redeemer!

As Yeshua spoke the words "I Am," the mob backed away and fell to the ground (John 18:6). Surely, they were overcome by the power of God! Nevertheless, Yeshua voluntarily gave Himself over to them in order to fulfill His purpose of redeeming humankind. Prior to this, whenever His enemies had desired to seize Him, they had never been able to do so. However, this was the appointed time so that the prophetic timetable be exactly fulfilled (Matthew 26:56).

On the Temple Mount

Yeshua asked that His disciples not be arrested along with Him. As He allowed Himself to be led away, the disciples fled in fear. Only Peter and John followed at a safe distance as the arresting party led Yeshua down the Mount of Olives and across the bridge to the "house" of the High Priest, Caiaphas. It has been generally assumed that this was the personal house of Caiaphas. However, an understanding of Jewish law reveals the actual location of the High Priest at this time.

According to Jewish law, the High Priest had to live on the Temple premises during the major feast days. This was to ensure ritual cleanness of the priest so that he would be able to carry out his duties and festival rituals. For this reason, underground chambers below the

Temple were provided to house, not only the High Priest and Assistant High Priest, but also many other priests (Figure 9).[21] According to the Bible, a courtyard was located near the chamber of the High Priest, Caiaphas— the same courtyard where Peter denied his Lord three times (Luke 22:55).

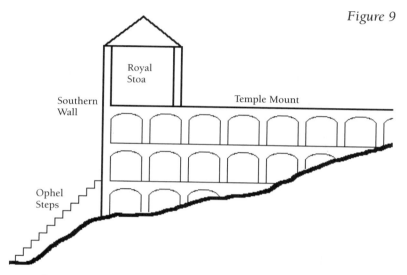

Figure 9

Temple Mount Vaults and Underground Chambers

Layered chambers were used for storage of items used in Temple rituals and ensured that the Temple itself did not touch defiled ground. In addition, underground chambers provided residential quarters for priests who performed Temple rituals and duties during their priestly course.

Yeshua was questioned first by Annas, the father-in-law and assistant to the High Priest, Caiaphas (John 18:13). He was then questioned by Caiaphas himself. At daybreak, Yeshua was taken to be tried by the Sanhedrin in the Chamber of Hewn Stones, the large council chamber at the southeast corner of the Temple.[22] There, conflicting testimony given by false witnesses was accepted as valid (Mark 14:56-59).

To these false accusations, Yeshua did not reply. To a direct question from Caiaphas, "Are You the Christ, the Son of the Blessed?", Yeshua responded, "I am; and you shall see the Son of Man sitting at the right hand of power, and coming with the clouds of heaven." This truthful statement evoked a judgment of blasphemy by the High Priest and all those present (Mark 14:64). And the uncontested sentence for blasphemy was death. Remarkably, this was to be the last judgment made by the Sanhedrin within the walls of the Chamber of Hewn Stone, for it was destroyed at the instant Yeshua breathed His last (Chapter 11)!

At the Antonia Fortress

In order to carry out a death sentence, the High Priest and Sanhedrin had to first obtain permission from the Roman authorities. For this reason, Yeshua was taken before the Roman governor, Pilate, in the Praetorium located inside the Antonia Fortress, just north of the Temple. The religious leaders took Him to the "hall of judgment" but did not go in for fear of becoming defiled (John 18:28). In their religiosity, they adhered to certain legalisms, yet violated the spirit of the Law for the sake of power and position, as they falsely condemned Yeshua.

Pilate asked what accusation they brought against Yeshua. Even at the initial stage of his involvement, Pilate revealed a reluctance to deal with this case. He told the religious leaders to "judge Him according to your law" (John 18:31). It seems he was trying to heed the warning given to him by his wife, who had experienced a prophetic dream concerning Yeshua the night before.

However, the religious leaders forced the issue by stating they could not lawfully perform execution without

Roman permission. When Pilate heard that the accused was a Galilean, he sent Him to King Herod in an attempt to abdicate all responsibility for this man's fate. Herod had heard of the amazing miracles Yeshua had performed and was most eager to become a firsthand witness. Yeshua's refusal to perform "signs and wonders" for Herod provoked cruel ridicule and abuse (Luke 23:9-11). After Herod and his men were through with Yeshua, He was returned to Pilate.

Pilate then interrogated Yeshua, asking, "Are you the King of the Jews," to which Yeshua responded, "My kingdom is not of this world: if my kingdom were of this world, then would my servants fight, that I should not be delivered to the Jews..." (John 18:36).

At this point, it is essential to clarify the meaning of the Greek words *hoi Ioudaioi,* translated "the Jews." According Malcolm Lowe, a Christian writer, editor and lecturer residing in Jerusalem:

> Sometimes *hoi Ioudaioi* means the Judean population in general, sometimes specifically their leaders....
>
> Moreover, John's Gospel says that the people of Judea stopped opposing Jesus. After he raised Lazarus from the dead, most of the people changed to admiring him. When John 19 is read carefully, one finds that the people had no role in the death of Jesus. Even those who call for the freeing of Barabbas are not a crowd of people, but just the chief priests and their officers.[23]

A careful reading of Scripture confirms that the Jewish people as a whole admired Yeshua and considered Him a prophet from God. It was the political and religious leadership who were threatened by Him and desired to kill Him. When Pilate asked Yeshua if He were King of the

Jews, he was referring to "the Jews," meaning the general Jewish population. When Yeshua answered Pilate, He refered to being delivered over to "the Jews," meaning the leadership, not the people. But who was the real power in the leadership at the time of Yeshua?

The Herodian dynasty was founded by Herod the Great, whose father was an Edomite (Idumean) and whose mother was a Nabatean Arab.[24] Recall that the Hasmonean dynasty which annexed Idumea compelled the Edomites to adopt Judasim. For this reason, Herod considered himself to be a Jew. However, the Pharisees, the spiritual leaders of the people, and the Jewish people never accepted Herod and his descendants as legitimate rulers. In fact, Herod required assistance from Rome to become installed as King of the Jews.

Not only were the Edomites the actual political power at that time, but the religious leadership was totally under their control. This was accomplished by controlling the office of the High Priest, head of the priesthood and the Sanhedrin. Up until the time of Antiochus Epiphanes, the legitimate Zadokite line filled this life-long and hereditary position. However, Antiochus deposed the Zadokite line in order to install High Priests totally controlled by him. Likewise, the Herodian Edomites totally controlled the office and filled it with illegitimate priests based solely upon political considerations. The term of office was considerably shortened and given to the highest bidder.[25] The resulting corruption of the high priesthood spread throughout the priestly aristocracy, which was mostly Sadducean at the time. The Jewish people knew that the High Priest was nothing more than a corrupt puppet of the political regime and that the Sanhedrin was controlled by a corrupt leadership. (For an in-depth study of this subject, see *The Crucifixion—The Edomite Connection* by Peter A. Michas.)

With this understanding, let us return to Pilate's questioning of Yeshua. His final response to Pilate was that He had come to bear witness to the truth (John 18:37), to which Pilate responded, "What is truth?" Judging Yeshua an innocent man, Pilate still had one possible hope of releasing Him even though the priests had found Him guilty.

At Passover, the people could choose to release one man condemned to die. Pilate offered Yeshua as that man but the corrupt religious leaders and their associates chose Barabbas. The people were not present and so not represented. Scripture clearly indicates that the Jewish people as a whole accepted Yeshua as a prophet from God, and that it was the chief priests (the religious leadership) and the rulers (the Edomite leadership) who were responsible for condemning and crucifying Him:

> ...And they said to Him, "The things about Jesus the Nazarene, who was a prophet mighty in deed and word in the sight of God and all the people, and how the chief priests and our rulers delivered Him up to the sentence of death, and crucified Him" (Luke 24:19, 20).

A decision to override them could easily have turned very ugly and very violent. Unable to afford the risk of revolt against Rome, Pilate washed his hands of the entire affair, in accordance with Jewish law (Deuteronomy 21:6-8).

GOD'S PASSOVER LAMB AND THE "SUFFERING SERVANT"

Yeshua, God's Passover Lamb—innocent of any sin—was delivered as a substitute sacrifice for the sins of humanity. He had undergone the four days of examination by the religious leaders and the people, and shown Himself to be without sin. Rather, sin was shown in those who unjustly condemned Him.

Isaiah's prophecies concerning the "Suffering Servant" were fulfilled in Yeshua the Messiah (Isaiah 53):

v. 3   He was despised and forsaken of men, A man of sorrows, and acquainted with grief; And like one from whom men hide their face, He was despised, and we did not esteem Him.

v. 4   Surely our griefs He Himself bore, And our sorrows He carried; Yet we ourselves esteemed Him stricken, Smitten of God, and afflicted.

v. 5   But He was pierced through for our transgressions, He was crushed by our iniquities; The chastening for our well-being fell upon Him, And by His scourging we are healed.

v. 6   All of us like sheep have gone astray, Each of us has turned to his own way; But the Lord has caused the iniquity of us all To fall on Him.

v. 7   He was oppressed and He was afflicted, Yet He did not open His mouth; Like a lamb that is led to slaughter, And like a sheep that is silent before its shearers, So He did not open His mouth.

Each carefully selected Passover lamb was slaughtered that day in preparation for the Passover meal, as the people observed it in the evening of the 15th of Abib (Wednesday evening). In this way, God's masterful Hand is evident as His Son observed the originally ordained Passover date (the 14th of Abib) and yet was able to become God's Passover Lamb. According to Mark 15:25, Yeshua was crucified at the third hour (9 am) but did not die until the ninth hour (3 pm).

The first-century Jewish historian Josephus records that the Passover lambs were sacrificed between 3 and 5 p.m.[26] Therefore, Yeshua died just before the sacrifices began. In other words, He was the fulfillment of the Passover Lamb and, thereafter, no other animal sacrifice was either necessary or efficacious. In all regards, the symbolic meaning is as powerful as it is precise according to God's Master Plan!

ON THE MOUNT OF OLIVES AT GOLGOTHA

Just as meaningful as the time of Yeshua's sacrifice was the site of His sacrifice. As previously discussed in Chapter 3, the Mount of Olives was the site of the most holy sin sacrifice, the Red Heifer. In addition, the ashes of all sin sacrifices performed in the Temple (including those on Yom Kippur, the Day of Atonement) had to be mingled with the ashes of the Red Heifer in order to be acceptable. Clearly, this altar was of supreme importance to God in accepting the ultimate sin sacrifice for all humankind's sin.

This altar was first built by Adam, at God's command, on the summit of the Mount of Olives. As Yeshua was led to the site of the crucifixion, He followed the same pathway as the Red Heifer—from the Temple Mount, across the Kidron bridge, and up to the summit.

The summit of the Mount of Olives is 2,660 feet above sea level,[27] the highest point directly east of the Temple Mount on Mount Moriah, which is 2,418 feet above sea level.[28] Because the entire Israelite nation was required to be in Jerusalem for Passover, the city and the slopes of the Mount of Olives were covered with people. Some scholars estimate that 80,000-100,000 pilgrims were added to the city's population of 150,000-200,000—a total of over 200,000 massed together in one spot.[29] Beyond doubt, the sacrifice of God's Lamb was witnessed by all Israel.

From Adam to Abraham, this altar was rebuilt at God's command. When Abraham lovingly placed his only son as a sacrifice on this same summit, God intervened, providing a substitute sacrifice. This was a foreshadowing of the ultimate sacrifice for all humanity's sin yet to come. Abraham gave a profoundly prophetic reply to Isaac's question, "Where is the sacrifice?" From the original Hebrew, Abraham said:

GOD WILL PROVIDE HIMSELF AS THE LAMB[30]

That prophecy was fulfilled in Yeshua—God incarnate! God's infinite and eternal nature by definition exceeds our finite and temporal attempts to comprehend and explain Him. Nevertheless, God communicates the truth about the Messiah to us in a way we can understand, through the use of literal and symbolic pictures. As we delve into the Word of God and the Holy Spirit enlightens us, the true Messiah's identity is revealed beyond any shadow of a doubt!

From the time of David, Golgotha ("the place of the skull") remained the place "outside the camp," where God was worshipped and where the Red Heifer and other sin sacrifices were brought. As discussed in Chapter 6, the authors believe that David planted a branch from Tree of Life here, under God's direction. The almond tree that grew from this branch bore the body of the Messiah, who is the Fruit that gives eternal life!

THE MEANING OF YESHUA'S FINAL WORDS

Just before Yeshua died, He cried out: "My God, My God, Why hast Thou Forsaken Me!" and "It is finished!" (Mark 15:34; John 19:30). These words are often misinterpreted to mean that somehow God the Father abandoned His Son. Nothing could be further from the truth and the profound meaning of these words is restored once they are put back into the Hebraic context.

According to Hebraic understanding, a reference to the first and last words of a particular text denotes the entire text. With this understanding, Yeshua's final words are of the utmost significance. In Hebrew, He cried out the first and last words of Psalm 22. The Jewish witnesses, especially the priests, knew what that Psalm contained: a detailed prophetic picture of the crucifixion, written one thousand years before by David! Truly, Yeshua was testifying that He is the prophetic fulfillment of Psalm 22!

Prophetic details concerning the timing and site of the crucifixion reveal the identity of the true Messiah. The evidence is overwhelming and yet there is still more powerful evidence to identify Yeshua as the fulfillment of the Law in every aspect and detail. In the next two chapters, we will see through the eyes of the witnesses during that most terrible and awesome day, two thousand years ago…

Notes

1. Philip Birnbaum, *Encyclopedia of Jewish Concepts*, p. 581.
2. Birnbaum, p. 581.
3. Jack Finegan, *The Archaeology of the New Testament*, p. 91.
4. W. E. Vine, *Vine's Expository Dictionary of Old and New Testament Words*, Vol. 1, p. 198.
5. Dr. Zvi Faier, Translator, *The Torah Anthology*, Vol. 13, p. 398.
6. Merrill C. Tenney, Editor, *The Zondervan Pictorial Encyclopedia of the Bible*, Vol. 4, p. 587.
7. Archibald Thomas Robertson, *Word Pictures in the New Testament*, Vol. 5, p. 220.
8. *The Zondervan Pictorial Encyclopedia of the Bible*, Vol. 3, p. 206.
9. Rabbi A. J. Rosenberg, Translator, *The Book of the Twelve Prophets*, Vol. 2, p. 362.
10. Rosenberg, Vol. 2, p. 362.
11. Vine, Vol. 1, p. 122.

12. Rosenberg, Vol. 2, pp. 376-377.

13. Rosenberg, Vol. 2, pp. 378-380.

14. Rosenberg, Vol. 2, p. 379.

15. *The Zondervan Pictorial Encyclopedia of the Bible*, Vol. 2, pp. 202-203; Vol. 3, p. 41.

16. *The Zondervan Pictorial Encyclopedia of the Bible*, Vol. 2, p. 204.

17. *The Zondervan Pictorial Encyclopedia of the Bible*, Vol. 2, p. 204; Vol. 3, pp. 41-42.

18. Rabbi Aryeh Kaplan, Translator, *The Torah Anthology*, Vol. 12, p.158.

19. Alfred Edersheim, *The Temple: Its Ministry and Services* (1979 softcover edition), pp. 147-148. Joachim Jeremias, *Jerusalem in the Time of Jesus*, p. 210.

20. *The Torah Anthology*, Vol. 4, p. 91.

21. Edersheim, pp. 52-54. Meir Ben-Dov, *In the Shadow of the Temple*, pp. 91, 132.

22. *The Zondervan Pictorial Encyclopedia of the Bible*, Vol. 5, p. 271.

23. "Understanding John's Gospel (II)," *Christians and Israel*, p. 5.

24. Dr. Geoffrey Wigoder, Editor, *The New Standard Jewish Encyclopedia*, p. 436.

25. Rabbi Hersh Goldwurm, Adapter, *History of the Jewish People/The Second Temple Era*, p. 149.

26. Nahum M. Sarna, Commentator, *The JPS Torah Commentary: Exodus*, p. 55.

27. Finegan, p. 89.

28. Finegan, p. 110.

29. Ben-Dov, p. 75.

30. Phinehas Ben Zadok, *Which Day Is the Passover?*, p. 35.

10

THE HIDDEN MEANING OF PILATE'S INSCRIPTION

*And Pilate wrote an inscription also
and put it on the cross. And it was written,
"JESUS THE NAZARENE, THE KING OF THE
JEWS."...and it was written in
Hebrew, Latin, and in Greek*
(John 19:19-20).

The four gospel accounts of the crucifixion mention an inscription that was placed above the crucified Yeshua. It is generally assumed that these accounts refer to one and the same inscription. However, closer examination of the relevant passages reveals that more than one inscription was involved.

ONE ACCUSATION—ONE TITLE

Let us closely examine the gospel record in order to determine the number and type of inscriptions displayed above the Messiah's head:

And they put above His head the *charge* against Him which read, "THIS IS JESUS THE KING OF THE JEWS" (Matthew 27:37).

And the *inscription* [superscription] of the *charge* against Him read, "THE KING OF THE JEWS" (Mark 15:26).

Now there was also an *inscription* [superscription] above Him, "THIS IS THE KING OF THE JEWS" (Luke 23:38).

And Pilate wrote an *inscription* [title] *also*, and put it on the cross. And it was written, "JESUS THE NAZARENE, THE KING OF THE JEWS" (John 19:19) (emphasis added.)

Matthew and Mark state the *charge* against Yeshua. The Greek word translated "charge" comes from *aitia*, meaning "cause" or "accusation."[1] In addition, Mark and Luke refer to a "superscription," meaning the charge was written above Yeshua. The Greek word translated "superscription" is *epigraphe*.[2]

In contrast, John describes an *inscription* that was *written by Pilate in addition* to the charge. The word translated "inscription" in John 19:19 comes from the Greek word *titlon*, meaning "title."[3] Moreover, the fact that the Greek distinguishes between "title" and "accusation" also seems to confirm two separate inscriptions.

Another reason for suspecting two separate inscriptions can be perceived from the reaction of the religious leaders to Pilate's title. They became greatly agitated and demanded that Pilate reword it (John 19):

> v. 21 And so the chief priests of the Jews were saying to Pilate, "Do not write, 'The King of the Jews'; but that He said, 'I am the King of the Jews.' "
>
> v. 22 Pilate answered, "What I have written I have written."

Pilate was adamant about not changing one letter of the inscription. It was the only time during the entire affair that he dared go against the demands of the religious leaders. What was so significant about the wording of this inscription that the chief priests insisted it be changed? The authors believe that the chief priests responded with an inscription of their own to counteract Pilate's inscription. After two thousand years, is it possible to unlock the mystery of its meaning?

PILATE'S INSCRIPTION

John 19:20 states that Pilate's inscription was written in three languages: Hebrew, Latin, and Greek. Because the great majority of the Jewish people were in Jerusalem for Passover, and Yeshua was crucified in a public place, thousands must have read this inscription. For us to comprehend the profound meaning it conveyed, we must first recover the exact wording on the crossbar that day, almost two thousand years ago. We must also have a fundamental grasp of how subtle changes in the Greek and Hebrew language can result in a significant change in meaning.

The original Greek of Pilate's inscription, as recorded in John 19:19, is:

IHΣOYΣ O NAZΩPAIOΣ O BAΣIΛEYΣ TΩN
IOYΔAIΩN[4]

Because Greek is the language in which the New Testament was preserved, we must reconstruct the Hebrew and Latin from the Greek. We must also arrive at the most accurate English translation from the Greek. Ultimately, understanding the Hebrew is the key to unlocking the hidden meaning of the inscription.

First, note that there are slight variations among English translations. For example, both King James Version (KJV) and New International Version (NIV) translate:

189

JESUS OF NAZARETH, THE KING OF THE JEWS

In contrast, both New American Standard Bible (NASB) and Amplified Bible (AB) versions translate:

JESUS THE NAZARENE, THE KING OF THE JEWS

Realizing that seemingly insignificant variations may obscure profound meaning in the original language, it is necessary to reconstruct the original Hebrew from the Greek text. For purposes of our discussion, note that transliteration refers to converting the letters of one alphabet into the corresponding letters of another alphabet, while translation refers to converting from one language into another language. We will begin by examining the inscription, word for word:

1. The name "Jesus" (*Iesus*) is the English transliteration of the Greek. The English transliteration of the Hebrew name is *Yeshua*, meaning "Salvation."

2. The word translated "Nazareth" in some English translations and "Nazarene" in others is accurately translated from the original Greek as *Nazarene*.[5] The actual Hebrew word, transliterated into English, is *Hanatzri*.

3. The original Hebrew word translated "King" seems to be the source of great upset among the Jewish leaders. The current Hebrew text translates the Greek word as *Melech*. However, it seems unlikely that this *form* of the Hebrew word created the problem since the religious leaders themselves used it to mock Yeshua (John 19:21).

4. The key to solving the problem which Hebrew word was used for "King" in the original Hebrew inscription comes from understanding the correct usage of the Greek letter, *omicron* (O), in the original Greek inscription. Generally, the omicron translates as "the."[6] However,

there are other possible translations depending upon the context.[7]

The "O" appears twice in the Greek inscription above: between *Yeshua* and *Nazarene,* then between *Nazarene* and *King.* Note the differences in how the omicron is translated in the English translations above. In the KJV and NIV, the first omicron is translated *of;* the second omicron is translated *the.* In the NASB and AB, both first and second omicrons are translated *the.* Judging by the reaction of the religious leaders, it seems the translation of the second omicron is *and,* resulting in the following English translation of the inscription:

JESUS THE NAZARENE *AND* KING OF THE JEWS

If the correct translation of the omicron before the word *King* is "and," the correct form of the Hebrew word for *King (Melech)* is *Vemelech,* meaning *and King.* (Note that the article *and* is indicated by the prefix *ve-.*) This apparently minor change in both the English and Hebrew will in fact have profound implications in the meaning of the inscription.

5. The last two Greek words in the inscription translate into English as "of the Jews." In Hebrew, it is one word, which transliterates into English as *HaYehudim.*

THE INEFFABLE NAME OF GOD

In order to ascertain the hidden meaning of the inscription, it is essential to comprehend certain unique aspects of Hebrew writing. In Hebrew study, speaking or writing the first and last words of a written text implies the entire text. A good example of this is Yeshua words on the tree. He spoke the first and last words of Psalm 22 to refer to the entire text of Psalm 22. In doing so, He indicated that He was the fulfillment of its prophetic picture.

In the same manner, the Jewish scribes of that day used a method of interpretation whereby the first letters of a sequence of words were combined in order to discern further meanings. This was particularly true if the first letters of the words were enlarged for emphasis.

The Roman Catholic Church borrowed this idea when they placed the four letters *INRI* on the crucifix. These are the first letters of the four words that make up the inscription in Latin, the language of the Roman Catholic Church:

IESVS NAZARENVS REX IUDAEORVM

However, the hidden meaning is entirely lost unless one goes back to the original Hebrew. The religious leaders of the day would certainly have related to their own God-given language and herein lies the cause of their alarm. The original Hebrew is:

יֵשׁוּעַ הַנָּצְרִי וּמֶלֶךְ הַיְהוּדִים

The first letters of the four Hebrew words are:

יהוה

Before this mystery can be fully revealed, we must remember that Hebrew is read from right to left. In order to clarify this aspect, let us look at the Hebrew for the full inscription, transliterated into English (from left to right):

YESHUA HANATZRI VEMELECH HAYEHUDIM

Thus, the first letters of the four words are:

YHVH

YHVH—the Tetragrammaton—is none other than the Ineffable Name of God! It was considered too awesome and too sacred to even be spoken! Let us recall that the rod of God also carried the Ineffable Name of God. Just as the rod from the Tree of Life carried the name of God, so too the crucifixion tree, which grew from the rod, carried the name of God!

It was also a sign of who Yeshua was—the Lamb of God—the Lamb God prophetically promised to Abraham. To fully appreciate the symbolic importance, we must understand a Passover tradition that was practiced at this time. As Jews prepared for the Feast of Unleavened Bread, they acquired a copper name tag bearing the family name. This tag was hung around the Passover lamb's neck with a red rope to identify their sacrifice. So, too, God's Passover Lamb was clearly marked for all to see and understand that Yeshua is the ultimate Passover sacrifice for the sins of humankind, once, and for all time!

ADDITIONAL MEANINGS

Nothing can compare with the title YHVH. Nonetheless, additional meanings within the inscription can be found when examining the individual words. Even the name *Yeshua*, meaning "Salvation," is consistent with Yeshua's role as the Savior of humankind (Matthew 1:21). John the Baptist referred to Him as the Lamb of God that takes away the sins of the world (John 1:29).

As mentioned previously, the word *Vemelech* itself refers to the title of King. Yeshua was who He said He was and this was why Pilate could find no guilt in Him. Is it possible that Pilate's own confession of faith is to be found within the inscription he wrote to honor Yeshua?

Moreover, the word *Hanatzri* ("Nazarene") was a link to Old Testament prophecies concerning the future Messiah. Matthew referred to the fact that Yeshua resided in the city of Nazareth so "that what was spoken through the prophets might be fulfilled, 'He shall be called a Nazarene' " (Matthew 2:23).

In accordance with Hebraic thought, further meanings can be implied from the root of the word used. For example, *Hanatzri* comes from the root word *natzr*, meaning to "watch," "guard," "protect," and "keep." This meaning is expressed in Isaiah 27:3, where the Lord is described as the "watchman" or "keeper" of Israel, His vineyard:

v. 2   In that day, A vineyard of wine, sing of it!

v. 3   "I, the Lord, am its keeper; I water it every moment. Lest anyone damage it, I guard it night and day.

In the same way, the Lord is referred to as the "Watcher" and "Keeper" of human life (Job 7:20; Isaiah 27:3; Proverbs 24:12; Psalm 25:20-21).[8] Moreover, Yeshua, as Creator, is the Keeper and Preserver of the order of the entire universe. As Colossians 1 states:

v. 16   For by Him all things were created, in the heavens and on earth, visible and invisible, whether thrones or dominions or rulers or authorities—all things have been created by Him and for Him.

v. 17   And He is before all things, and in Him all things hold together.

Another very interesting connection is found in God's promise to David (II Samuel 7):

v. 12   "When your days are complete and you lie down with your fathers, I will raise up your descendant after you, who will come forth from you, and I will establish his kingdom....

v. 16   "And your house and your kingdom shall endure before Me forever; and your throne shall be established forever."

The word translated "descendant" comes from a Hebrew word derived from the same root, *natzr*. By this, God spoke through the prophet Nathan, to foretell that the Messiah would be David's descendant and establish the Throne of David forever. This promise was confirmed by the prophet Isaiah (Isaiah 11):

> v. 1 Then a shoot will spring from the stem of Jesse, and a branch from his roots will bear fruit.

Here, again, we have reference to the root word *natzri*, in the word *netzre*, from which the word "branch" is translated. The meaning is that the ancestral branch of Jessie, the father of David, will give rise to the Messiah. Yeshua was the fulfillment of this prophecy and that of Zechariah 6:

> v. 12 "Then say to him, 'Thus says the Lord of hosts, "Behold, a man whose name is Branch, for He will branch out from where He is; and He will build the temple of the Lord.
>
> v. 13 "Yes, it is He who will build the temple of the Lord, and He who will bear the honor and sit and rule on His throne. Thus, He will be a priest on His throne, and the counsel of peace will be between the two offices." '

This same Messiah is the Savior of all humankind because the root of Jesse includes all believers (Isaiah 60):

> v. 21 "Then all your people *will be* righteous; They will possess the land forever, the branch of My planting, The work of My hands, That I may be glorified."

At His second coming, Yeshua HaMashiach (Jesus the Messiah) will be revealed as Yeshua ben David (Yeshua, son of David) and fulfill His role as the Messiah who comes to set up His Kingdom in triumph. At the time of His crucifixion, however, He fulfilled the role of the Messiah as the Suffering Servant, Yeshua ben Joseph (Isaiah 53).[9]

That Yeshua is God is revealed in the profound meaning of the crucifixion inscription. Beyond this, many awesome signs were displayed as further confirmation that Yeshua was God incarnate. We will now examine those supernatural events that were witnessed by a vast crowd and the Roman centurion assigned to supervise the crucifixion...

Notes

1. James Strong, *The New Strong's Exhaustive Concordance of the Bible*, #156. W. E. Vine, *Vine's Expository Dictionary of Old and New Testament Words*, Vol. 1, p. 181.

2. Strong, #1923. Vine, Vol. 4, p. 93.

3. Henry G. Liddell and Robert Scott, *A Greek-English Lexicon*, p. 1799.

4. Alfred Marshall, *The Interlinear KJV-NIV Parallel New Testament in Greek and English*, p. 333.

5. Merrill C. Tenney, Editor, *The Zondervan Pictorial Encyclopedia of the Bible*, Vol. 4, pp. 387-388.

6. George C. Divry, *Divry's Modern English-Greek and Greek-English Desk Dictionary*, p. 611.

7. Liddell and Scott, pp. 1193-1195.

8. R. Laird Harris and others, *Theological Wordbook of the Old Testament*, Vol. 2, pp. 594-595.

9. F. F. Bruce, *The New Testament Development of Old Testament Themes*, pp. 68-99.

11

THE WITNESS OF THE CENTURION

Now the centurion, and those who were with
him keeping guard over Jesus, when they saw
the earthquake and the things that were
happening, became very frightened and said,
'Truly this was the Son of God!'
(Matthew 27:54).

As Yeshua suffered in agony on the tree, it was the Roman centurion's business to see to it that order was maintained. The centurion was a trained killer with little or no regard for human life, a man steeped in the pagan religion of the day. Yet, this human being with a heart of stone, who just a few hours earlier had been gambling for the Lord's garments, was instantly transformed by the remarkable events that transpired when Yeshua died.

While hanging on the tree, Yeshua was ridiculed by certain members of the crowd, including the chief priests, scribes, and elders; even the criminals crucified next to Him joined in (Matthew 27:39-44). Nonetheless, when the Lord breathed His last, the multitudes went away beating their breasts (Luke 23:48). At the same time, the centurion at the foot of the crucifixion tree was fearfully making his confession of faith (Matthew 27:54). What life-shattering experiences caused the dramatic spiritual conversion of these witnesses at the scene of the crucifixion?

DARKNESS FALLS AT NOON

Before discussing the supernatural events at Yeshua's death, it should be mentioned that an ominous darkness fell from noon until the time of His death (Matthew 27):

> v. 45 Now from the sixth hour [noon] darkness fell
> upon all the land until the ninth hour [3 pm].

The word "darkness" comes from the Greek word *skotos,* which generally refers to spiritual darkness.[1] Most often a physical darkness has been imagined and this can also be understood to be involved. However, the predominant nature of this darkness has to do with evil spiritual forces. Just as evil, oppressive forces pervaded the land at the time of the crucifixion, so too an evil spiritual atmosphere pervaded the location of the tomb prior to the resurrection (Chapter 12).

THE VOICE OF GOD

Scripture relates that Yeshua spoke with "a loud voice" just before dying (Matthew 27):

> v. 46 And about the ninth hour [3 pm] Jesus cried
> out in a loud voice...
> v. 50 And Jesus cried out again with a loud voice,
> and yielded up His spirit.

Considering His physical condition, it is probable that this was no ordinary voice, but rather a voice supernaturally empowered by God.

In verse 50, the Greek word translated "loud" comes from the root word *megas,* meaning "great" in form, size, or measure.[2] In this case, the authors believe it refers to a voice of supernatural quality. Likewise, the same word refers to the supernatural voices of the angels (Revelation 5:2, 12).

This word is also associated with other supernatural phenomena described in the New Testament. These include the "strong" wind of the storm that Yeshua miraculously calmed on the Sea of Galilee (John 6:18), and the falling of stars from the sky by a supernatural event likened to a "great" wind (Revelation 6:13). Again, the word is used to describe the disciples' miraculous catch of fish through the power of their Master (John 21:11); the mystery of Christ's relationship to the Church (Ephesians 5:32); and the stone that was supernaturally rolled away from the tomb at Yeshua's resurrection (Matthew 27:60).

Moreover, this Greek word is used to characterize both God (Titus 2:13) and Yeshua, the "great" High Priest (Hebrews 10:21). As Yeshua fulfilled the role of our eternal High Priest in His sacrifice for our redemption, He was empowered to speak with the voice of God because He is God, and His last words were a testimony to the prophetic fulfillment of God's Word in Psalm 22 (Chapter 9).

This event seems to parallel God's empowering of the High Priest on the Day of Atonement:

When the High Priest recited the Tetragrammaton [the name of God] on Yom Kippur [Day of Atonement] it could be heard at a very great distance. This was a great miracle, like when the Torah was given, as it was written, "Moses spoke and God answered in a voice" (Exodus 19:19). God made Moses' voice so strong that all 600,000 Israelites could hear it. Similarly, the same was true of the High Priest. *God would make his voice so loud so that all the people could hear it* (emphasis added).[3]

Yeshua, who is *The* High Priest, spoke with a voice so powerful that it reverberated from the Mount of Olives. Biblical and historical sources seem to show that the only damage sustained during the "earthquake" at the time of the crucifixion was limited to the Temple and the tombs located on the Mount of Olives. Was the great voice of God, as spoken by Yeshua as He faced the Temple, the actual cause of the ground's shaking?

THE TEARING OF THE VEIL

The tearing of the Temple veil, another of the many miraculous events associated with the crucifixion, occurred at the exact moment of Yeshua's death. Most Biblical commentators say that it was the veil in front of the Holy of Holies that was rent in two. However, there were actually two veils in the Second Temple: one in front of the Holy Place, at the eastern entrance to the Temple, and another separating the Holy Place from the innermost (and westernmost) Holy of Holies. Besides the veil at the entrance to the Holy Place, there was also a very large set of wooden doors behind this outer veil. Therefore, if the inner veil was torn, this would not be evident to witnesses outside the Temple.

Scripture is very specific in stating that it was the veil of the Temple that was rent from top to bottom:

> And behold, the veil of the temple was torn in two from top to bottom, and the earth shook; and the rocks were split (Matthew 27:51).

> And the veil of the temple was torn in two from top to bottom (Mark 15:38).

> ...and the veil of the Temple was torn in two (Luke 23:45).

According to Josephus, a great veil hung over the entrance (Porch) to the outer Temple so that no one could see inside the Holy Place.[4] This huge, exterior veil was beautifully embroidered in blue, white, scarlet, and purple.[5] Actually, the veil is better described as a curtain or rug, for it measured 82.5 feet in height and 24 feet in width![6] Josephus does not give its thickness, but it can be assumed to be at least as thick as the original veil in front of the Holy of Holies, which was "one handbreadth [three inches] in thickness."[7] Due to its great size, the veil of the Temple was easily visible from the summit of the Mount of Olives.

Historical evidence indicates that an earthquake fractured the supporting beam (lintel), to which the veil was attached, causing the veil to tear—at the precise moment Yeshua expired! Robertson states:

> Josephus (*War* VI. 299) tells of a quaking in the temple before the destruction and the Talmud tells of a quaking forty years before the destruction of the temple [in 70 C.E.]. Allen suggests that *'a cleavage in the masonry of the porch, which rent the outer veil and left the Holy Place open to view, would account for the language of the Gospels, of Josephus, and of the Talmud'* (emphasis added).[8]

As the earth shook, the thirty-ton lintel was fractured, ripping the huge veil in two:[9]

> And behold, the veil of the temple was torn in two from top to bottom, and the earth shook; and the rocks were split (Matthew 27:51).

Furthermore:

> ...early Jewish records show that the doors of the Holy Place (in front of which this curtain was suspended) mysteriously opened of their own accord in AD 30 (the year in which Christ was crucified)... (*Yoma* 39b).[10]

From the summit of the Mount of Olives, the centurion and everyone else there had a clear, unobstructed view of the front of the Temple (Figure 3). They could easily see the magnificent veil split asunder and the doors to the Temple thrown open! What they witnessed was the symbolic removal of the spiritual separation that existed between God and humanity. Human beings no longer required a Levitical High Priest as their mediator to God. From that time forward, each believer was given direct access to God through Yeshua, the eternal High Priest, and the only mediator between man and God.

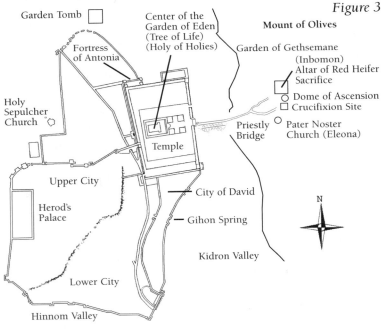

Figure 3

Garden Tomb

Center of the
Garden of Eden
(Tree of Life)
(Holy of Holies)

Mount of Olives

Fortress
of Antonia

Garden of Gethsemane
(Inbomon)
Altar of Red Heifer
Sacrifice

Holy
Sepulcher
Church

Dome of Ascension
Crucifixion Site

Priestly
Bridge

Pater Noster
Church (Eleona)

Temple

Upper City

City of David

N

Herod's
Palace

Gihon Spring

Kidron Valley

Lower City

Hinnom Valley

Jerusalem Site Map

According to the Mishna (Middot 2.4):

All the walls that were there [on the Temple Mount] were high, with the exception of the eastern wall, so that the [High] Priest who burned the [red] heifer stood on the top of the Mount of

Olives and was able to see directly into the entrance of the Sanctuary when the blood was sprinkled.

The rending of the Temple veil allowed God's High Priest, Yeshua—symbolized by the Red Heifer—to see directly into the entrance of the Sanctuary as His blood was shed!

THE EARTHQUAKE

The collapsing lintel not only tore the Temple veil but also destroyed the Chamber of Hewn Stone, the council chamber of the Sanhedrin located at the southeastern side of the Temple. From this time forward, the Sanhedrin was forced to convene at another location on the Temple Mount. Consequently, no one else would ever be tried in the place where Yeshua had been so unjustly convicted![11]

It seems possible that the Kidron bridge may have also collapsed or become impassable at this time. According to Josephus, when the Romans launched an attack against Jerusalem forty years later, there was no direct access to the city from the Kidron Valley.[12] This seems to indicate that the bridge was no longer passable at this time. Since the Kidron bridge was required to ensure a ritually clean path for all sin sacrifices brought from the Temple to the Mount of Olives, its absence would invalidate any such sacrifices.

In this regard, it is certainly remarkable that for forty years, from the crucifixion to the destruction of the Temple, there were supernatural signs that the Yom Kippur (Day of Atonement) sacrifices were no longer acceptable to God (Yoma 39b). One sign was that the scarlet wool of the scapegoat no longer miraculously turned to white, indicating the forgiveness of sins. Another was that the lot selecting the goat for God was, against the odds, drawn by the High Priest's left (inauspicious) hand on every Yom Kippur during this period of time. These were not the only signs occurring at this time to indicate Israel's impending doom (see Chapter 13).

THE GRAVES OPEN

As the ground continued to shake:

v. 52   ...the tombs were opened; and many bodies of the saints who had fallen asleep were raised;

v. 53   and coming out of the tombs after His resurrection they entered the holy city and appeared to many.

Again, what better place to witness the opening of the graves than on the Mount of Olives, where the graves, including those of some of the prophets, were located? Note that though the graves were opened at this point, the dead did not resurrect until Yeshua resurrected. At that time, they became witnesses to many in Jerusalem of what had transpired. Forming the luminescent cloud around Yeshua, they ascended with Him into Heaven forty days later.

At some future time, believers (whether in Heaven or on Earth) will hear and respond to the Lord's voice. As Hebrews 12 states:

v. 26   And His voice shook the earth then, but now He has promised, saying, 'Yet once more I will shake not only earth, but also the heaven.'

And in 1 Thessalonians 4:

v. 16   For the Lord Himself will descend from heaven with a shout, with the voice of the archangel, and with the trumpet of God, and the dead in Christ shall rise first.

v. 17 Then we who are alive and remain shall be caught up together with them in the clouds to meet the Lord in the air, and thus we shall always be with the Lord.

This is what is referred to as the "Rapture" or "catching up" of the Bride of Messiah. At this time, all believers receive an incorruptible spiritual body and will be with the Lord forever.

THE GLORY OF GOD

In almost every case that the voice of God is recorded in the Bible, the glory of God is present as well. The manifestation of the *Shekinah* (Divine Presence) occurred initially on Mount Sinai when God spoke to the people (Exodus 19:18-21). At the transfiguration, Yeshua became radiant as a cloud formed around Him and the voice of God said: "This is My beloved Son, listen to Him!" (Mark 9:3-7).

Accordingly, though it is not recorded in the gospels, it seems likely that there may have been a manifestation of God's glory as Yeshua gave up His Spirit (Matthew 27:50; Luke 23:46; and John 19:30). Even so, it is likely that only selected individuals were able to perceive this manifestation of God's power and presence (Acts 9:3-7).

Without exception, the human response to the Shekinah is one of awe and sometimes fear so great that it results in falling to the ground (Matthew 17:6; John 18:6; Matthew 27:54; 28:4). As Yeshua died, the centurion and other witnesses may have been allowed to see (or sense in some way) the luminescence of His Spirit as it left His earthly body. Assuredly, such an experience would be life-changing. According to Luke 23:48, as those witnessing all these events returned to the city, they beat their breasts—to this day an act of repentance among the Jews.

In the following chapter, we will deal with the next event in which God's glory was revealed—the resurrection. Though the disciples must have witnessed the supernatural occurrences surrounding the crucifixion, they were nevertheless totally overwhelmed by grief and despair at the loss of their Lord. Three days later, something happened that suddenly and dramatically transformed their lives forever...

Notes

1. Henry G. Liddell and Robert Scott, *A Greek-English Lexicon*, p. 1615. W. E. Vine, *Vine's Expository Dictionary of Old and New Testament Words*, Vol. 1, p. 268.

2. Vine, Vol. 2, p. 173.

3. Rabbi Aryeh Kaplan, *The Torah Anthology*, Vol. 11, p. 369.

4. Merrill C. Tenney, Editor, *The Zondervan Pictorial Encyclopedia of the Bible*, Vol. 5, p. 646.

5. Whiston, *Josephus Complete Works*, p. 555 (*Wars of the Jews*, V, 5, 5). *The Jewish Encyclopedia*, Vol. 12, p. 85.

6. William Whiston, Translator, *The Life and Works of Flavius Josephus*, p. 784.

7. Rabbi Dr. H. Freedman and Maurice Simon, Editors, *The Midrash*, Vol. 3, p. 559. *The Zondervan Pictorial Encyclopedia of the Bible*, Vol. 3, p. 29.

8. Archibald Thomas Robertson, *Word Pictures in the New Testament*, Vol. 1 p. 235.

9. Ernest L. Martin, *Secrets of Golgotha*, p. 17.

10. Martin, pp. 16-18.

11. Martin, p. 231.

12. Whiston, *Josephus Complete Works*, p. 557 (*Wars of the Jews*, V, 6, 2).

12

SABBATH—THE DAY OF THE RESURRECTION

*In the end of the Sabbath, as it began to
dawn toward the first day of the week, came
Mary Magdalene and the other Mary to see
the sepulchre (Matthew 28:1, KJV).*

Let us now pick up the chronology of events from the
day after the crucifixion up to and including the day
of the resurrection:

15TH OF ABIB (Sunset Wednesday to Sunset Thursday)

Yeshua's body was placed in a newly hewn tomb on
the Mount of Olives late in the day— sometime before
sunset—on Wednesday (the 14th of Abib). Though a very
heavy roll stone had been placed over the entrance of the
tomb, the religious leaders feared that the disciples might
attempt to remove the body. Therefore, the next day they
went to Pilate and said (Matthew 27):

> v. 63 …"Sir, we remember that when He was still
> alive that deceiver said, 'After three days I am
> to rise again.'

> v. 64 "Therefore, give orders for the grave to be made secure until the third day, lest the disciples come and steal Him away and say to the people, 'He has risen from the dead', and the last deception will be worse than the first."
>
> v. 65 Pilate said to them, *"You have a guard; go, make it as secure as you know how."*
>
> v. 66 *And they went and made the grave secure, and along with the guard they set a seal on the stone* (emphasis added).

Note Pilate's statement: "You have a guard." Pilate did not post a Roman guard at the tomb but instead directed the religious leaders to use their own Temple Guard for this purpose. It is highly unlikely that a Roman Guard would have been ready to admit they fell asleep at their posts (Matthew 28:13).[1] The Temple Guard was made up of Levites, assisted by priests, who also acted as Temple Police.[2] It was also the Temple Guard who made the arrest of Yeshua.

16TH OF ABIB (Sunset Thursday to Sunset Friday)

Mark 16:1 tells us that Friday, the day after the Passover Sabbath, Mary Magdalene, Mary (the mother of James), and Salome bought spices to complete the preparation of the body:

> And when the Sabbath [Passover Sabbath] was over, Mary Magdalene, and Mary the *mother* of James, and Salome, bought spices, that they might come and anoint Him.

Due to the hasty circumstances of the burial, there was insufficient time for complete preparation of the body before placing it into the tomb. Because of Passover (sunset Wednesday to sunset Thursday), they were not able to buy the necessary spices to complete the process until Friday.

It is important to note that the traditional Friday crucifixion and Sunday resurrection does not seem to allow adequate time for the women to buy spices. There was barely sufficient time to place the body in the tomb due to the fact that Passover Sabbath was fast approaching. Mary Magdalene and Mary were at the tomb when the body was placed inside. It does not seem likely that there would have been sufficient time for them to go from the tomb to the market to make such purchases when everyone was getting ready for Passover.

However, given that the crucifixion actually occurred on Wednesday, it can easily be seen how the women waited until after the completion of the Passover Sabbath. The next day, Friday, provided sufficient time to make the necessary purchases before the onset of the weekly Sabbath on Friday evening.

17TH OF ABIB (Sunset Friday to Sunset Saturday)

The next day, Saturday, was the weekly Sabbath. As will become clear, it was on this day that the Lord resurrected. The proof of this is found in Scripture by referring to the original Greek text. One may ask, "What difference does it make?" The answer to this question is that God set up His prophetic timetable for the purpose of revealing the identity of the true Messiah. With an accurate understanding of the timing of the crucifixion and the resurrection, the identity of the true Messiah is revealed and confirmed.

Remember what Yeshua said to the scribes and Pharisees who asked Him for a sign (Matthew 12):

> v. 38 Then some of the scribes and Pharisees answered Him, saying, "Teacher, we want to see a sign from You."
>
> v. 39 But he answered and said to them, "An evil and adulterous generation craves for a sign;

and *yet* no sign shall be given to it but the
sign of Jonah the prophet;

v. 40 *for just as* JONAH WAS THREE DAYS AND THREE
NIGHTS IN THE BELLY OF THE SEA MONSTER, *so
shall the Son of Man be three days and three
nights in the heart of the earth* (emphasis
added).

As clearly stated in Scripture, the sign of Jonah speci-
fied a period of three days and three nights. The traditional concept of a Friday crucifixion and a Sunday morning resurrection fails to satisfy the requirement of three
nights (Chapter 8). The question is: If Yeshua is Who He
claims to be, why the discrepancy? Unless we have an
accurate understanding of the timing of key events, we
cannot hope to adequately answer this legitimate question concerning a central issue.

The answer is explicitly given in the original Greek
text of every passage dealing with the day of the resurrection. Therefore, an accurate translation of the original
Greek is absolutely essential in this study.

THE BASIS FOR A SUNDAY RESURRECTION

Sunday is the traditional day celebrated as the day of
the resurrection and is supported by English translations
referring to "the first day of the week." Even so, the KJV
of Matthew 28:1 seems to imply that the resurrection
actually occurred on Sabbath (Saturday):

In the end of the Sabbath, as it began to dawn
toward the first *day* of the week, came Mary
Magdalene and the other Mary to see the sepulchre (emphasis added).

If Mary Magdalene came to the tomb "in the end of
the Sabbath" and the resurrection had already occurred,
then Sabbath must be the actual day of the resurrection.

However, confusion arises due to alternate English translations of this same passage. Most other English versions translate the phrase "the end of the Sabbath" as "after the Sabbath":

> Now *after the Sabbath*, as it began to dawn toward the first day of the week, Mary Magdalene and the other Mary came to look at the grave (emphasis added).

The difference between the words "end of" and "after" is one day. How, then, can we be certain which day is correct—Saturday or Sunday? Only by referring back to the original Greek text can we correctly answer this question.

WHAT DOES THE GREEK SAY?

For this study, the Nestle's Greek New Testament is used for the Greek text because it is considered to be a very reliable text.[3] The *Concordant Literal New Testament* is used to clarify the literal translation of relevant passages. We will closely examine the relevant passages of the four Gospel accounts, beginning with Matthew. In Matthew, it will be necessary to include the resurrection in the context of previous verses (Matthew 27:66; 28:1):

> v. 66 And [on Thursday] they went and made the grave secure, and along with the guard they set a seal on the stone.
>
> v. 1 Now after ["end of" KJV] the Sabbath, as it began to dawn toward the first *day* of the week, Mary Magdalene and the other Mary came to look at the grave.

The first problem that must be addressed deals with verse numbers and punctuation:

> Neither the chapter numbers, verse numbers, nor the punctuation are inspired. Numbering for verses was begun in the sixteenth century, and for

chapters in the thirteenth century.... The Original contained no conventional marks of punctuation, such as periods, commas, colons, question marks and exclamation points. These have been added by the translators, and are therefore *not infallible*.[4]

In addition, the "oldest manuscripts of the New Testament are *uncial* texts, that is all letters were capitals,"[5] without spaces between the individual words. The authors believe that Matthew 28:1 is a good example of the error that can result given the very difficult task of the translator under these conditions.

Before continuing with this thought, let us refer to the literal meaning of the original Greek for the phrase at the beginning of the sentence. The Greek words translated as "now after (end of) the Sabbath" are:

'Οψὲ δὲ σαββάτων

The Greek, transliterated into English:

opse de Sabbaton

Opse can mean "end," "late in" or "late on."[6] *De* can mean "and," "but," or "now."[7] But the only meaning for *Sabbaton* is "Sabbath."[8] However, even though most English versions translate "Sabbath" in the singular form, the Greek word is actually plural ("Sabbaths"). The reason for this is not clear until the entire sentence is separated into two sentences expressing two separate thoughts. The *Concordant Literal New Testament* provides the best literal translation of Matthew 28:1, showing the separation of the two sentences:

> Now it is the evening of the sabbaths. At the lighting up into one of the sabbaths came Mary Magdalene and the other Mary to behold the sepulcher.[9]

The first sentence notes the passage of time from the posting of the Temple Guard at the sealed tomb on Thursday (Matthew 27:66) to the morning of the weekly Sabbath. Thursday evening marked the passing of the Passover Sabbath and Friday evening marked the passing of the eve of the weekly Sabbath. The above literal translation shows that there is a separation of thoughts: the first relating to the passage of time, the second relating to the women coming to the tomb after the resurrection.

Therefore, using the second sentence as the starting point for Matthew 28:1, let us now compare the NASB English translations for all four Gospel accounts (emphasis added):

As it began to dawn toward *the first day of the week*, Mary Magdalene and the other Mary came to look at the grave (Matthew 28:1).

And very early on *the first day of the week*, they came to the tomb when the sun had risen (Mark 16:2).

Now after He had risen early on *the first day of the week*, He first appeared to Mary Magdalene, from whom He had cast out seven demons (Mark 16:9).

But on the *first day of the week*, at early dawn, they came to the tomb, bringing the spices which they had prepared (Luke 24:1).

Now on *the first day of the week* Mary Magdalene came early to the tomb, while it was still dark, and saw the stone already taken away from the tomb (John 20:1).

According to the English translation, all four Gospel accounts state that the resurrection occurred on "the first day of the week." However, this is not the literal translation from the Greek. In order to understand the correct literal translation, let us first examine the Greek text.

213

For Mark 16:2, Luke 24:1, and John 20:1, the Greek words translated as "the first day of the week" are:

μια των σαββατων

The English transliteration of the Greek is:

mia ton Sabbaton

Word for word, the literal English meanings are: *mia* means "one,"[10] *ton* means "of the,"[11] and *Sabbaton* means "Sabbaths."[12] Accordingly, the literal translation is:

one of the Sabbaths

One may wonder how the literal translation, "one of the Sabbaths," has been transformed into "the first day of the week." This issue will be discussed later in the chapter. But for now, let us continue by comparing the above with the Greek translated as "the first day of the week" in Matthew 28:1 and Mark 16:9.

For Matthew 28:1, the Greek is:

ἐις μιαν σαββατων

The English transliteration is:

eis mian Sabbaton

The first word, *eis*, used as a preposition, has various meanings, including "to," "in," "at," "into," "upon," and "on."[13] The second word, *mian*, a form of *mia* and the feminine form of the word *(h)eis*, means "one."[14] The last word, *Sabbaton*, is plural, meaning "Sabbaths." Therefore, the literal meaning of this Greek phrase is:

on one (of the) Sabbaths

Note that the words "of the" are understood and so appear in parenthesis.

For Mark 16:9, the Greek is:

πρώτη σαββάτου

The English transliteration is:

proti Sabbatou

Proti comes from the root word *protos*, meaning "first."[15] *Sabbatou* is in the singular form, "Sabbath."[16] Therefore, the literal translation is:

first Sabbath

Without exception, a literal translation of the original Greek in each of the Gospel accounts refers to Sabbath (Saturday) as the day of the resurrection. Specifically, reference is made to "one of the Sabbaths" which is a direct reference to the seven weekly sabbaths between Passover and Pentecost.[17] The resurrection occurred on the first of these seven weekly sabbaths. This is probably the reason Mark 16:9 refers specifically to "the first Sabbath." Importantly, using the phrase "one of the Sabbaths" also clearly distinguishes between the annual Passover Sabbath and the weekly Sabbath.

TESTING THE CONCEPT OF "ONE OF THE SABBATHS"

Further support for both the literal translation and the understanding that "one of the Sabbaths" refers to one of the seven weekly sabbaths between Passover and Pentecost is found in Acts 20:6-7, according to the *Concordant Literal New Testament* translation:

v. 6   Yet we sail off from Philippi *after the days of unleavened bread*, and came to them in Troas in five days, where we tarry seven days.

v. 7   Now on *one of the sabbaths*, at our having

> gathered to break bread, Paul argued with them, being about to be off on the morrow (emphasis added).[18]

Unfortunately, most English versions mistranslate *mia ton sabbaton* as "the first day of the week" instead of the literal meaning, "one of the sabbaths." Two exceptions are *The Interlinear Bible*[19] and the *The Interlinear KJV-NIV Parallel New Testament in Greek and English*,[20] which both use the literal translation "one of the sabbaths." The context confirms the accuracy of the literal translation by referring to "the days of unleavened bread," meaning Passover/Feast of Unleavened Bread. This ties "one of the sabbaths" to the seven weekly sabbaths between Passover and Pentecost.

Also, according to the *Concordant Literal New Testament* translation, reference is made to "one of the Sabbaths" in I Corinthians 16:2:

> On *one of the sabbaths* let each of you lay aside by himself in store that in which he should be prospered, that no collections may be occurring then, whenever I may come (emphasis added).[21]

Unfortunately, the Greek, *kata mian sabbatou*, is incorrectly translated as "first day of every week" (or some minor variation thereof) in most English versions. However, reading the passage in context reveals a reference to Pentecost, confirming the literal translation of "one of the sabbaths" as referring to one of the seven weekly Sabbaths between Passover and Pentecost.[22]

The literal translation is logical and consistent with an accurate timetable of events and the Hebraic picture. However, lacking an accurate timetable and Hebraic understanding, a real dilemma arises. For how could Yeshua have fulfilled the sign of Jonah, given a Friday crucifixion and a Saturday resurrection?

Generally, a Friday crucifixion and Sunday resurrection is justified by insisting that three days—Friday, Saturday, and Sunday—can be counted in a way (partial days counting as whole days) to make the claim that the prophecy was fulfilled. Nevertheless, in doing so, the "three nights" requirement is disregarded. In order to turn the Saturday resurrection into a Sunday resurrection, an idiomatic usage of the Greek is claimed. But if the literal translation fits the prophetic timetable and the Hebraic context, how can an idiomatic interpretation be justified, especially when it fits neither?

QUESTIONING THE IDIOMATIC INTERPRETATION

In the times of Yeshua, the Jews referred to the days of the week in terms of their position, for example, "first day," "second day," "third day," etc. Only the seventh day had a name, "Sabbath" (Shabbat), referring to the day of rest. This is in accordance with the Biblical account of creation. In the first century, the Greeks also followed this basic system of naming the days of the week, except when referring to the seventh day as *Sabbaton*, and the first day as "the Lord's Day." The names of the days of the week as used today derive from the Latin system of naming each day in honor of Roman gods, who were associated with the sun, moon, and five planets known at that time.[23]

In the Greek language, there exist words that mean "first," "day," and "week." They are respectively, *protos*[24], *(h)emera*[25], and *ebdomas*.[26] Therefore, the phrase "first day of the week" could easily be expressed in a literal fashion. This being the case, why would the New Testament writers resort to an idiom rather than a clear, literal meaning, especially regarding such a crucial event?

With regard to the possible use of an idiomatic expression, let us consider the following. Today a single

Greek word, *Kuriaki* (κυριακη), refers directly to "the Lord's Day," which is understood to be Sunday, the first day of the week.[27] The use of this single Greek word seems to have derived from the Greek words *Kuriaki emera* (κυριακη ἡμέρα) and can be found in Revelation 1:

> v. 10 I was in the Spirit *on the Lord's day,* and I heard behind me a loud voice like the *sound* of a trumpet,

The literal meaning of the two Greek words translated "the Lord's day" is "imperial day."[28] According to Robertson, "the Lord's Day" was the name given to the first day of the week in honor of the Roman Emperor.[29] Therefore, it was already in use at the time of Yeshua. At some time later, the expression was picked up by Christians and applied to Yeshua. We therefore have a historical basis for validating its meaning. However, the authors are not aware of any such validation for an idiomatic usage of "one of the Sabbaths" to mean "first day of the week."

HISTORICAL BACKGROUND

Of interest and importance in this inquiry are the historical developments that affected the Church and its members during the early centuries of Christianity:

> For the first three centuries of the Christian era *the first day of the week was never confounded with the sabbath*; the confusion of the Jewish and Christian institutions was due to declension [falling away] from apostolic teaching (emphasis added).[30]

Early Christians observed the Sabbath according to the Biblical Commandment. The Biblical Sabbath observance continued until the time of Constantine when Sunday, "the Lord's Day," was substituted for Sabbath. The Church Council of Nicea (325):

widened the breach between Christianity and Judaism by forbidding the celebration of the Christian Sabbath on Saturday and tried to prevent the coincidence of Easter and Passover.[31]

At this point, the authors wish to emphasize that they are not attacking the practice of Sunday worship. As Mark 2:28 literally states from the Hebrew, Yeshua is "Lord Sabbath" and as such, the Sabbath rest is in Him. However, the authors are attempting to present an accurate picture of how Yeshua did fulfill foundational Biblical prophecies concerning the Messiah. In doing so, facts must be presented and an understanding of the historical development of Christianity is imperative.

The third century was especially critical for the development of Christianity. At that time, Constantine understood the advantage of using religion as a powerful and effective political tool to unite the Roman Empire. He is credited with legitimizing Christianity; however, an enormous price was paid in terms of compromising truth. Under his influence, Christianity was mixed with paganism.[32] Pagans were allowed to become Christians and yet keep their pagan beliefs and customs. Even the religious leadership became infiltrated with pagan priests. And Constantine himself retained the pagan high priest's title, Pontifex Maximus.[33]

The previous persecutions of Christians had eliminated a great number of true believers—both in the leadership and in the laity—who were unwilling to compromise their faith. As a result, those strictly adhering to the truth were overshadowed by those with greater political power and influence. Thus, the foundational truths were weakened and the Church moved farther and farther away from its Hebraic roots.

The adoption of the Lord's Day in honor of Yeshua was an example of how pagan concepts were incorporated into the religious system of the Church. Unfortunately, in the process of "Christianizing" paganism, Christianity itself became more and more paganized. Pagan feast days were substituted for God's Biblical Feast Days and, in the process, the prophetic timetable was lost. In the same way, the truth of a Sabbath resurrection was obscured and Sunday, the Lord's Day, substituted in its place.

Had the early translators understood Scripture within its Hebraic context, the literal meaning of "one of the Sabbaths" would certainly have been better comprehended. Even the traditional concept of a Friday crucifixion may have resulted from a limited understanding of the Biblical Feast Days. For example, how would John 19:31 have been interpreted:

> The Jews therefore, because it was the *day of preparation*, so that the bodies should not remain on the cross *on the Sabbath (for that Sabbath was a high day)*, asked Pilate that their legs might be broken, and that they might be taken away (emphasis added).

The Day of Preparation has been interpreted as preparation day for the weekly Sabbath. However, Scripture clearly states that that Sabbath was a "High Day," a reference to the first day of the Feast of Unleavened Bread, not the weekly Sabbath. No distinction was made between the Passover "preparation day," the day the Passover lambs were sacrificed, and preparation for the weekly Sabbath. Likewise, no distinction was made between the approaching Passover Sabbath as opposed to the weekly Sabbath.

Since Friday was chosen as the day of the crucifixion, the translators were faced with a serious dilemma if they literally interpreted the passages dealing with the day of the resurrection. For how could Yeshua fulfill the sign of Jonah if He were crucified on Friday and resurrected on the following day? Adopting an "idiomatic" interpretation of the Greek rather than accepting its literal meaning concealed this blatant inconsistency.

REFUTING THE IDIOMATIC INTERPRETATION

In the Hebrew, there are two related (derived from the same root word), but clearly distinct, Hebrew words for "Sabbath" and "week." The Hebrew word *Shabbath*,[34] "Sabbath," refers to weekly or annual Sabbaths. In contrast, the Hebrew word *shabuwa*[35] (other forms: *shabua* and *shebuah*) refers to a period of seven days ending with the Sabbath.

The Greek version of the Old Testament, the Septuagint, makes a clear distinction between the Hebrew words for "Sabbath" and "week." In Exodus 24:22, Deuteronomy 16:10, and II Chronicles 8:13, the "Feast of Weeks" (Pentecost) is mentioned. According to *The Jewish Encyclopedia*, "Feast of Weeks" transliterates from the Hebrew as *Hag Shab'ot*; in Greek, it is:

$$\text{ἑορτὴ ἑβδομάδων}^{36}$$

The English transliteration of the Greek is:

eorte ebdomadon

The first word, *(h)eorte*, translates as "feast" or "festival" and is also used in the New Testament, including seventeen times in John's Gospel.[37] The second word, *ebdomadon*, is plural and refers to a period of seven days. It translates as "weeks" and is a form of the word *ebdomas*, meaning "week."[38] This is a definitive case where there is a clear distinction between the Hebrew words for "Sabbath" and "week" in the Greek text.

Given a clear distinction, how could the same word (*Sabbaton*) be inconsistently translated one place as

"Sabbath," and another place as "week," even within the same sentence (Matthew 28:1)? The answer seems to be that the translators interpreted this and other related passages within the context of later tradition rather than within the original Hebraic context.

The authors would like to address one final passage which has been cited as an example of the idiomatic usage of the word "Sabbath" to mean "week." It is found in Luke 18:

> v. 12 I fast twice a week; I pay tithes of all that I
> get.

The Greek word *Sabbatou* has been translated as "week." Let us compare the NASB version above with the *Concordant Literal New Testament* translation below:

> I am fasting twice of a sabbath. I am taking
> tithes from all whatever I am acquiring.[39]

Here, the literal translation of the word "sabbath" is used. Also, a period, rather than a semi-colon, divides the Greek into two separate thoughts.

The authors agree that the literal translation of "Sabbath" is correct and that two main thoughts are being expressed. However, based upon an alternative literal translation, the break seems to come before, not after, the word "Sabbath." In order to clarify this point, let us focus on the first three Greek words before the word "Sabbath":

νηστεύω δὶς του

The English transliteration is:

nesteuo dis tou

The first word translates as "I fast" or "I am fasting." The second word, *dis*, as an adverb, can be translated as "twice" or "doubly."[40] The third word, *tou*, can be used as a pronoun or a preposition. As a pronoun, it can mean "him" or "it"; as a preposition, it can mean "of the."[41] In the context of the passage, the authors believe the accurate translation for this word is "him." Translated, the English is:

> I am fasting doubly as him. Sabbath, I am taking tithes from all whatever I am acquiring.

Putting the meaning back into context, the Pharisee is comparing himself to the tax collector mentioned in the same passage. In a self-exalting prayer, he thanks God, believing he is more righteous than others because he fasts more and tithes more.

An understanding of the Hebraic context confirms the placement of the period before "Sabbath." First, tithes were generally brought to the Temple on Sabbath. Paul's instructions to believers to set aside their offerings on Sabbath is in agreement with this practice (see literal translation of I Corinthians 16:2, above section "Testing the Concept of 'One of the Sabbaths' ").

In addition, if the period were placed after Sabbath, it would indicate that the Pharisee fasted on Sabbath. But it is clear that Jews were not, as a general rule, permitted to fast on Sabbath. In fact, if a fast day happened to coincide with a Sabbath, it was usually deferred (held prior to or following the Sabbath). The only fast day that could not be deferred was Yom Kippur, Day of Atonement.[42]

Furthermore, understanding the Jewish concept of fasting can also be used to show that the idiomatic interpretation is incorrect. According to this notion, the Pharisee fasted twice a week. However, excessive fasting was forbidden and even considered sinful because it harms the body.[43] Fasting was done on certain days and on certain occasions but consistent fasting twice a week was not practiced and likely falls under the category of "excessive" fasting.

THE TIME OF THE RESURRECTION

The original Greek text clearly establishes Sabbath as the actual day of the resurrection. Generally, the Gospel accounts (emphasis added below) indicate that the resurrection occurred sometime before dawn:

As it began to *dawn* on one of the Sabbaths, Mary Magdalene and the other Mary came to look at the grave (Matthew 28:1).

And *very early* on one of the Sabbaths, they came to the tomb when the sun had risen (Mark 16:2).

Now after He had risen *early* on one of the Sabbaths, He first appeared to Mary Magdalene, from whom He had cast out seven demons (Mark 16:9).

But on one of the Sabbaths, at *early dawn*, they came to the tomb, bringing spices which they had prepared (Luke 24:1).

Now on one of the Sabbaths, Mary Magdalene came *early* to the tomb, *while it was still dark*, and saw the stone taken away from the tomb (John 20:1).

The literal translations of all Gospel accounts indicate an early morning resurrection. Words including "dawn," "very early," "early dawn," and "while it was still dark" support this literal interpretation.

However, an idiomatic interpretation of "as it began to dawn" in the KJV version of Matthew 28:1 may be mistaken to indicate that the resurrection occurred on Sabbath, just before sunset:

In the end of the Sabbath, as it began to dawn toward the first day of the week, came Mary Magdalene and the other Mary to see the sepulchre (Matthew 28:1, KJV).

According to the idiomatic interpretation, "as it began to dawn" refers to sunset, the beginning of a new day, in keeping with Jewish thought. However, this interpretation does not seem to fit Matthew's later story about the guards who were told by the chief priests to lie about the disappearance of Yeshua's body:

...Say ye, His disciples came by *night*, and stole him away while we slept (Matthew 28:13).

The Greek word translated "night" is *nektos* and cannot be confused with "day" or "daylight."[44] According the the chief priests' concocted scenario, the disciples stole the body at night while the guards slept. This is compatible with a predawn resurrection. Moreover, Mark makes a specific reference to the sun as having risen (16:2). Here, the Greek word translated "sun" is *eliou* and refers to the literal sun.

Lastly, after all the events of that momentous day, John 20:19 reports Yeshua's appearance to His fearful disciples in the evening of the Sabbath. Again, the Greek (*mia sabbaton*) literally translates as "one of the sabbaths" (*Concordant Literal New Testament*):

v. 19 It being, then, *the evening of that day, one of the sabbaths*, and the doors having been locked where the disciples were gathered together, because of fear of the Jews, Jesus came and stood in the midst and is saying to them, "Peace to you!"

v. 20 And saying this, He shows them His hands also, and His side. The disciples, then rejoiced at perceiving the Lord (emphasis added).[45]

What a message of peace and joy to all disciples of Yeshua—past, present, and future—for the believer's faith (trust) is built upon an unshakable foundation of truth that Yeshua is the Messiah!

REFUTING OTHER POSSIBLE OBJECTIONS

The Day After the Sabbath

Scripture is clear that the resurrection occurred on Sabbath. A Sabbath resurrection also fits the actual timetable of Passover events, a timetable that is confirmed by the Hebrew calendar for the year 30 C.E.[46] (The year 30[47] is considered by most scholars to be the year of the crucifixion because it fits historical data. One such historical fact is that the Temple is known to have been destroyed in 70 C.E., forty years after the crucifixion.)

A Sunday crucifixion is sometimes said to be supported by the offering of the omer on the day after Sabbath. The omer was the first of the barley harvest. The harvest of first fruits covered the period of time called the omer, from the day after Passover until the day of Pentecost (Shavuot), fifty days later. In this symbolic picture, Yeshua is the first of the First Fruits, culminating in the harvest on Pentecost, symbolizing the birth of the Church, as evidenced by the indwelling of the Holy Spirit in true believers.

During the time of Yeshua, there was a sharp controversy between the Pharisees and the Sadducees as to the meaning of "the day after the Sabbath." First let us refer to Scripture for the relevant passage (Leviticus 23):

> v. 10 "Speak to the sons of Israel, and say to them, 'When you enter the land which I am going to give to you and reap its harvest, then you shall bring in the sheaf of the first fruits of your harvest to the priest.

> v. 11 'And he shall wave the sheaf before the LORD for you to be accepted; *on the day after the sabbath* the priest shall wave it (emphasis added).

According to the Sadducees, Sabbath refers to the weekly Sabbath, meaning that the omer was to be waved on the Sunday following Passover. However, the Pharisees (rabbis) interpreted Sabbath to refer to the Passover Sabbath, meaning that the omer was to be waved on the day following Passover.[48] At the time of Yeshua, the Jewish people followed the Pharisees and accepted their interpretation. Even though the Sadducees controlled the priestly aristocracy, the Pharisees controlled the observance of Temple rituals. Paul himself was a Pharisee who followed the Pharisaic interpretation and he ties Yeshua's resurrection to the First Fruits of the omer (I Corinthians 15:20, 23).

This brings us to the question: How did Yeshua fulfill the wave offering? According to the Pharisaic tradition, the omer would have been waved on Friday, the day after Passover, which was on Thursday in the year 30 C.E. However, Yeshua did not resurrect until Sabbath. The authors believe the reason is that Yeshua had to fulfill the sign of Jonah. The three days and three nights that He spent in Sheol do not seem to be counted as part of the timetable. The concept of ordinal versus cardinal time seems to be involved. Cardinal time is time as we measure time. Ordinal time is time as God measures time.

In this regard, it is noteworthy that God ordained specific dates on the Hebrew lunar calendar for the following Biblical Feast Days: Passover-14th of Nisan; Feast of Unleavened Bread-15th of Nisan; Rosh HaShanah-1st of Tishri; Yom Kippur-10th of Tishri; and Sukkot-15th of Tishri (see Leviticus 23). But when it came to the wave offering of the omer, God did not designate a specific day of the month but referred to the day after the (Passover) sabbath as the day to offer the omer and to begin counting fifty days until Pentecost. Therefore, the date of

Pentecost was dependent upon the counting of the omer, rather than being a fixed date. Perhaps the reason God did not specify a date on the calendar has to do with the sign of Jonah.

If this is the case, God's ordinal timetable stopped at Yeshua's death on the tree and did not start again until Yeshua's resurrection from the grave. On such an ordinal timetable, Yeshua, symbolized by the omer, was offered to God the day after Passover—on the weekly Sabbath—at His ascension into Heaven. It is interesting to note that the ground shook both at the death and resurrection of Yeshua. Could this shaking be represented by the waving of the omer? It is also very significant that, as the first of the First Fruits (I Corinthians 15:20, 23), Yeshua rose on the first of the seven Sabbaths between Passover and Pentecost, the period of time referred to as First Fruits.

According to Jewish tradition, the omer was cut on the eve following Passover eve:

> After the omer was cut, it was brought to the Temple Hall...and beaten with fresh reeds, so as not to crush the barley completely. Then it was winnowed and carefully picked over. After that, the barley was singed over fire in a vessel. This vessel made out of copper and perforated so that the fire could singe the barely.[49]

This picture does seem to fit what happened during Yeshua's arrest, trial, flogging, and crucifixion. Yeshua followed the original Passover timetable and was "cut off" at His death on Wednesday. He had been judged (copper symbolizes judgment) and was innocent of any sin. Yet the chief priests and Sanhedrin sentenced Him to death.

The actual timetable also has great significance for what happened at Pentecost, following Yeshua's acension.

Both the KJV and Amplified Bible state in Acts 2:1 that the day of Pentecost had *fully* come. As stated above, Pentecost came on the fiftieth day of the omer, as counted from the day after Passover. In the year of the crucifixion (30 C.E.), the fiftieth day fell on Friday, the 6th of Sivan. However, Pentecost was actually observed for a two-day period, including the fiftieth and fifty-first day of the omer.

Therefore, it seems that Scripture is referring to the second day of Pentecost, the fifty-first day of the omer, on the 7th of Sivan. On this day was fulfillment of what God said in Jeremiah 31:33:…"I will put My law within them, and on their heart I will write it…." According to the Talmud, God gave the Ten Commandments on the 7th of Sivan, the fifty-first day of the omer,[50] and this day fell on Sabbath.[51] The Holy Spirit (Ruach HaKodesh) wrote God's commandments on stone tablets.

On the Pentecost following Yeshua's resurrection and acsension, the Holy Spirit wrote the commandments on the very heart (soul/spirit) of believers who accepted Yeshua as Messiah. This fulfillment also came on the 7th of Sivan, the fifty-first day of the omer, and on Sabbath! It is interesting to note that this day was the fifty-first day of the omer, based upon the Pharisaic method of counting, but was actually the fiftieth day of the omer, based upon counting from the day of Yeshua's resurrection!

The Emmaus Road Incident

Another possible objection to a Sabbath resurrection might be made based upon the fact that two of the disciples, Cleopas and Simon, traveled the day of the resurrection to Emmaus, seven miles from Jerusalem (Luke 24:13-35). If it were Sabbath, would they not be violating the Law by going more than a Sabbath Day's journey from Jerusalem? According to the NASB translation:

And behold, two of them were going that very day to a village named Emmaus, which was about seven miles from Jerusalem (Luke 24:13).

In fact, the disciples traveled in the twilight hours of Saturday evening, beginning about 6 pm, *after* the Sabbath. It would have taken them about two hours to walk from Jerusalem to Emmaus. During the journey, Yeshua joined them and they talked together until they reached Emmaus, by which time it had grown darker. After realizing that Yeshua had appeared to them, they returned immediately to Jerusalem to tell the other disciples. Since Passover always falls on a full moon, the moon would still have been bright enough for them to make the return journey that same evening.

Having established Sabbath as the true day of the resurrection, there remain other significant questions surrounding the death and resurrection of Yeshua. Where was He during those three days and three nights? And after His resurrection, where was He going and for what purpose? Answering these questions provides deeper insight as to the Messiah's role in our salvation...

Notes

1. Joachim Jeremias, *Jerusalem in the Times of Jesus*, p. 180.

2. Alfred Edersheim, *The Temple: Its Ministry and Services* (1979 softcover edition), pp. 147-148.

3. Alfred Marshall, *The Interlinear KJV-NIV Parallel New Testament in Greek and English*.

4. *Concordant Literal New Testament with the Keyword Concordance*, p. 612.

5. *Concordant Literal New Testament*, p. 619.

6. W. E. Vine, *Vine's Expository Dictionary of Old and New Testament Words*, Vol. 2, p. 312.

7. Vine, Vol. 3, p. 120.

8. Henry G. Liddell and Robert Scott, *A Greek-English Lexicon*, p. 1579.

9. *Concordant Literal New Testament*, p. 86.

10. Vine, Vol. 3, p. 137.

11. George C. Divry, *Divry's Modern English-Greek and Greek-English Desk Dictionary*, p. 714.

12. Liddell and Scott, p. 1579.

13. Divry, p. 488.

14. Vine, Vol. 3, p. 137.

15. Vine, Vol. 2, p. 103.

16. *Concordant Literal New Testament*, p. 135.

17. *Concordant Literal New Testament*, "Greek-English Keyword Concordance," p. 253.

18. *Concordant Literal New Testament*, p. 336.

19. Jay P. Green, Sr., Translator-Editor, *The Interlinear Bible*, p. 843.

20. Marshall, p. 413.

21. *Concordant Literal New Testament*, p. 419.

22. Archibald Thomas Robertson, *Word Pictures in the New Testament*, Vol. 3, p. 338. Robertson states that this episode occurred a year before the one described in Acts 20:6-7.

23. *The World Book Encyclopedia*, Vol. 21, p. 146.

24. Vine, Vol. 2, p. 103.

25. Vine, Vol. 1, p. 270.

26. Divry, 380.

27. Divry, p. 569.

28. Marshall, p. 725.

29. Roberston, Vol. 6, p. 290.

30. Vine, Vol. 3, p. 312.

31. Dr. Geoffrey Wigoder, Editor, *The New Standard Jewish Encyclopedia*, p. 214.

32. Ralph Edward Woodrow, *Babylon Mystery Religion*, p. 49.

33. Dr. Tim Dowley, Editor, *The History of Christianity*, p. 140.

34. James Strong, *The New Strong's Exhaustive Concordance of the Bible*, #7676.

35. Strong, #7620.

36. *The Jewish Encyclopedia*, Vol. 9, p. 592.

37. Vine, Vol. 2, p. 86.

38. Liddell and Scott, p. 466.

39. *Concordant Literal New Testament*, p. 196.

40. Liddell and Scott, p. 436.

41. Divry, p. 707.

42. Philip Birnbaum, *Encyclopedia of Jewish Concepts*, p. 650.

43. Birnbaum, p. 651.

44. Liddell and Scott, p. 1183.

45. *Concordant Literal New Testament*, p. 279.

46. HaYom On-line Hebrew Calendar, A. G. Reinhold, 14 Fresh Pond Place, Cambridge, MA 02138-4430, Copyright © 1994. See also Jewish calendar, Jerusalem One web site.

47. Merrill C. Tenney, Editor, *The Zondervan Pictorial Encyclopedia of the Bible*, Vol. 1, p. 1041.

48. Michael Strassfeld, *The Jewish Holidays: A Guide and Commentary*, p. 49.

49. Rabbi Aryeh Kaplan, Translator, *The Torah Anthology*, Vol. 12, p. 159.

50. Strassfeld, p. 71.

51. Rabbi Aryeh Kaplan, *The Torah Anthology*, Vol. 6, p. 156.

13

YESHUA—ETERNAL HIGH PRIEST

And having been perfect, He became to all those who obey Him the source of eternal salvation, being designated by God as a high priest according to the order of Melchizedek (Hebrews 5: 9-10).

In the previous chapter, the importance of establishing the fact that Yeshua resurrected after three days and three nights in prophetic fulfillment of the sign of Jonah was discussed. But where was Yeshua during this period of time and what was He doing?

After His resurrection, Yeshua told Mary Magdalene that she was not to touch him (John 20):

> v. 17 Jesus said to her, "Stop clinging to Me, for I have not yet ascended to the Father; but go to My brethren, and say to them, 'I ascend to My Father and your Father, and My God and your God.'

What did Yeshua mean that she was not to cling to Him? And for what purpose was He to ascend to the Father? This first ascension is clearly distinct from His second ascension into Heaven as recorded in Acts 1:9-11.

Certainly, Yeshua must have performed something of the utmost significance at this time. Nevertheless, He did return to spend the next forty days with His disciples, continuing to witness and to instruct them before ascending once more into Heaven.

Yeshua's actions can only be understood in the context of God's commandments concerning sin atonement. Of central importance is Yeshua's fulfillment of His role as eternal High Priest. In order to see the complete picture, we must go back to the crucifixion.

THE CRUCIFIXION—THE PATTERN OF THE MENORAH

Regarding the crucifixion, certain symbolic meanings and patterns are revealed when viewed from the Hebraic perspective. One such pattern is that of the menorah. As previously mentioned, the menorah, the golden seven-branched candelabrum kept in the Holy Place of the Temple, represented the Tree of Life (Chapter 5). And a miraculously budding branch of this tree, called Aaron's rod, was planted on the Mount of Olives by David and grew into the crucifixion tree (Chapters 6 and 7).

In this symbolic parallel, Yeshua represents the fruit of the Tree of Life. Accepting His sacrifice for atonement of sin provides the only way of salvation and eternal life. Thus, the Tree of Life is seen to be both literally and symbolically connected to the crucifixion and what Yeshua did for us in His sacrifice.

Another pattern of the menorah emerges from the crucifixion tree: the body of Yeshua forming its central shaft, surrounded by six outstretched arms of the three as they hung on the tree. Even as Yeshua claimed to be the light of the world, the menorah represents this truth (John 8):

v. 12 Again therefore Jesus spoke to them, saying,

"I am the light of the world; he who follows Me shall not walk in the darkness, but shall have the light of life.

THE ROLE OF THE HIGH PRIEST IN SIN ATONEMENT

The symbolic meaning of Passover pointed to Yeshua, and was fulfilled in His sacrifice as God's Passover Lamb for the redemption of all humankind. But Yeshua's fulfillment of the symbolic meaning of God's Holy Days is not limited to Passover. Yom Kippur, the Day of Atonement, also conveys significant patterns fulfilled by Messiah as well.

The Day of Atonement is the holiest day of the year for the Jews. It is a time of fasting and seeking God's forgiveness for one's sins. During Temple times, sacrifice was made for the sins of the entire Israelite nation for the whole preceding year. It was the only day of the year when the High Priest entered the Holy of Holies to offer sacrifice: first for his own sins and then for the sins of the nation.

As we examine the meaning of the activities of this most holy and awesome day, unique parallels emerge in relation to the work of Yeshua in His death, resurrection, and ascension. The entire picture shows that He is the Messiah anointed by God and the eternal High Priest who continually intercedes for us in Heaven (Figure 10). However, complete fulfillment of this Biblical Feast Day in regard to the nation of Israel is yet to take place at the Lord's Second Coming.

THE PARALLEL OF THE TWO GOATS

God explained the law of atonement to Moses in Leviticus 16. Before the High Priest could make the sin sacrifice for the people, he had to first sacrifice a young bull for his own sins and those of the other priests. Only

Figure 10

The Anointing of Yeshua by the Holy Spirit

A dove in the hovering posture, with wings pulled forward, forms the Hebrew letter kaf. This letter represents the pattern in which the anointing oil was poured on the head of a high priest or king, the oil symbolizing the Holy Spirit. This is what is referred to in Matthew 3:16:

"And after being baptized, Jesus went up immediately from the water; and behold, the heavens were opened, and He saw the Spirit of God descending as a dove, coming upon Him."

The "Spirit of God descending as a dove" refers to the Holy Spirit looking like a dove, i.e., resembling a dove's wings in the form of the Hebrew letter kaf. It means that the Holy Spirit descended over Yeshua in the shape of the kaf to symbolize His anointing by the Holy Spirit of God as High Priest and King. Not since the destruction of Solomon's Temple had a king or high priest been anointed.

after this sacrifice was he allowed to enter the Holy of Holies on the Day of Atonement. In contrast, Yeshua required no such sacrifice for He alone is sinless.

The sin sacrifice for the Israelite nation was selected by casting lots to select the goat for the sin offering to God and the scapegoat, the carrier of Israel's sins into the wilderness of Azazel. The two goats were required to be taken from the community, purchased at the same time, and alike in appearance, size, and value.[1] A lottery process then determined which goat would be "for God" and which goat would be "for Azazel."

According to this selection process, the two goats were brought before the High Priest: one stood to the right of the High Priest, the other stood to his left. The High Priest then placed his hands into a box which contained two identical tablets of gold. One lot was engraved with the name of God, the other with the name of Azazel. Next, the High Priest drew out one of the lots with his right hand and placed it over the head of the goat to his right. Likewise, he drew the other lot with his left hand and placed it over the head of the goat on the left.[2] This was the manner of designation for each goat.

The goat selected for God was then taken to be sacrificed, its blood offered for the sins of the people in the Holy of Holies by the High Priests. (It should be emphasized at this point that God ordained sacrifices to Him to be carried out in the most humane way possible in order to prevent suffering of the animal.)

The goat chosen as the scapegoat became the bearer of the sins of the people. A skein of scarlet thread was tied between its horns and the High Priest placed both hands on this goat, confessing the sins of the people. According to Scripture, God commanded that the scapegoat be released in the wilderness:

"And the goat shall bear on itself all their iniq-uities to a solitary land; and he shall release the goat in the wilderness" (Leviticus 16:22).

The scapegoat was led out through the Eastern Gate, over the Kidron bridge, into the Judean wilderness to a place called Azazel: a high, rocky precipice. This desolate desert area was considered to be a place of demons.[3] The name Azazel also referred to the master of evil spirits of the wilderness.[4] At the place of Azazel, part of the scarlet wool tied to the goat's horns was removed and attached to a rocky protrusion on the cliff. Previously, a piece of this same scar-let wool had been attached to the door of the Temple.

Although Scripture states that the goat was to be released in the wilderness, by tradition the scapegoat was cast over the high cliff. As its body shattered against the rocks, it was reported that the scarlet wool on the rocky cliff, as well as that on the door of the Temple, miracu-lously turned from red to white. This sign was interpreted as symbolizing the forgiveness of sins, according to Isaiah 1:18: "If your sins are like scarlet they shall become as white as snow."

A parallel can be seen between the two goats and the two criminals who were crucified on the same tree with Yeshua. Yeshua is the eternal High Priest whose hands stretched out over the heads of the two criminals crucified at His sides, just as the High Priest held his hands over the two goats. One man turned to God in repentance; the other man refused to turn to God for forgiveness (Luke 23):

> v. 39 And one of the criminals who were hanged *there* was hurling abuse at Him, saying, "Are You not the Christ? Save Yourself and us!"

> v. 40 But the other answered, and rebuking him said, "Do you not even fear God, since you are under the same sentence of condemnation?

v. 41 "And we indeed justly, for we are receiving what we deserve for our deeds; but this man has done nothing wrong."

v. 42 And he was saying, "Jesus, remember me when You come in Your kingdom!"

v. 43 And He said to him, "Truly I say to you, today you shall be with me in Paradise."

By their own freewill choices, the individuals determined to whom they belonged: God or Azazel. The individual who repented of his crimes and asked Yeshua to remember Him in His Kingdom (Heaven) belonged to God. Surely, this man recognized Yeshua as the true Messiah. On the other hand, the unrepentant man challenged Yeshua to prove He was the Messiah by saving them from a physical death. His concern was only for his physical condition, not his spiritual condition.

Though humanity's sin was imputed to Yeshua, He could not retain sin because He is holy and sinless. From II Corinthians 5:21, we know that Yeshua, Who was sinless, bore the penalty for our sins. Thus, we are given His righteousness when we accept His offering for our sins. This passage has been translated as "He [God] made Him [Yeshua] who knew no sin *to be* sin on our behalf, that we might become the righteousness of God in Him." The words "to be" are italicized because they do not appear in the original Greek text. Hank Hannegraff gives an excellent explanation to clarify the meaning of this passage:

Let's take a closer look at the word "sin" ....First, scholars agree that the word "sin" in this passage is used in an abstract sense. They are virtually unanimous in pointing out that the phrase "to become sin" as used here is a *metonym* (a word or phrase substituted for another associated word or phrase) for Christ "bearing the penalty for our

239

sins." ...Scripture does say that man's sin was laid to the account of Christ (see Isaiah 53:4, 5). To put it another way, our sins were imputed to Christ and His righteousness is imputed to us. *Clearly, the Levitical concepts of substitution and imputation are the background of 2 Corinthians 5:21. Jesus did not literally become sin; sin was imputed to Him.* The Bible insists that the sacrifice of Christ was a sufficient substitutionary offering *precisely* because it was a sinless sacrifice (emphasis added).[5]

Yeshua did not literally become sin, but the totality of humanity's sin (both past and future), was imputed to Him on the tree. Because Yeshua was sinless and could not retain sin, the authors believe the sin was sent back to Satan by means of the man who chose Satan as his master. Azazel represents the abode of Satan and, significantly, it is the same place where Yeshua was tempted by Satan (Luke 4:1-2).

As mentioned above, the miraculous turning of the wool from scarlet to white indicated God's acceptance of the Yom Kippur sacrifice for sin atonement. Significantly, the Talmud (Yoma 39b) records that the wool no longer turned from red to white during the forty-year period from the crucifixion to the destruction of the Temple. This confirms Yeshua's sacrifice as total fulfillment of the Yom Kippur sin sacrifice. Thereafter, God did not recognize man's animal sacrifices for sin.

The Talmud (Yoma 39b) also records that every year, for forty consecutive years before the destruction of the Temple, the High Priest drew the lot for God in his left hand. Just as drawing God's lot in the right hand was considered an auspicious sign, drawing it in the left hand was considered an ominous sign. For this lot to be drawn in the left hand on forty consecutive Yom Kippur's was against the odds of random chance and struck fear into the hearts of the Jewish people. These were not the only ominous signs occurring at this time.

Two other signs reported by the Talmud (Yoma 39b) occurred in the Temple. In one, the westernmost light of the menorah, which is thought to be the light used to light the other lights, refused to burn. According this pattern, Yeshua, positioned closest to the west on the crucifixion tree, is represented by the "servant candle" or *shamash*, which was used to light the other candles of the menorah. In addition, the doors of the Temple began to open by themselves. The rabbis interpreted this sign as fulfillment of Zechariah 11:1, "Open your doors, O Lebanon, that a fire may feed on your cedars," which prophesied the destruction of the Temple by fire. Forty years later, the Romans totally destroyed the Temple with fire.

YESHUA DESCENDS INTO SHEOL PARADISE

The fate of the unrepentant man, represented by the scapegoat, was to go to a place of desolation and separation from God. On the other hand, the repentant man who asked Yeshua to remember him in His kingdom was given a promise that he would be in Paradise that very day! In order to understand what Yeshua meant, we must refer to the story of the rich man and Lazarus in Luke 16:19-31.

The Biblical picture shows that the souls of the dead went to a temporary underworld holding place, called Sheol (the Greeks called it Hades, from which we get the word Hell). The souls of the righteous, those who trusted God and accepted His plan of salvation, were in the part of Sheol called Paradise, also referred to as "Abraham's bosom." The souls of those who rejected God and His plan of salvation were in the part of Sheol called Torment. From the story of the rich man who died and went to Sheol Torment, it is clear that though he could see and call out to Abraham on the other side in Paradise, there was no way to cross the great chasm that separated Sheol Torment from Sheol Paradise.

Yeshua promised the repentant man that he would be in Paradise that day, meaning that their spirits would go to Sheol Paradise, not Sheol Torment. Yeshua never died spiritually, He only gave up His earthly body. Then His spirit descended into Sheol Paradise where He brought the good news of His sacrifice for sin to those who trusted God for their salvation. Prior to Yeshua's sacrifice, there was no sin atonement that could allow these souls to be brought into the presence of God. After Yeshua's sacrifice, they could now join their Savior and be taken into Heaven. However, there was a period of forty days after the resurrection that many of these spirits bore witness of Yeshua to the living in Jerusalem (Matthew 27:52):

> v. 51   And behold, the veil of the temple was torn in two from top to bottom, and the earth shook; and the rocks were split,
>
> v. 52   and the tombs were opened; and many bodies of the saints who had fallen asleep were raised;
>
> v. 53   and coming out of the tombs after His resurrection they entered the holy city and appeared to many.

Note that even though the graves were opened at the time of Yeshua's death, the saved did not rise until Yeshua resurrected. For the forty days that Yeshua continued to appear to His disciples before His ascension into Heaven, the risen spirits also gave testimony among the living. Given this fact, it seems strange that any could deny the witness of those who had come back from the dead. Nevertheless, this clearly demonstrates the truth of Abraham's response to the rich man's plea to send a witness from Sheol to his five brothers (Luke 16):

v. 29 "But Abraham said, 'They have Moses and the Prophets; let them hear them.'

v. 30 "But he said, 'No, Father Abraham, but if someone goes to them from the dead, they will repent!'

v. 31 "But he said to him, 'If they do not listen to Moses and the Prophets, neither will they be persuaded if someone rises from the dead.'"

The condition of a person's heart determines whether he/she acknowledges God, repents and accepts God's plan of salvation. Denying the reality of the spiritual realm has eternal consequences. Those who reject God are held in Sheol Torment until the final judgment. The consequences are eternal separation from God. In today's world of advanced science and technology, supernatural occurrences are often rationalized away because they do not fit the "rational" mind-set. It is not too difficult to see that even if the dead came back to be a witness of the truth of Yeshua HaMashiach, many would still reject their need of His redemptive sacrifice.

YESHUA'S FIRST ASCENSION

Before Yeshua's ascension to Heaven forty days after His resurrection, He had ascended to Heaven the first time, on the day of His resurrection. Let us again refer to the words He spoke to Mary Magdalene (John 20):

v. 17 Jesus said to her, "Stop clinging to Me, for I have not yet ascended to the Father ...."

What did Yeshua mean by telling Mary Magdalene she was not to "cling to Him" before He ascended?

Symbolically, He meant that the previous fellowship that had existed among them in the earthly, physical sense was now to be superseded by fellowship in the heavenly, spiritual sense. She was not to cling to things past but look toward those things, not of the physical world, but of the spiritual world.

And in a literal sense, the time had come for the Son to ascend to God the Father in Heaven for the purpose of finalizing the sacrifice of His blood for the atonement of humankind's sins. According to the Law of Atonement, no one could accompany the High Priest into the Sanctuary (Leviticus 16:17). The New Covenant in His blood is spoken of in detail in Hebrews 9:

v. 11 But when Christ appeared as a high priest of the good things to come, He entered through the greater and more perfect tabernacle, not made with hands, that is to say, not of this creation.

v. 12 and not through the blood of goats and calves, but through His own blood, He entered the holy place once for all, having obtained eternal redemption,

v. 13 For if the blood of goats and bulls and the ashes of a heifer sprinkling those who have been defiled, sanctify for the cleansing of the flesh,

v. 14 how much more will the blood of Christ, who through the eternal Spirit offered Himself without blemish to God, cleanse your conscience from dead works to serve the living God?

v. 15 And for this reason He is the mediator of a new covenant, in order that since a death has taken place for the redemption of the transgressions that were *committed* under the first covenant, those who have been called may receive the promise of the eternal inheritance.

Thus, we can know from Scripture that Yeshua entered the heavenly Holy of Holies as the heavenly High Priest and the only Mediator between man and God. He fulfilled His role as Savior by applying His blood in the heavenly sanctuary which was the pattern for the earthly sanctuary. To continue to quote from Hebrews 9:

v. 22 And according to the Law…all things are cleansed with blood, and without shedding of blood there is no forgiveness.

v. 23 Therefore it was necessary for the copies [the earthly Tabernacle/Temple] of the things in the heavens to be cleansed with these [earthly sacrifices], but the heavenly things themselves with better sacrifices than these.

v. 24 For Christ did not enter a holy place made with hands, a mere copy of the true one, but into heaven itself, now to appear in the presence of God for us;

v. 25 nor was it that He should offer Himself often, as the high priest enters the holy place year by year with blood not his own.

v. 26 Otherwise, he would have needed to suffer often since the foundation of the world; but now once at the consummation of the ages He has been manifested to put away sin by the sacrifice of Himself.

v. 27 And inasmuch as it is appointed for men to die once and after this comes judgment,

v. 28 so Christ also, having been offered once to bear the sins of many, shall appear a second time for salvation without reference to sin, to those who eagerly await Him.

Clearly, the Bible teaches that there is a spiritual reality upon which the earthly Tabernacle/Temple and the earthly sacrifices were patterned. These things were symbolic of the reality of the Messiah to come, Who by His work would accomplish what no earthly sacrifice by earthly priests could—atonement for all humankind's sins once and for all time. By examining the pattern of the earthly sacrifices instituted by God to point to His Messiah, we should be able to understand, even if in a limited way, the essence of what Yeshua did at the time of His first ascension into Heaven. (For an in-depth discussion of the symbolic pattern of the Tabernacle vessels in regard to the crucifixion, see Appendix II.)

First, let us understand the reason why blood was required for sin atonement. According to Leviticus 17:

> v. 11 For the life of the flesh is in the blood, and I [God] have given it to you on the altar to make atonement for your souls; for it is the blood by reason of the life that makes atonement.

It was because of this unique quality of harboring life that God accepted blood as atonement for sin. The spiritual fellowship experienced by Adam and Eve with their Creator was perfect before sin entered the world. Then, "By one man sin came into the world and death by sin" (Romans 5:12). The spiritual separation between humankind and God began at this time and continues because "All have sinned and fallen short of the glory of God" (Romans 3:23). In truth, God did not prefer the sacrifice of animals; rather, He preferred that man not sin (Psalms 40:6).[6] But man is not capable of avoiding sin, as Scripture states and human experience clearly shows.

The shedding of the blood of animals provided a temporary substitute for atonement but was insufficient to provide a perfect and complete atonement and restoration of man to his Creator. The blood of the sinless Messiah, however, was sufficient as a perfect and complete sacrifice to bridge the gap between man and God for all time. This sacrifice is offered to each one as a free gift of God. Nevertheless, God allows each individual the freewill choice to accept or to reject His sacrifice for sin.

In the Tabernacle and First Temple, the High Priest entered the earthly Holy of Holies on Yom Kippur and sprinkled blood once on the Mercy Seat (the cover of the Ark) and seven times in front of the Ark of the Covenant. In the Second Temple, the Ark had been lost so that the Holy of Holies was empty; therefore, the High Priest sprinkled the blood on the Foundation Stone upon which the Ark had rested. Through His own blood, Yeshua entered the heavenly Holy of Holies on the day of His res-urrection as the sole Mediator between man and God and through His redemptive work restored fellowship between man and his Creator.

From that time forward, every human being has direct access to God through Yeshua. There is no other mediator or co-mediator required, heavenly or earthly, for this rela-tionship. In fact, to choose a route other than the one pro-vided by God is in direct conflict with God's plan of sal-vation and, as such, is futile and without efficacy. God desires a direct personal relationship and has provided the way. It is up to each individual to accept or reject this gift of God's grace.

YESHUA'S ASCENSION TO THE HEAVENLY THRONE

For forty days after His resurrection, Yeshua appeared to His disciples and continued to teach them. He also promised them that the Holy Spirit would be sent to enable them to continue the work He had commissioned them to do (Acts 1):

> v. 8 but you shall receive power when the Holy Spirit has come upon you; and you shall be My witnesses both in Jerusalem, and in all Judea and Samaria, and even to the remotest part of the earth.
>
> v. 9 And after He had said these things, He was lifted up while they were looking on, and a cloud received Him out of their sight.
>
> v. 10 And as they were gazing intently into the sky while He was departing, behold, two men in white clothing stood beside them;
>
> v. 11 and they also said, "Men of Galilee, why do you stand looking into the sky? This Jesus, who has been taken up from you into heaven, will come in just the same way as you have watched Him go into heaven.

The word "cloud" in verse 9 comes from the Greek word *nephele*, but is not referring to an ordinary water vapor cloud. This word and other forms of the same word appear in several New Testament passages dealing with the Shekinah (Mark 9:7; Luke 9:34; I Corinthians 10:1; Revelation 14:14). The Shekinah (Glory Cloud) is a physical manifestation of the Divine Presence. The Hebrew Bible (Old Testament) describes the cloud by day and pillar of fire by night which enveloped the Holy of Holies of the Tabernacle and extended above it, guiding the Israelites as it moved from place to place in the wilderness. The Shekinah was also present in Solomon's Temple where it rested above the Mercy Seat of the Ark of the Covenant in the Holy of Holies.

The Glory of God shown around Yeshua and the body of believers He had brought out of Sheol Paradise. This great multitude of believers included all those who had accepted Yeshua as Lord and Savior—from Adam and Eve to the repentant man on the crucifixion tree, including the Patriarchs, the Prophets, the anointed Kings, and ordinary individuals. Their spiritual bodies rose with Yeshua in the Shekinah as He ascended to take (Hebrews 8):

> v. 1 …His seat at the right hand of the throne of the Majesty in the heavens,
>
> v. 2 a minister in the sanctuary, and in the true tabernacle which the Lord pitched, not man.

This, however, was not the only such appearance of the Divine Presence associated with Yeshua. The New Testament account of the transfiguration describes another occurrence (Matthew 17):

> v. 5 While he [Peter] was still speaking, behold a bright cloud overshadowed them; and behold, a voice out of the cloud, saying, "This is my beloved Son, with whom I am well-pleased; listen to Him!"

The "bright cloud" enveloping Yeshua and the disciples was the Shekinah. Its presence was a sign and a witness of His identity and mission.

The Shekinah is also referred to in passages dealing with the "catching up" (called the Rapture), when all those having a personal relationship and commitment to the Lord will be taken out of the world before the Tribulation (1 Thessalonians 4):

> v. 17 Then we who are alive and remain shall be caught up together with them in the clouds to meet the Lord in the air, and thus we shall always be with the Lord.

For believers, the hope of the "catching up" is alive and exciting. When it happens, those believers who are ready and receptive to Messiah's return for them will hear the call to join Him in the air. Their physical bodies will be instantaneously transformed into incorruptible spiritual bodies and they will join Yeshua in the Shekinah, with the entire heavenly body of believers who will likewise be given spiritual bodies at this same instant of time. The Bride—the entire body of believers—will then ascend into Heaven with the Bridegroom Yeshua for the Marriage Feast of the Lamb.

At the end of the Tribulation, the Bride will return to Earth with the Messiah at the Second Coming—in the Shekinah (Mark 13):

> v. 26 And then they will see the Son of Man coming in clouds with great power and glory.

"Coming in clouds with great power and glory" refers to the Shekinah. It will be a brilliant luminosity which will pierce the spiritual and physical darkness which is prophesied to pervade Earth just prior to the Second Coming. It will be witnessed by all those who have survived the Tribulation, wherever they may be on the planet.

At the time of Yeshua's ascension, the presence of the Glory Cloud gave witness to the One who sent Him. As He ascended into Heaven with the multitudes of the saints (believers), the luminous brilliance that enveloped them was a testament of God's power and glory. The disciples were overwhelmed and awe-struck by what they witnessed. Yet two of the saints, who stood by before likewise ascending, proclaimed that a day would come when Yeshua would return in this same Glory Cloud...

Notes

1. Rabbi Aryeh Kaplan, *The Torah Anthology*, Vol. 11, p. 338.
2. Kaplan, Vol. 11, p. 338.

3. Kaplan, Vol. 11, p. 348.

4. Merrill C. Tenney, Editor, *The Zondervan Pictorial Encyclopedia of the Bible*, Vol. 1, p. 426.

5. Hank Hannegraff, *Christianity in Crisis*, p. 159.

6. Dr. Zvi Faier, Translator, *The Torah Anthology: The Book of Tehillim*, Vol. 2, p. 110.

14

UNITY OF FATHER/SON/SPIRIT OF THE HOLY ONE

*"Hear, O Israel! The LORD is our God, the
LORD is one! (Deuteronomy 6:4)*

"I and the Father are one" (John 10:30).

THE DEITY OF YESHUA

The greatest and most profound event of human history is the revelation of God in the person of Yeshua HaMashiach (the Messiah). According to the apostle John (John 1):

v. 1　In the beginning was the Word, and the Word was with God, and the Word was God.

v. 2　He was in the beginning with God.

v. 3　All things came into being by Him, and apart from Him nothing came into being that has come into being.

Yeshua is referred to as "the Word." In Jewish thought, the Word (Torah) of God is the same as God. Therefore, before time began, Yeshua existed as God, with God. He existed before the world was created and, through Him, all things were created. And God became flesh in order to reveal the mystery of man's redemption (John 1):

> v. 14 And the Word became flesh, and dwelt among us, and we beheld His glory, glory as of the only begotten from the Father, full of grace and truth.
>
> v. 15 John [the Baptist] bore witness of Him, and cried out, saying "This was He of whom I said, 'He who comes after me has a higher rank than I, for He existed before me.' "

And according to Colossians 1:

> v. 16 For by Him all things were created, both in the heavens and on earth, visible and invisible, whether thrones or dominions or rulers of authorities—all things have been created by Him and for Him.
>
> v. 17 And He is before all things, and in Him all things hold together.

Not only was the universe created by the Word, Yeshua, but it is held together moment to moment by Him. This is not a case of an impersonal God or force creating a universe that is subsequently left to "run" on its own, as a wound-up clock. The Creator is intimately connected to His creation and in total control of it at all times.

Yeshua is referred to as the firstborn of all creation (John 1:15). This does not mean "born" in the way that a human being is born. Rather, it means that He is preeminent in position over the creation and always existed. Furthermore, His deity is revealed in the "I AM" declarations He made during his ministry (John 6:35; 8:12; 10:7, 9, 11, 14; 11:25; 14:6; 15:1, 5). As God incarnate, He came to redeem all humankind, and there is no other way to God except through the Son:

..."I am the way, and the truth, and the life; no one comes to the Father, but though Me" (John 14:6).

By the "I AM" statements, Yeshua implicitly and explicitly identifies Himself with the I AM-YHVH of the Old Testament (John 4:25-26; 8:18, 24, 58; 13:19). This unity is one of essence, power and operation. The works of Yeshua reveal this unity, for they are always in accordance with the will of the Father:

Jesus answered them, "I told you, and you do not believe; the works that I do in My Father's name, these bear witness of Me (John 10:25).

"I and the Father are one" (John 10:30).

..." the Father is in Me, and I in the Father" (John 10:38).

Matthew also testifies to the incarnation of God:

BEHOLD, THE VIRGIN SHALL BE WITH CHILD, AND SHALL BEAR A SON, AND THEY SHALL CALL HIS NAME IMMANUEL," which translated means, "GOD WITH US" (Matthew 1:23).

It is clearly tied to the Old Testament prophecy of Isaiah:

Therefore the Lord Himself will give you a sign: Behold, a virgin will be with child and bear a son, and she will call His name Immanuel (Isaiah 7:14).

Thus, deity and humanity existed in the person of Yeshua. In an analogous way, as God dwelt among His people in the Tabernacle, God, in the person of Yeshua, dwelt in a flesh-body "tabernacle" among men.

UNITY OF FATHER/SON/SPIRIT OF THE HOLY ONE

The unity of Yeshua HaMashiach with God the Father and the Holy Spirit has never been clearly understood from the doctrine of the Trinity. However, Scripture is clear that God is a unity or oneness that cannot be divided:

> "Hear, O Israel! The LORD is our God, the LORD is one! And you shall love the LORD your God with all your heart and with all your soul and with all your might" (Deuteronomy 6:4, 5).

The above Scripture is referred to in Hebrew as the *Shema Yisrael*. It is the Jewish confession of faith that sums up the first and second commandments of the Ten Commandments.[1] It emphasizes the unity of God. To understand the true relationship of God the Father, God the Son, and God the Holy Spirit, it is essential to preserve this concept of oneness.

God is *echad*, "one." Father, Son, and Spirit of the Holy One are one in essence and operation. (Note: To better express the Spirit of God from the Hebraic perspective, we will use the words "the Spirit of the Holy One" rather than "Holy Spirit" or "Holy Ghost.") Never is there a separation of one from the others, nor an independent will or action seen in operation. This essential unity is not well-explained or understood from the trinity concept but can be better explained and understood from a Hebraic perspective.

One of the problems with the trinity concept is that paganism had its own trinity of three individual gods, a polytheistic relationship. This concept was adapted to the Father, Son, and Holy Spirit, which are not three individual gods. The pagan concept fails to properly explain the Godhead, and has been the source of much confusion as well as a stumbling block to those who recognize its polytheistic flavor.

Old Testament as well as New Testament references reveal the essential unity of Father, Son, and Spirit of the Holy One. This understanding comes from a Hebraic understanding of Scripture and is not in conflict with the oneness of God.

The aspect of Father may be simply understood as the Will of God. The aspect of Son may be understood as the Word of God. The aspect of Spirit of the Holy One may be understood as the Power of God. The perfect will of the Father is embodied in and performed by the Son, through the power of the Spirit.

In the process of creation, as well as the plan of salvation, the oneness of God and interrelation of Father, Son, and Spirit is revealed. It was God the Father's will that the cosmos be created. It was God the Son who created the cosmos through the power of the Spirit. It was God the Father's will that salvation be brought to humankind. It was God the Son who brought salvation to humankind through the power of the Spirit (Colossians 1: 15-22).

To say God is three "persons" opens the door to misunderstanding God. God is Spirit and cannot be reduced to the concept of a person. While the Father, Son, and Spirit are spirit in nature, only the Son became incarnate and therefore took on a flesh body in the form of man. At no time in Scripture is God the Father spoken of in any other form than Spirit and Truth. The Spirit of the Holy One is the very essence of the power of God the Father and not some separate entity.

From this, we can understand that "God created man in His own image" refers to the spirit of God being breathed into man, not that God has a physical body in the identical form of man. The very essence of the life-giving force of God was breathed into the soul of man. This does not make man a "little god," but an eternal living being. Once God's life-giving force was breathed into the soul of man, man's soul meshed together with this eternal life-giving spirit and will one day either return to its

Creator or live eternally with the fallen angelic spirits. While the Son took on a flesh body, the Father and Spirit have never taken on a flesh body form and cannot properly be referred to as "Persons."

The Son gave up His physical flesh, bone, and blood body and was resurrected in a flesh and bone body, an incorruptible spirit body (Luke 24:39). This is the type of body that is promised to those who trust in the sacrifice of God's Son for the sins of humanity. For flesh and blood cannot inherit the Kingdom of God and the corruptible must die so that the spirit can take on a incorruptible spirit body (1 Corinthians 15:50). The spirits of those who die in the Lord go to be with the Lord, for to be absent from the body is to be present with the Lord (2 Corinthians 5:8). The spirit body is not acquired until God the Father has the Son call through the Spirit His Bride. At this "catching up," referred to as the Rapture, believers already in heaven, as well as those on earth, will be transformed (metamorphosed) into their spiritual bodies which will never age or die (1 Corinthians 15:50-58; 1 Thessalonians 4:15-17).

The person of Yeshua HaMashiach does therefore exist in a bodily form. But this aspect of God is the only one to take on the form of a body and therefore can properly be understood as a "Person." Let us examine, verse for verse, John 1:1-4, for a better understanding of the revelation that God the Son became flesh:

v. 1   In the beginning was the Word, and the Word was with God, and the Word was God.

The "Word" is referring to the Hebrew word "Torah," or the first five books of the Old Testament. Every word concerning the promised Messiah in the Torah is embodied in Yeshua's physical presence. Yet at the same time, He is still one with God, never separated. "The Word/Torah was with God." This expression reveals that what is in the Torah and what the Torah is, was always with God. "The Word was God." Everything that is in the Torah reveals everything man requires to comprehend God on his level. Every nature of God and His relationship to man is revealed in the living, breathing Torah. The very word "Torah" means "The Instructions of God" for man.

v. 2   He was in the beginning with God.

Yeshua was in the beginning with God, *Elohim* in Hebrew. Significantly, this word is plural. In the Old Testament Hebrew, the Tetragrammaton (YHVH) is translated LORD and refers to Yeshua. Therefore, "the Lord your God" is a reference to "YHVH/LORD your Elohim." This shows that YHVH is a oneness with the plurality of Elohim. Elohim consists of: 1.) EL, the Father, representing judgment alone (Father without mercies), 2.) YHVH, the Son, representing infinite mercy (Son without judgment), and 3.) The Spirit of the Holy One, the very essence of the power emanating from EL through YHVH.

v. 3   All things came into being by Him, and apart
        from Him nothing came into being that has
        come into being.

"All things came into being by Him." When looking at Genesis 1:1, the word used in the creation is Elohim, yet in just a few verses it changes to YHVH. Yeshua, being YHVH, is in Elohim, even as creation was a mere thought in EL's mind. Once the will of EL is revealed to YHVH, YHVH brings forth this will at which time the Spirit of the Holy One is there also, emanating from EL through YHVH as the very power of Elohim in full manifestation of the fullness of God to bring about creation. Therefore Scripture does say that pre-incarnate Yeshua/YHVH was present at creation and that the cosmos was created by Him, as He was the one who spoke forth the will of EL, upon which the power of EL through YHVH brought about the physical act. At no time is Elohim/God separable! "And apart from Him nothing came into being." Without this union there could be no creation and creation would cease to exist if it could be separated.

> v. 4   In Him was life, and the life was the light of men.

"In Him was life." Without YHVH, there is no life. "And the life was the light of men." With Him being YHVH, the mercies of Elohim, in Him alone is life and He alone is the light of this life.

John 1:10, 14 is also of relevance in this discussion:

> v. 10   He was in the world, and the world was made through Him, and the world did not know Him.

> v. 14   And the Word became flesh, and dwelt among us, and we beheld His glory, glory as of the only begotten from the Father, full of grace and truth.

Verse 10 is crystal clear that God the Son existed before creation, not as a being created by God, but part of the very essence of God. Even though the Creator entered the world in a flesh body, most of humanity did not recognize Him. Verse 14 refers to the Word becoming flesh "as of the only begotten from the Father." This is an analogy and does not mean that the Son was conceived as a human being is conceived. A picture can be developed from the Hebrew as to the way in which the Son was brought forth from the Father.

The Hebrew word *rachem* means "womb." It can also be understood to refer to the deepest and purest form of love and compassion that exists, as the love of a mother for her child, the child that she carried in her womb and to whom she gave birth. The plural form of the word *rachem* is *rachamim* and means "mercies," not as one mercy, but in the plural signifying the infinite mercies of God.

It was from the "womb" of God that the Son came forth (John 17):

v. 7 "Now they have come to know that everything Thou hast given Me is from Thee;

v. 8 for the words which Thou gavest Me I have given to them; and they received them; and *truly understood that I came forth from Thee*, and they believed that Thou didst send Me (emphasis added).

It was God the Father's will that the Son not only create the cosmos but in fact enter His creation for the purpose of revealing and fulfilling God's plan of salvation to the world. In doing so, God was revealing the depth of His love, His infinite mercies, in His Son Yeshua. The very nature of YHVH is embodied in the Son. YHVH refers to God the Son, the mercies of God, and the Redeemer of humankind.

In Genesis 22:8, God revealed His ultimate plan for the salvation of mankind:

v. 8 And Abraham said, "God will provide for Himself the lamb for the burnt offering, my son."...

In the parallel of Abraham and Isaac, God was revealing the basic plan of salvation: the sacrifice of His much beloved Son. The original Hebrew is accurately translated:

God will provide Himself as the lamb

Yeshua HaMashiach is that promised Lamb of God, sent as the sacrifice for the sins of humanity, to bring humankind back into a personal relationship with God. John 3:16-17 says it all!

v. 16 "For God so loved the world, that He gave His only begotten Son, that whoever

believes in Him should not perish, but have
eternal life.

v. 17 "For God did not send the Son into the
world to judge the world, but that the world
should be saved through Him."

YHVH manifested in the flesh in Yeshua HaMashiach.
What the sacrifice of animals could not accomplish was
accomplished in the one sacrifice, once and for all, by
Yeshua Himself, according to the will of God the Father.
There is no salvation by any other means other than what
God Himself provided in the sacrifice of His Son.

GOD'S PURPOSE OF CREATION

Before sin entered creation, there was no need of a
mediator to God. God had formed man in His own spiritual image and communion was direct. However, God did
not create robots or puppets, but freewill beings with the
choice of obedience or disobedience.

Man's choice to rebel against God resulted in a painful
and tragic spiritual separation from his Creator. The
effects can be seen from that time until today, including
all evil that exists in the world. But why did God give man
free will if it could result in evil?

The answer to the above question is fundamentally
tied to the answer to another question: "Why did God
create the world?

Obviously, it would be utterly naive to believe
that we could ever fully answer this question....

Yet, we can understand God's reasons to the
extent that they have been revealed by Him in the
Torah. The account of creation ends with the
words, "God saw everything that He had made,
and it was very good" *(Genesis 1:31)*. This and
similar passages teach us that God's purpose in
creation was to do good. In order to express His

love and goodness, God had to create a world....

But since God is infinitely and ultimately good, it would stand to reason that if He wanted to give good to His creation, it would have to be the highest possible good. What is that? What is the highest ultimate good?

The answer should be perfectly obvious. This ultimate good is God Himself. God thus created a world to which He could give of Himself.

But how is this possible? In what way can God give of Himself? How can a mere man partake of God?...

It is for this reason that God gave man free will. If man did not have free will, he would be poles apart from God. He would be little more than a robot or puppet....In giving man free will, God gave him the ability to imitate God and thus ultimately partake of Him.

Therefore, just as God chose good as a matter of free will, so can man. But in order for this choice to be real, God had to create the opposite of good. He therefore created the possibility of evil, so that man would be free to choose between good and its opposite. God Himself speaks of this when He tells His prophet, "I form light and create darkness, I make peace and create evil—I am God; I do all these things" (*Isaiah 45:7*).

God's ultimate purpose, however, is to do good, and to bring about a world "where all is good." The destiny of evil is to be transformed ultimately into good."[2]

ONE GOD–ONE PATH TO GOD

At the core of every human being is the need for spiritual healing and union with one's Maker. This search for

God and union with God is revealed in all forms of spiritual and religious pursuits in our world today. But which path truly leads to God?

For those who insist that "all paths lead to God," God's Word is clear:

> For there is one God, and one mediator also between God and men, the man Christ Jesus, who gave Himself as a ransom for all, the testimony borne at the proper time (1 Timothy 2:5-6).

> There is a way which seems right to a man, but its end is the way of death (Proverbs 14:12).

> "Enter by the narrow gate; for the gate is wide, and the way is broad that leads to destruction, and many are those who enter by it. For the gate is small and the way is narrow that leads to life, and few are those who find it" (Matthew 7:13-14).

The loving Creator who made us, and provided the only solution to spiritual isolation resulting from the sinful human condition, has not left us in spiritual darkness as to which path to take. The absolute perfection of God's Master Plan leads to the true Messiah, the only mediator between man and God. The sinless God-Man Messiah, Yeshua ben Joseph (the Suffering Servant of Isaiah 53), paid the price for each human being's sins so that each person could be restored spiritually to God. And the Messiah will come again, as Yeshua ben David, to establish the Davidic Kingdom God promised, thus fulfilling the dual aspects of the Messiah.

Since there is only one true path to God, God ensured that the identity of the true Messiah would be clearly revealed to those who earnestly seek God in spirit and in truth. God laid out every detail of His Master Plan in such a way as to point to the only true Messiah, in no uncertain terms. God has provided the truth for each of us to seek. However, He allows us the free choice to seek and accept that truth.

"But an hour is coming, and now is, when the true worshipers shall worship the Father in spirit and truth; for such people the Father seeks to be His worshipers" (John 4:23).

Again therefore Jesus spoke to them, saying, "I am the light of the world; he who follows Me shall not walk in the darkness, but shall have the light of life" (John 8:12).

It is the authors' prayer that this book provides the reader with a solid foundation in spiritual truth that leads to the only true Messiah and eternal life with God:

"For God so loved the world, that He gave His only begotten Son, that whoever believes in Him should not perish, but have eternal life. For God did not send the Son into the world to judge the world, but that the world should be saved through Him" (John 3:16-17).

For the believer, a solid foundation in spiritual truth leads to a greater understanding and trust in God and closer personal relationship through Yeshua. For the skeptic or unbeliever, an understanding of spiritual truth will hopefully lead to the individual choice to accept God's gift of salvation and commitment to a personal relationship with Yeshua.

YESHUA—THE ALEPH TO TAV

The purpose of this book has been to reveal the beauty, logic, and precision of God's Master Plan. From the first light of creation, the Light of Messiah, every detail of God's plan of salvation reveals, beyond a shadow of a doubt, the existence of a personal and loving God. And this perfect plan of salvation is brought to completion in Yeshua, the Messiah:

Who has performed and done this, calling the generations from the beginning? I, the LORD, am first, and will be with the last (Isaiah 41:4).

When the LORD refers to Himself as "the first and the last," He is showing Himself to be the source and end goal of all creation. The word *Lord* comes from the Hebrew *Adon*. Recall that whenever the Tetragrammaton, YHVH, the Ineffable Name of God, appeared in Scripture, it was considered too sacred to be spoken. Because of this, the word Adon was substituted in its place. Therefore, in the Isaiah passages quoted above and below, Lord refers to YHVH, embodied in Yeshua:

Thus says the LORD, the King of Israel, and his [God's] Redeemer, the LORD of hosts: I am the first and I am the last; besides me there is no god (Isaiah 44:6).

Listen to me, O Jacob, and Israel, whom I called: I am He; I am the first, and I am the last (Isaiah 48:12).

In the Book of Revelation, the Lamb of God, Yeshua HaMashiach, refers to Himself as "the Alpha and the Omega." This is identical in meaning to "the first and the last," as it refers to the first and last letters of the Greek alphabet, Greek being the language in which Revelation was written. Had this book been written in Hebrew, however, He would have said: "I am the Aleph and the Tav." This is its real meaning, which can only be adequately expressed in the Hebrew language. The idiom, "from aleph to tav," refers to:

something that is expressed or analyzed in its entirety....the very order of the letters represents profound... concepts. The use of an alphabetical sequence to praise God, or describe a person or concept, denotes totality and perfection.[3]

From this, we are to understand that Yeshua embodies spiritual totality and perfection. In Yeshua is the completion of God's Master Plan of redemption for humankind. All who come to Him will find spiritual completion and perfection.

"I am the Alpha [Aleph] and the Omega [Tav]," says the Lord God, who is and who was and who is to come, the Almighty" (Revelation 1:8).

Then he said to me, "It is done! I am the Alpha [Aleph] and the Omega [Tav], the beginning and the end. To the thirsty I will give water as a gift from the spring of the water of life" (Revelation 21:6).

"I am the Alpha [Aleph] and the Omega [Tav], the first and the last, the beginning and the end" (Revelation 22:13).

Notes

1. Philip Birnbaum, *Encyclopedia of Jewish Concepts*, p. 620.
2. Rabbi Aryeh Kaplan, *Tzitzith: A Thread of Life*, pp. 55-57.
3. Rabbi Michael L. Munk, *The Wisdom in the Hebrew Alphabet*, p. 34.

APPENDIX 1

ALTERNATIVE SITES FOR GOLGOTHA—DO THEY SATISFY BIBLICAL AND HISTORICAL CRITERIA

All the evidence previously discussed supports the Mount of Olives as the actual site of the crucifixion and resurrection. Nevertheless, Catholic and Protestant traditions hold to alternative sites, the Church of the Holy Sepulcher and Gordon's Tomb respectively. Let us, therefore, do a comparative analysis of the Biblical, historical, and archaeological facts in order to assess the accuracy of these competing claims for the authentic site of Yeshua's death and resurrection.

For the purpose of this discussion, it should be remembered that the sites of the crucifixion and burial are in close proximity to each other, based upon the Scriptural record (John 19:41).

THE CHURCH OF THE HOLY SEPULCHER

In 326 C.E., the site of the Church of the Holy Sepulcher was selected by the Roman Emperor

Constantine as the site of the crucifixion, based upon visions and dreams which he had experienced. Although Constantine is credited with making Christianity the religion of the Roman Empire, the preponderance of the evidence suggests that he used religion as a political tool to strengthen the Empire, rather than that he was truly spiritually converted. (In fact, Constantine was not baptized until he was on his deathbed.) This understanding is essential in order to ascertain the validity of visions and dreams Constantine experienced.

The site of the Church of the Holy Sepulcher is located west of the Temple area, facing the back of the Temple building (Figures 3, 11). In addition, a wall was located between this area and the Temple at the time of the crucifixion. If the crucifixion had taken place here, it would have been impossible for the centurion and others to have seen the veil at the entrance of Temple tear, as described in Scripture (Matthew 27:51-54).

For the same reason, Yeshua would not have been "in the presence" of God as His sentence was executed. In other words, He would not have been facing the entrance to the Temple, where God's presence resided.

Another problem with this site is the fact that it lies well within the 2000-cubit distance from the Temple area. The crucifixion took place outside the 2000-cubit perimeter at the place called "outside the camp," a specific site just outside the city on the Mount of Olives. Furthermore, no new tombs or gardens were allowed inside the 2000-cubit area, referred to as "within the camp," at the time of Yeshua.[1]

GORDON'S TOMB

The Protestant alternative to the Catholic crucifixion site is called Gordon's Tomb. It was proposed by British

General Gordon in 1883 and based upon the notion that by superimposing an imaginary skeleton on the city of Jerusalem, the place where the skull fell indicated the crucifixion site. In this area, Gordon selected a hill with eye-like openings, thinking this fit the meaning of "place of the skull." It is important to note that these eye-like features are due to subsequent erosion and did not exist two thousand years ago. It is also important to note that the Hebrew words, *ha rosh*, translated as "the skull," do not refer to a literal skull but instead to "the top" or "the summit." In other words, it refers to a high, exposed area.

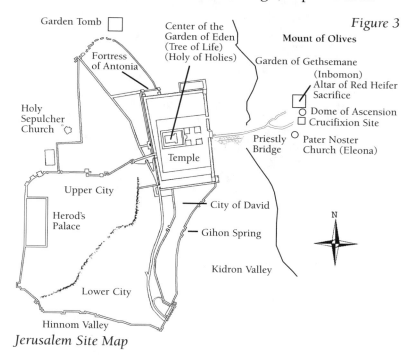

Figure 3

Garden Tomb

Center of the Garden of Eden (Tree of Life) (Holy of Holies)

Mount of Olives

Fortress of Antonia

Garden of Gethsemane (Inbomon)

Altar of Red Heifer Sacrifice

Holy Sepulcher Church

Dome of Ascension

Crucifixion Site

Priestly Bridge

Pater Noster Church (Eleona)

Temple

Upper City

City of David

Herod's Palace

Gihon Spring

N

Kidron Valley

Lower City

Hinnom Valley

Jerusalem Site Map

Like the Church of the Holy Sepulcher, Gordon's Tomb does not meet the basic Biblical requirement of providing a vantage point of the Temple so that the veil of the

Figure 11

Antonia Fortress

Rock Quarry

The Site of the Church of the Holy Sepulcher

Site of the Church of the Holy Sepulcher, as it appeared at the time of the crucifixion. A rock quarry was located here, just outside the city's western wall. An additional wall surrounded the Temple area. From this location, it would have been impossible to see the veil at the eastern entrance to the Temple.

Temple could be seen to tear from top to bottom. This is because the site is located north of the Temple, away from the eastern entrance where the veil hung (Figure 3). Some claim that the fact Gordon's Calvary is to the north of the Temple shows its authenticity since the Mishna states the most holy sacrifices were slaughtered on the north side of the Temple altar. However, the Mount of Olives more fully satisfies the Mishna requirement, as discussed below.

The final blow to the authenticity of this site, however, is based upon recent archaeological evidence. According to an article in *Biblical Archaeology Review*, Gordon's tomb is located in one of a network of burial chambers which were hewn during the First Temple period, some eight to nine hundred years before Christ.[2] Yet the Gospel of John clearly states that the body of Yeshua was placed in a "new tomb in which no one had yet been laid" (John 19:41).

First Temple period burial chambers can be differentiated from Second Temple period burial chambers based upon the basic layout of the chambers and distinctive architectural features, including the type of chisel marks. In addition, certain archaeological artifacts closely associated with the original tombs are clearly from the First Temple period. Furthermore, "not a single tomb from Second Temple times has been found in this area."[3] Finally, this area was located within the city limits during the time of the Second Temple, where, according to legal restrictions, no cemeteries were allowed.[4]

THE MOUNT OF OLIVES

As thoroughly discussed in Chapter 3, the Mount of Olives as the crucifixion site is consistent with all Biblical, historical, and archaeological data (Figure 5).

The *ha rosh*, or summit, of the Mount of Olives afforded the best vantage point, as it was even higher than Mount Moriah, where the Temple was located. The site is approximately one-half mile east of the front of the Temple, and the huge veil at the Temple entrance would have been clearly visible to the witnesses of the crucifixion. In addition, Yeshua would have faced "the presence of God" in the Temple as He faced the entrance of the Temple from the crucifixion tree.

Figure 5

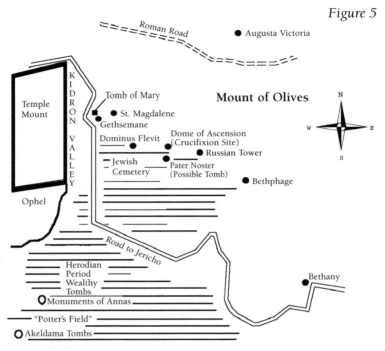

Mount of Olives Site Map

As previously mentioned in the discussion on Gordon's Calvary, the Mishna states that the most holy sacrifices were to be slaughtered on the north side of the Altar[5], which was located directly in front of the Temple. However, the Mishna also states that the most holy sacrifices slaughtered *above* the Altar fully satisfy this requirement.[6] In this regard, the Red Heifer Altar on the summit of the Mount of Olives is *above* the Altar on the Temple Mount.

The holiest of all sacrifices, the Red Heifer, was sacrificed at the summit of the Mount of Olives at the Red

Heifer Altar. From this altar, the High Priest could look across the Kidron Valley to the Temple on Mount Moriah. And because the Temple was oriented toward the east, it was possible to look directly into the Sanctuary while the blood of the red heifer was sprinkled on the Mount of Olives.[7] Yeshua Himself looked into the Sanctuary at the moment the Temple veil was rent—the moment He gave up His life.

The Red Heifer Altar was the highest point opposite the Temple. Many sacrifices were taken up to this particular site and mixed with the ashes of the red heifer for many forms of sin offerings. Moreover, the Red Heifer Sacrifice was the holiest of all sacrifices. Therefore, the Red Heifer Altar was above all other sacrificial altars, not only in a physical sense but also in a spiritual sense as well. The mysterious spiritual significance of the red heifer has never been fully explained.[8] However, it was understood that the ashes of the red heifer, mixed with the living water of the Gihon spring, were required to cleanse one from ritual uncleaness according to the Biblical laws of purity and impurity.

There is only one way that all the sacrificial laws could have been fulfilled by Yeshua. He was not only the sin and guilt offering, but He was also the holiest of all sacrifices, represented by the Red Heifer. Therefore, He had to offer Himself at the place of the red heifer sacrifice so as to comply with the law of sin and guilt offerings on the north as well as to fulfill the red heifer sacrifice at the same place. Only one place in all of Jerusalem satisfies all the sacrificial requirements in every way—the Mount of Olives.

It is noteworthy that Eusebius, the top theologian and church historian living at the time of Constantine, wrote that the Mount of Olives was the only place considered holy by the Christians and, in fact, Christian pilgrims came from all over the world to worship at a cave/crypt located near its summit.[9]

The "House of God," the headquarters for the Christian Church in Jerusalem, was located on the Mount of Olives until it was destroyed in 303 C.E.[10] And during the time of Constantine, the Eleona Church was built over the site of the cave/crypt because Christians considered it such a holy place. In 614, the Eleona Church was destroyed and, in 1868, the Pater Noster ("Our Father") Church was built on this same site.[11] The following table provides a comparative summary of the three sites, clearly demonstrating that the Mount of Olives is the only site which satisfies all Biblical, historical, and archaeological criteria:

Notes

1. Ernest L. Martin, *Secrets of Golgotha*, p. 157.
2. Gabriel Barkay, "The Garden Tomb: Was Jesus Buried Here?", pp. 40-57.
3. Barkay, p. 51.
4. Barkay, p. 52.
5. Philip Blackman, *Mishnayoth Kodashim*, Vol. 5, p. 36 (Zevachim 5:1).
6. Blackman, Vol. 5, p. 41 (Zevachim 6:1).
7. Leen Ritmeyer, "The Ark of the Covenant—Where It Stood in Solomon's Temple," pp. 54, 70.
8. Philip Birnbaum, *Encyclopedia of Jewish Concepts*, p. 241.
9. Martin, p. 73.
10. Martin, p. 138.
11. Jack Finegan, *The Archaeology of the New Testament*, p. 97.

Comparison Chart of Three Sites			
BASIS AND CRITERIA	HOLY SEPULCHER	GORDON'S CALVARY	MOUNT OF OLIVES
Basis of site selection	Constantine's visions & dreams	Gordon's imaginary skeleton	Biblical, historical & archaeological data
Fits "ha rosh"	No	No, skull-like appearance due to much later erosion	Yes, "skull" meaning "summit" or "top" of Mount of Olives
Could veil be seen?	No	No	Yes
In "the presence of God"?	No	No	Yes
Near the place called "outside the camp"?	No	No	Yes
In a "garden" (tree orchard)?	Gardens not allowed within city limits at the time of Yeshua.	Gardens not allowed within city limits at the time of Yeshua.	Yes
New tombs nearby?	No	No	Yes (only location where new tombs allowed at this time)
Possible to witness opening of tombs?	No	No	Yes (tombs nearby and clearly visible)
Satisfies all sacrificial requirements?	No	No	Yes

APPENDIX 2

THE CRUCIFIXION TREE AND THE PATTERN OF THE TABERNACLE VESSELS

It is mind-boggling to realize that the pattern of the earthly Tabernacle was based upon its heavenly counterpart. John's vision, as recorded in the Book of Revelation, alludes to the heavenly Tabernacle-Temple:

And the temple of God which is in heaven was opened; and the ark of His covenant appeared in His temple... (Revelation 11:19).

After these things I looked, and the temple of the tabernacle of testimony in heaven was opened, (Revelation 15:5).

In-depth study of the earthly Tabernacle reveals that it symbolically portrayed God's Messiah and redemptive plan for humankind. Even the pattern contained in the configuration of the Tabernacle vessels was reflected in the crucifixion of the Messiah, Yeshua.

The most holy of the Tabernacle articles was the Ark of the Covenant (Exodus 25:10-22), which was placed within the Holy of Holies where God's presence dwelt. It contained the Ten Commandments and was covered by the

Mercy Seat. A veil (Exodus 26:31-37) formed a partition between the Holy of Holies and the eastern chamber called the Holy Place (Exodus 40):

> v. 20 And he [Moses] took the testimony [Ten Commandments] and put it into the ark, and attached the poles to the ark, and put the mercy seat on top of the ark.

> v. 21 And he brought the ark into the tabernacle, and set up the veil for the screen, and screened off the ark of the testimony, just as the LORD had commanded Moses.

In the Holy Place were three articles: the Table of Showbread (Exodus 25:23-30), the Menorah (Exodus 25:31-40), and the Altar of Incense (Exodus 30:1-10). Their positioning was based upon precise instructions from God (Exodus 40):

> v. 22 Then he [Moses] put the table in the tent of meeting, on the north side of the tabernacle, outside the veil.

> v. 23 And he set the arrangement of bread in order on it before the LORD, just as the LORD had commanded Moses.

> v. 24 Then he placed the lampstand [menorah] in the tent of the meeting, opposite the table, on the south side of the tabernacle.

> v. 25 And he lighted the lamps before the LORD, just as the LORD had commanded Moses.

> v. 26 Then he placed the gold altar in the tent of meeting in front of the veil;

> v. 27 and he burned fragrant incense on it, just as the LORD had commanded Moses.

Outside the tent of the Tabernacle which covered the Holy of Holies and the Holy Place, was an area called the Court of the Israelites. Here, there were two more articles, the Brazen Altar (Exodus 27:1-8) and the Brazen Laver (Exodus 30:18-21). (Note that the laver and altar were actually made of copper, which symbolizes judgment.)

And he [Moses] set the altar of burnt offering before the doorway of the tabernacle of the tent of meeting, and offered on it the burnt offering and the meal offering, just as the LORD had commanded Moses. And he placed the laver between the tent of meeting and the altar, and put water in it for washing (Exodus 40:29-30).

The arrangement of the Tabernacle articles discussed above can be seen to parallel the body of Yeshua as it was nailed to the Crucifixion Tree, a branch from the Tree of Life (Figure 12). In essence, the elements of the Tabernacle symbolized the Messiah:

1. The Mercy Seat represented the propitiatory covering which was sprinkled with blood as payment for sin. Yeshua is the propitiation for our sins (I John 4:10).

2. The Ark of the Covenant, containing the Ten Commandments, symbolized the Law given to Moses by God on Mount Sinai. Yeshua said He came to earth to fulfill, not abolish, the Law (Matthew 5:17).

3. The Table of Showbread held the twelve loaves of consecrated bread. Yeshua said He is the Bread of Life (John 6:35).

4. The Menorah illuminated the Holy Place. Yeshua said that He is the Light of the World (John 8:12).

5. The Altar of Incense contained the coals which were lit by the fire of God to consume the sacred incense. The incense represented the prayers of the people to God. Yeshua is the only Mediator between man and God (1 Timothy 2:5).

6. The Brazen Laver was filled with living (flowing, not stagnant) water for the purification of the priests. Yeshua is the Living Water that gives eternal life (John 4:10-14).

7. The Brazen Altar burned the sacrifices as judgment for sin. Yeshua is the Judge of the living and the dead (Acts 10:42).

Clearly, God designed the Tabernacle and every vessel it contained as a symbolic picture of the Messiah to come. Just as clearly, Yeshua fulfills the picture of the true Messiah in every prophetic detail and symbolic meaning.

Figure 12

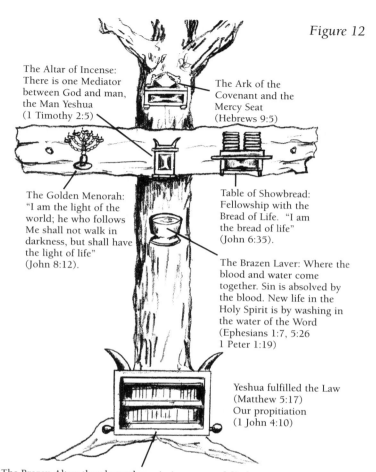

The Altar of Incense:
There is one Mediator
between God and man,
the Man Yeshua
(1 Timothy 2:5)

The Ark of the
Covenant and the
Mercy Seat
(Hebrews 9:5)

The Golden Menorah:
"I am the light of the
world; he who follows
Me shall not walk in
darkness, but shall have
the light of life"
(John 8:12).

Table of Showbread:
Fellowship with the
Bread of Life. "I am
the bread of life"
(John 6:35).

The Brazen Laver: Where the
blood and water come
together. Sin is absolved by
the blood. New life in the
Holy Spirit is by washing in
the water of the Word
(Ephesians 1:7, 5:26
1 Peter 1:19)

Yeshua fulfilled the Law
(Matthew 5:17)
Our propitiation
(1 John 4:10)

The Brazen Altar: the place where sin is consumed (Judgment Fire, Acts 10:42).

And being found in appearance as a man, He humbled
Himself by becoming obedient to the point of death, even
death on a tree (Phillipians 2:8).

"And I, if I be lifted up from the earth, will draw all men to
myself." But He was saying this to indicate the kind of death
by which He was to die. The multitude therefore answered
Him, "We have heard out of the Law that the Messiah is to
remain forever; and how can You say, 'The Son of Man must
be lifted up'? Who is this Son of Man?" (John 12:32-34).

The Crucifixion Tree and the Pattern of the Tabernacle Vessels

BIBLIOGRAPHY

The Apocrypha of the Old Testament (KJV). New York: American Bible Society, (no date given).

Bader, Gershom (translated by Solomon Katz). *The Encyclopedia of Talmudic Sages* (1993 softcover edition). Northvale, NJ: Jason Aronson Inc., 1988.

Barkay, Gabriel. "The Garden Tomb: Was Jesus Buried Here?" *Biblical Archaeology Review*, 12:2 (March/April 1986) 40.

Ben Amir, Jacob. "Fresh Water Was Discovered in the Northern Part of the Dead Sea." *Globes*, 2354 (March 26, 1993) Israel.

Ben-Dov, Meir (translated by Ina Friedman). *In the Shadow of the Temple*. New York: Harper & Row, Publishers, 1982.

Ben-Yehuda, Ehud, Editor. *Ben-Yehuda's Pocket English-Hebrew/Hebrew-English Dictionary*. New York: Pocket Books, 1961, 1964.

Ben Zadok, Phinehas. *Which Day is the Passover?* Kibbutz Ir-Ovot, Israel: A Voice Crying in the Wilderness, 1988.

Birnbaum, Philip. *Encyclopedia of Jewish Concepts*. New York: Hebrew Publishing Company, 1979.

Blackman, Philip. *Mishnayoth* (second edition). New York: Judaica Press, Inc., 1983.

Blech, Rabbi Benjamin. *The Secrets of Hebrew Words*. Northvale, NJ: Jason Aronson Inc., 1991.

Braun, Moshe. *The Jewish Holy Days: Their Spiritual Significance*. Northvale, NJ: Jason Aronson Inc., 1996.

Bruce, F. F. *The New Testament Development of Old Testament Themes*. Grand Rapids, MI: Wm. B. Eerdmans Publishing Co., 1977.

Bushwick, Rabbi Nathan, Translator. *The Book of Joshua*. Brooklyn, NY: Moznaim Publishing Corporation, 1990.

The Comparative Study Bible. Grand Rapids, MI: Zondervan Publishing House, 1984.

Concordant Literal New Testament with the Keyword Concordance. Canyon Country, CA: Concordant Publishing Concern, 1983.

Dake, Finis Jennings. *Dake's Annotated Reference Bible*. Lawrenceville, GA: Dake Bible Sales, Inc., 1963.

Divry, George C., Editor. *Divry's Modern English-Greek and Greek-English Desk Dictionary*. New York: D. C. Divry, Inc., Publishers, 1982.

Dowly, Tim, Editor. *The History of Christianity* (revised edition). Batavia, IL: Lion Publishing Corporation, 1990.

Edersheim, Alfred. *The Temple: Its Ministry and Services* (softcover edition). Grand Rapids, MI: Wm. B. Eerdmans Publishing Co., 1979.

Edersheim, Alfred. *The Temple: Its Ministry and Services* (updated hardcover edition). Peabody, MA: Hendrickson Publishers, Inc., 1994.

Encyclopedia Judaica (corrected edition). Jerusalem: Keter Publishing House Jerusalem Ltd., (no date given).

Faier, Dr. Zvi, Translator. *The Book of Tehillim/Psalms* (five volumes). Brooklyn, NY: Moznaim Publishing Corporation, 1989 .

Faier, Zvi, Translator. *Malbim: Beginning and Upheaval*. Jerusalem: Hillel Press, 1978.

Faier, Dr. Tzvi, Translator. *The Torah Anthology* (volume 13). New York: Maznaim Publishing Corporation, 1982.

Feuer, Rabbi Avrohom Chaim. *The ArtScroll Tanach Series: Psalms* (two volumes). Brooklyn, NY: Mesorah Publications, Ltd., 1977, 1985.

Finegan, Jack. *The Archaeology of the New Testament*. Princeton: Princeton University Press, 1969.

Frankel, Ellen and Teutsch, Betty Platkin. *The Encyclopedia of Jewish Symbols*. Northvale, NJ: Jason Aronson Inc., 1992.

Freedman, Rabbi Dr. H. and Simon, Maurice, Editors. *The Midrash: Exodus* (volume 3). London: Soncino Press, 1951.

Goldwurm, Rabbi Hersh, Adapter. The ArtScroll History Series, *History of the Jewish People: The Second Temple Era*. Brooklyn, NY: Mesorah Publications, Ltd., 1982.

Green, Jay P., Sr., Translator-Editor. *The Interlinear Bible*. Grand Rapids, MI: Baker Book House, 1981.

Hanegraaff, Hank. *Christianity in Crisis*. Eugene, OR: Harvest House Publishers, 1993.

Harris, R. Laird, Archer, Gleason L., Jr., and Waltke, Bruce K., Editors. *Theological Wordbook of the Old Testament* (two volumes). Chicago: Moody Press, 1980.

Jeremias, Joachim. *Jerusalem in the Time of Jesus* (1975 softcover edition). Philadelphia, PA: Fortress Press, 1969.

The Jewish Encyclopedia. New York: Funk & Wagnell's Company, 1916.

Kaplan, Rabbi Aryeh, Translator. *The Torah Anthology* (volumes 1, 2, 4, 6, 9, 11, 12). Brooklyn, NY: Moznaim Publishing Corporation, 1977, 1978, 1979, 1981, 1982.

Kaplan, Rabbi Aryeh, Translator. *The Torah Anthology: Passover Haggadah*. Brooklyn, NY: Maznaim Publishing Corporation, 1978.

Kaplan, Aryeh. *Tzitzith: A Thread of Light*. New York, NY: National Conference of Synagogue Youth/Union of Orthodox Jewish Congregations of America, 1984.

Liddell, Henry G. and Scott, Robert. *A Greek-English Lexicon* (ninth edition). Oxford: The Clarendon Press, first published 1843; first ninth edition 1940; 1985.

Lowe, Malcolm. "Understanding John's Gospel (II)." *Christians and Israel*, 5:2 (Spring 1996) 5.

Marshall, Alfred. *The Interlinear KJV-NIV Parallel New Testament in Greek and English.* Grand Rapids, MI: Zondervan Publishing House, 1975.

Martin, Ernest L. *Secrets of Golgotha.* Portland, OR: ASK Publications, 1988.

Mounce, William D. *Basics of Biblical Greek.* Grand Rapids, MI: Zondervan Publishing House, 1993.

Munk, Rabbi Michael L. *The Wisdom in the Hebrew Alphabet* (second edition). Brooklyn, NY: Mesorah Publications, 1983.

The New Testament in Hebrew and English. Cambridge: University Press, 1966.

Nun, Mendel. *The Sea of Galilee and Its Fisherman in the New Testament.* Kibbutz Ein Gev, Israel: Kinnereth Sailing Co., 1989.

Richman, Chaim. *The Holy Temple of Jerusalem.* Jerusalem: The Temple Institute and Carta, 1997.

Ritmeyer, Leen. "The Ark of the Covenant—Where It Stood in Solomon's Temple." *Biblical Archaeology Review,* 22:1 (January/February 1996) 46.

Robertson, Archibald Thomas. *Word Pictures in the New Testament* (six volumes). Grand Rapids, MI: Baker Book House, 1930.

Rosenberg, Rabbi A. J., Translator. *The Book of II Kings.* New York: The Judaica Press Inc., 1985.

Rosenberg, Rabbi A. J., Translator. *The Book of Samuel 1.* New York: The Judaica Press Inc., 1988.

Rosenberg, Rabbi A. J., Translator. *Twelve Prophets* (two volumes). New York: The Judaica Press Inc., 1986, 1988.

Sarna, Nahum M., Commentator. *The JPS Torah Commentary: Exodus.* New York: The Jewish Publication Society, 1991.

Sarna, Nahum M., Commentator. *The JPS Torah Commentary: Genesis.* New York: The Jewish Publication Society, 1989.

Sauer, James A. "The River Runs Dry—Biblical Story Preserves Historical Memory." *Biblical Archaeology Review*, 22:4 (July/August 1996) 52.

Slotki, Rev. Dr. I. W. *The Soncino Books of the Bible: Isaiah*. New York: The Soncino Press, 1949.

Strassfeld, Michael. *The Jewish Holidays: A Guide and Commentary*. New York: Harper & Row, 1985.

Strong, James. *The New Strong's Exhaustive Concordance of the Bible*. Nashville: Thomas Nelson Publishers, 1990.

Tenney, Merrill C., Editor. *The Zondervan Pictorial Bible Dictionary*. Grand Rapids, MI: Zondervan Publishing House, 1963, 1964, 1967.

Tenney, Merrill C., Editor. *The Zondervan Pictorial Encyclopedia of the Bible* (five volumes). Grand Rapids, MI: Zondervan Publishing House, 1975, 1976.

The Torah Anthology (multi-volume set). Brooklyn, NY: Maznaim Publishing Corporation, 1977.

Unterman, Alan. *Dictionary of Jewish Lore and Legend*. London: Thames and Hudson Ltd., 1991.

Vine, W. E. *Vine's Expository Dictionary of Old and New Testament Words*. Old Tappan, NJ: Fleming H. Revell Company, 1981.

Weissman, Rabbi Moshe. *The Midrash Says* (five volumes). Brooklyn, NY: Benei Yakov Publications, 1980.

Whiston, William, Translator. *Josephus, Complete Works*. Grand Rapids, MI: Kregel Publications, 1960, 1978, 1981.

Whiston, William, Translator. *The Life and Works of Flavius Josephus*. New York: Holt, Rinehart and Whiston (no date given).

Wigoder, Dr. Geoffrey, Editor. *The New Standard Jewish Encyclopedia* (new revised edition). New York: Facts on File, 1992.

Williams, Larry. *The Mountain of Moses*. New York: Wynwood Press, 1990.

Woodrow, Ralph Edward. *Babylon Mystery Religion*. Riverside, CA: Ralph Woodrow Evangelistic Association, Inc., 1966, 1990.

The World Book Encyclopedia. Chicago: World Book, Inc., 1985.

Yadin, Yigael. *The Temple Scroll*. New York: Random House, 1985.

Zlotowitz, Rabbi Meir, Translator. *The ArtScroll Tanach Series: Genesis* (two volume edition). New York: Mesorah Publications, Ltd., 1986, 1988.

Zodhiates, Spiros, Th.D., Editor. *The Hebrew-Greek Key Study Bible—New American Standard*. Chattanooga, TN: AMG Publishers, 1984, 1990.

The Zondervan Pictorial Encyclopedia of the Bible (five volumes). Grand Rapids, MI: Zondervan Publishing House, 1976.

Index for Significant Events on
Mount Moriah and Mount of Olives

Mount Moriah	Mount of Olives
Tree of Life Gen. 2:9	Tree of the Knowledge of Good & Evil Gen. 2:9; 3:3
Center of the Garden of Eden Gen. 2:9; 3:3	Adam & Eve's Exit From Garden of Eden Gen. 3:23
City of Salem where Melchi-Tzedek Ruled Gen. 14:18	East Door to Garden of Eden Gen. 3:24
Land of Moriah Gen. 22:2	Adam's Sacrificial Altar TA Vol. 1, p. 281
The Temple (House of God) 2 Chr. 3:1-2	Abel's Sacrificial Altar Gen. 4:4 • TA Vol. 1, p. 287
Presence of Glory Cloud of God 2 Chr. 5:11-14 • 2 Chr. 7:1-3	Noah's Sacrificial Altar Gen. 8:20 • TA Vol. 1, p. 375
Threshing Floor of Ornan the Jebusite 1 Chr. 5:18-26 - 600 Shekels of Gold • 2 Chr. 3:1	Abraham's Sacrificial Altar Gen. 22:9 • TA Vol. 2, p. 332
Yeshua's Dedication & Circumcision Luke 2:21-38	Threshing Floor of Araunah the Jebusite 2 Sam. 24:18-25 - 50 Shekels of Silver
High Priest's Chamber, Courtyard & Trial John 18:15-40	Red Heifer Sacrifice (Outside the Camp) Num. 19:1-10 • Ex. 29:14 Lev. 4:21; 16:11
Temple Mount (Courtyard of Israelites) Acts 2:1-13	King David's Ascent (Absalom's Rebellion) 2 Sam. 15:30-32 - Ha Rosh
Baptism of 3000 Acts 2:41	Location (Crucifixion, Burial & Resurrection) Matt. 27:33 • Mark 15:22 - Golgotha (Skull) • John 19:17 - Place of the Skull • Luke 23:33 - Calvary (Place of the Skull) • Matt. 27:54 Veil Witnessed by Centurian • Heb. 13:11-13 - Outside the Camp (Gate)
King's Throne of Rulership Ezek. 43:1-12 • Rev. 20, 21, 22	
TA = Torah Anthology	Location of the Ascension Acts 1:9-12 • Luke 24:50-52
	Location of the Lord's Return Zech. 14:3-8

NOTES

NOTES

NOTES

NOTES

NOTES

NOTES

NOTES

NOTES

NOTES

NOTES

NOTES

NOTES

Additional copies of *The Rod of an Almond Tree in God's Master Plan* are available directly from Messengers of Messiah International Ministries. Quantity order discounts available.

Messengers of Messiah
P.O. Box 125
Troy, IL 62294
Tel. 618-667-1022

Contact Messengers of Messiah for:

- Free Catalog of Tapes and Books
- Updates of New Tapes and Books
- Tape Subscription Information

Visit Messengers of Messiah's Web Site at:
http://www.ezl.com/~peterm/

- E-mail Bible Study
- Real Audio Files
- Newsletters
- Subscription Information
- Tape & Book Catalog
- Information Updates
- On-line Tour of Israel:
over 100 photos plus 40 pages of text

Web site: http://www.
messengers-of-messiah.org/
E-mail: peterm@messengers-
of-messiah.org